CAMBRIDGE LIBRARY COLLECTION

Books of enduring scholarly value

Travel and Exploration in Asia

This collection of travel narratives, mainly from the nineteenth century, records the impressions of Europeans who visited China, Japan, South and South-East Asia. Some came as missionaries, others as members of trade or diplomatic missions, or as colonial administrators. Some were straightforward tourists, and one or two arrived as prisoners or shipwrecked sailors. Such accounts of travellers' experiences in exotic locations were eagerly received by European readers.

Nine Years in Nipon

The Scottish doctor Henry Faulds (1843–1930) is best remembered for his role in the history of fingerprinting. His strong religious faith had first led him to missionary work in India and then, from 1874, in Japan. He worked there as a surgeon in the mission hospital at Tsukiji, near Tokyo, where he also established a medical school and a school for the blind. It was his discovery of the impressions of thumbprints on ancient Japanese pottery which led to his development of a fingerprinting system and his championing of it as a forensic tool. The present work, part-travelogue, part-journal, was first published in 1885. It remains an engaging account of Japanese life, customs, geography and natural history, interwoven with discussions of topics such as education, language, and the future of the country. There are characterful line drawings throughout. Faulds' *Dactylography* (1912) is also reissued in the Cambridge Library Collection.

T0371585

Nine Years in Nipon

Sketches of Japanese Life and Manners

HENRY FAULDS

CAMBRIDGE
UNIVERSITY PRESS

CAMBRIDGE
UNIVERSITY PRESS

University Printing House, Cambridge, CB2 8BS, United Kingdom

Cambridge University Press is part of the University of Cambridge.

It furthers the University's mission by disseminating knowledge in the pursuit of
education, learning and research at the highest international levels of excellence.

www.cambridge.org
Information on this title: www.cambridge.org/9781108081627

© in this compilation Cambridge University Press 2015

This edition first published 1885
This digitally printed version 2015

ISBN 978-1-108-08162-7 Paperback

NINE YEARS IN NIPON.

ON THE TOKAIDO

NINE YEARS IN NIPON:

SKETCHES OF JAPANESE LIFE AND MANNERS.

BY

HENRY FAULDS, L.F.P.S.,

Surgeon of Tsukiji Hospital, Tokio; Member of the Royal Asiatic Society.

ALEXANDER GARDNER,
12 PATERNOSTER ROW, LONDON; AND PAISLEY.

1885.

TO MY FATHER

THIS WORK IS AFFECTIONATELY DEDICATED.

PREFACE.

So many works have of late been written on Japan that perhaps the best apology for publishing a new one is that the public seem to wish for more.

My aim has been to give in language as free as possible from pedantic jargon such an account of Nipon and its people as may instruct, without unduly boring my readers. A great deal more might have been written than I have here attempted, but fortunately strict limits were imposed upon me, and I sincerely hope that useful and interesting things only have found admission.

I have been obliged to omit, most reluctantly, a large section in which I intended to give some account of the religious and moral systems which prevail in Japan, but, should this work succeed in finding a moderate measure of public approbation, I hope soon to expand my notes on these subjects into a separate volume.

CONTENTS.

NINE YEARS IN NIPON.

CHAPTER I.

Introductory.

The Land—Its Contour—The Four Great Islands—Inland Sea—Rivers and Canals—Coast—Lighthouses—Harbours—The Black Stream—Climate —*Flora* and *Fauna*—Races.

APAN is the name usually given by English writers to a fertile and populous group of four great islands associated with a number of smaller ones, which lies in the far East almost where our artificial day begins, and whose people may perhaps therefore, not unreasonably, hope to form a natural link between those of East and West. Its area is rather greater than that of the United Kingdom, and may be about 150,000 square miles, much of which still lies waste and uncultivated, though apparently capable of tillage. About one-fourth is forest land. Japan is washed on the east by the sluggish rollers of the Pacific, and on the west by the seas of Japan and

A

Okhotsk. The most westerly point is within an hour
or two's sail of the Asiatic continent, and eastwards
it is about 5000 miles distant from San Francisco.
Comprising the crescent-shaped mainland, or largest
island, which is not definitely named like the others—
Kiushiu, Shikoku, Yesso, the Kurile Islands, and many
others—it lies stretched from 24° to 50° 40′ N. lat., and
from 124° to 156° 38′ E. long,—that is, speaking roughly,
it lies diagonally in, and north of, the sub-tropical belt,
and has northern points corresponding with Paris and
Newfoundland on the one hand and southern ones placed
like Cairo, Madeira, and the Bermudas ; or again, it cor-
responds pretty nearly in latitude with the eastern coast
line of the United States, adding Nova Scotia and Newfoundland; and the contrasts of climate in the latter
island and in Florida are probably not more remarkable
than those which are observed in the extreme northern
and southern regions of Japan.

By the almost U-shaped Suez canal route the distance
is nearly 12,000 miles from Liverpool, but by the slightly
arched San Francisco route the distance is greatly
lessened, much of it being practically still further
shortened by railway so that the journey can be accomplished in a month.

The general shape of the mass formed by the four great
islands, which lie closely together separated only by the
narrowest straits, has often been poetically compared by
native writers to the curved form of a dragon-fly in flight.
Perhaps to the common-place mind of the western bar-
barian it may suggest the less romantic idea of a hen's
foot with partly outstretched claws!

The four islands are—

1. KIUSHIU ("the nine counties"), of an irregular double-wedge shape ; its obtuse wedge lying to the north and the acuter one to the south, the mass being placed nearly at right angles to the so-called mainland. The Bungo Nada, a dangerous strait opening from the Inland Sea into the Pacific, separates it from the next, or

2. SHIKOKU ("the four provinces"), an irregular crescent lying southward from and parallel to the western part of the "mainland," having its concavity turned southward to the Pacific, while its convexity forms the southern boundary of the Inland Sea.

3. The (strictly-speaking) unnamed HONDO, or HONSHIU, or mainland is considerably larger than the other three islands combined. It is almost divided into two

portions by the large fresh water Lake Biwa and two corresponding deep indentations on the north and south
coasts respectively, or the bays of Wakasa and Owari.
The western or smaller portion lying east-west is something like a human foot with its toes pointing westward,
the hollow of the arch forming the north boundary of the
Inland Sea.   The remaining portion is somewhat like an
inverted axe, its handle pointing due north and the blade
touching the western portion just described.

4. YESSO, the northernmost island, lies close to the
mainland, being separated from it by Tsugaru strait, which
can be crossed in an hour or so.   It bears no very fanciful
resemblance to a gigantic ray fish, steering eastward, with
contorted tail pointing to the mainland.

The chain of smaller islands trends from S.W., by N.E.,
forming a broken sinuous line with Saghalien—no longer
politically a part of Japan—and the Aleutian islands.

Saghalien was a possession of some value, and in 1875
was ceded to Russia in return for the comparatively worth-
less Kurile islands, where sea-otters are obtained.   The
act of cession was very unpopular in Japan.   The island
is said now to contain about 4000 exiles chiefly of the
male sex.   They are sent by sea from Odessa, and the
fatality on the way has been great.

The Japanese government seem to have a fairly good
claim to the small but interesting group of Loochoo
(Liu-chiu) islands, but it is hotly contested by China.
The people have more natural affinity in language and
customs to Japan than to China, and would be more
benefited by control from Tokio than from Pekin.

The Bonins, called Ogasawara, were recently ceded by the British to Japan.

The most striking geographical feature of Japan is the Inland Sea, which is certainly one of the beauties of the world. It is a long irregularly-shaped arm of the sea, with tides and rapid currents, of variable width and no great depth, studded with innumerable thickly-wooded islands. It may be entered from the Pacific by two straits, —Linschoten strait and Bungo nada, the navigation of the latter in certain seasons being especially dangerous and difficult. On the northern side the Inland Sea is entered from the Sea of Japan through the strait of Shimonoseki, which very greatly resembles the Kyles of Bute in its narrow sinuous passage and surrounding scenery of most romantic beauty. This is practically the shortest way from Yokohama to Nagasaki, Mr. Griffis to the contrary notwithstanding, and is the route now taken by the mail steamers of the Peninsular and Oriental Steamship Company. This little question, however, led, in 1864, to much bloodshed and subsequent diplomacy, of which I shall have something to say in another chapter.

The crescent of the narrow mainland, if the largest of the islands may be so called, presents its convex side to the Pacific Ocean, while the concavity is turned towards the sea of Japan and the newly opened kingdom of Corea. It is pretty clearly divided into somewhat irregular north-western and south-eastern slopes, with well-marked climatic differences, by a grand central range of great height, broken here and there by the strongly marked individuality of a still living, or but recently extinct, volcano, the whole forming a rough back-bone flanked with many spur-like ranges, water-carved, and often beautifully terraced along the river valleys, but nowhere, so far as has yet been observed, showing any direct effects of glacial action.

The Central main line of railway is intended to run along the flanks of this rugged crest, far enough inland to be safe from attack by sea or destruction by flooding of the rivers, whose shifting beds form no very good formation for the long viaducts which would be required in another situation. Most of the larger rivers in the mainland curiously run a course tending almost north or south. The general contour of the land—its great narrowness—is such, indeed, that they must needs be short, but this direction gives them the greatest length possible. There are brief periods of excessively heavy rain, and so they are often then in fierce flood, carrying everything before them and leaving great plains of water-worn stones and gravel around their mouths, on which, after a time, soil has sometimes accumulated and great forests have grown. From their extreme shortness of course the chief commercial cities of Japan, even when placed on the banks of broad rivers, are always near enough to "taste the salt breath of the great wide sea."

The geological structure of many of the rocks has also been favourable to the formation of numerous most picturesque waterfalls, which attract the traveller and have from ancient times been warmly admired and eulogised by native artists and poets. The rivers at a short distance from their outlets are rendered navigable chiefly by the courage, enterprise, and ingenuity of the boatmen, who are amongst the most daring and skilful in the world.

Till recently little has been done to deepen river channels or protect their banks except in the interest of agriculture. In the lower reaches where broad alluvial plains of great fertility have been formed they are frequently intersected by numerous shallow canals for the most part of comparatively recent excavation, but some of them are many centuries old, and these, in the general absence of good roads, have been of immense service in keeping up cross communication throughout the country.

The detritus brought down by the heavy rains is, in some parts of the country, enormous, and is the result of the rapid weathering of certain exposed and easily disintegrated rocks. Those are nearly devoid of vegetation, and masses may be seen peeling off and visibly crumbling into dust. The beds of the rivers and the bordering tracts on each side in those regions have thus sometimes actually been raised above the average level of the surrounding country, and in crossing the bed of the river you have to climb up an embankment which has often been strengthened artificially by means of long "snake baskets" of bamboo, afterwards to be described.

Such *levées*, as geologists call them, are not unknown in other countries. They have been described to me by travellers as being common in the north of China, and there are examples in Italy and in the valley of the Mississippi.

One or two of the rivers of Japan, such as the Sumida —on the banks of which Tokio, the capital, lies, and which is almost as broad as the Thames at Westminster— are worthy of note, and at the present day many a fair modern craft on Western lines may be seen, under the cheerful tap of hammers, taking shape on their banks. Here it may be mentioned that any particular appelation given to a river in Japan holds good only for a limited part of its course, so that it changes its name perhaps four or five times from its birth amongst the cloud-capped, pine-shaded mountains to its final *nirvana* in the ocean. For example, the river which passes through the city of Osaka changes its name four times within the city limits!

The wide bays along the south-eastern coast are for the most part shallow, and a very slight elevation of the land would vastly increase the areas of the bordering plains, which are already very extensive. Such elevations have already notably taken place, as is shown by the presence of naturally deposited strata of recent sea-shells far above high water mark, while there are reliable indications that considerable elevation of the land has taken place even within the historic period.

In spite of their shallowness and rapid silting, some of the rivers of Japan are capable of being so improved as to admit of the passage of steam vessels of the largest size, and there are fine natural inlets and one or two spacious bays, which form natural harbours of great excellence.

To the wants of a large and progressive society, which nature has thus shown her readiness to favour, the Japanese Government are every year becoming more and more alive. What is still more promising, the people themselves, greatly more active than their neighbours in China, show a laudable desire to initiate and carry out such local improvements as may promise to secure the fullest advantage to the community from nature's lavish gifts.

One of the most interesting and characteristic features of the Industrial Exhibition held in Tokio, in 1882, was the splendid display of local maps and models illustrative of achieved or proposed undertakings in engineering, such as embankments, canals, breakwaters, etc. Many of them were of real value, showed scientific insight as to the economical application of ways and means, and were, as might have been expected, very attractive merely as works of art.

Owing to geologically recent elevations of land the coast is usually steep and even precipitous. Its chief natural features, such as sunken rocks, capes, straits, entrances to bays and harbours, and the mouths of rivers, are now well-marked out with beacons, lights or lighthouses of modern construction. Some of the latter are of superior merit, and speak eloquently to the approaching mariner of the progress made in the country since the recent Restoration. I sincerely hope, in the interests of science, that the lighthouse keepers may be encouraged to use the good opportunity they enjoy of observing and recording the flight of birds during their periods of migration ; while they might also, as has been proposed, assist in forming a *cordon* of meteorological observers which might give valuable warnings to fishermen and sailors of coming typhoons.

The government surveyors seem to have followed our own charts for the coastline to begin with, and they are proceeding rapidly and carefully to fill in all needful details as to the interior. At Yokoska, in Yedo Bay, where the chief docks are, the coast tide is said only to rise about four feet on an average. In spring tides it rarely exceeds six feet, and in general the height of the flood-tide is never very great.

In no mere Tennysonian dream, it may be said—

"   . . The mist is drawn
A lucid veil from coast to coast."

This renders navigation in summer dangerous and difficult, and fogs are deemed by experienced sailors to be the great scourge of Japan. Indeed, those malarious cloud-banks, laden with infectious germs, as they can almost now be proved to be, are probably as dangerous to the landsman as to the mariner. While the large area of land lying under shallow water during rice cultivation may have some share in the formation of those dangerous mists, we must seek for a wider and more general cause, and that is readily to be found in the great current (or rather currents) of warm water passing into a colder sea, which is called the *Kuro shiwo*, or Dark Tide or Current.*

The yearly evaporation at the tropics of fully fourteen or fifteen feet of ocean water, causes the great equatorial current of the Pacific which moves westward at first, then splits into two streams, one of which curves northward towards the colder waters of the sea of Japan, but gives off minor eddying currents running at 30 to 40 knots around the greater islands of the empire. Where the cold waters meet them condensation of the water-laden air takes place with the resulting formation of great cloud banks. The

---

* Not "Black River," as Réclus translates it in *The Ocean.* (English edition, p. 82.)

water appears to be of a deep, almost indigo blue colour, whence the name given to the stream by the Japanese. Fish occur in great numbers where the arctic current of fresher, lighter, and cooler water meets the warm salt stream from the south amidst great commotion. And these seem to be attracted by the myriads of minute organisms which the water there contains. The analogy of this great current to our own Gulf Stream has been pointed out, and there can be no doubt as to its great influence on the climate of Japan. A difference of from 8 to 10 degrees centigrade may be observed in passing from its waters to the cold currents from the north, and the effect of this on the superjacent atmosphere is very marked. Sudden and severe changes of temperature are often noticed on the southern coasts of Japan, and even in Yedo Bay. They are evidently due to eddies or branch currents from the great streams of cold and warm waters which interweave themselves in the neighbourhood.

In the northern island, which is rapidly being "colonised" since the Restoration, the extremes of temperature are somewhat greater than in England. In the vicinity of Tokio the winter is usually clear and mild, with occasional sharp frosts and heavy falls of snow. In summer the heat is intensely oppressive for three months or so. The *mean* temperature is of little practical importance. The thermometer not seldom records a heat of 88° to even 97° Fah. in the *shade*, and even at night the heat remains so high that sleep becomes impossible, the air being muggy and no breath of wind stirring. The greatest heat is usually from the middle of June to early in September, but there are often brief periods of hot weather even in

May. The cold in winter is much more severe on the north-western coasts, and the roads across the main island are often blocked with snow, so that communication is suspended for months.

In such a summary sketch as this, it is impossible to say almost anything of the fauna and flora of Japan. Thomé gives China and Japan a botanical district to themselves. The useful bamboo flourishes in all parts of the land, sugar cane and the cotton plant grow in the southern parts, tea almost everywhere. The tobacco plant, hemp, maize. or Indian corn, mulberry for silk-worm food, rice, wheat, barley, millet, buckwheat, potatoes, yams, are all cultivated. The beech, the oak, maples and pine trees, in rich variety ; azaleas, camelias, etc., grow in moor and forest. Some of the more characteristic plants are wistaria, salisburia, cryptomeria, chrysanthemums, and varieties of evergreens such as retinospora, now well known to all British gardeners. Many familiar wild flowers are to be gathered by hedgerow or mossy bank—such as violets, blue bells, forget-me-not, thyme, dandelion, and its allies. The woods are rich in ferns, amongst which the royal fern is conspicuous, orchids, creepers, lichens, mosses, fungi, and liverworts, while the aquatic flora is extensive. The beautiful lotus, though imported, may now fairly be considered as naturalised. There are many water-lilies, reeds, and rushes, some of which are of great utility.

The mammalia of Japan are not numerous. In ancient times, before the dawn of history, two species of dwarf elephants existed in the plains around Tokio. There are many monkeys *(Macacus)* in some parts, and even in extremely northern latitudes. Foxes abound, and are reverenced ; but it is said none are ever found in Shikoku. Wolves and bears are destructive in the north, and had at one time a more extensive field. There are wild antelopes, red deer, wild boars, raccoon dogs, badgers, otters, stoats, ferrets, bats (including a peculiar fruit bat), moles, shrews, and rats ; while the sea is specially rich in seals, sea-otters, and whales. The country has been found quite unsuitable for sheep, but goats thrive well, although not hitherto much favoured. Oxen are used for draught. Horses are small, but of fair quality, and the breed is being improved. The cats are often nearly tail-less. The dogs are of a low, half-wolfish breed. There are some three hundred birds known in Japan. Few of them are what we call song-birds, but the lark is at least one brilliant exception. Game birds are pretty plentiful, and are now protected.

Insects are very numerous—no traveller will dispute that—and Japan is now greatly courted by entomologists, who have done much within the last few years to increase our knowledge of the treasures Japan has to yield to science in that department. Locusts are often destructive, and mosquitoes are a great pest. Bees, the silkworm, and the wax-insect are, however, highly appreciated.

There are several kinds of lizards, a great variety of frogs, seven or eight snakes, including a deadly *cerastes*, and two or three kinds of tortoise. Edible turtles abound in the Bonins. The crustaceans are numerous and interesting, and of fish there is extraordinary variety, especially of marine species. Oysters are excellent and in great quantity, and Americans can revel in clam chowder. Cuttle-fish often rival the monsters described by Victor Hugo.

Mr. Blakiston, who has given careful attention to the subject, notes that Japan contains, besides a peculiar fauna, other elements of a tropical and Eurasian character. He proposes to account for the first imported element, reptiles, insects, and bats, by the application of Darwin's ingenious supposition that drifted ancestors might reach such an island home through the aid of such a current as the Black Stream. The Eurasian larger mammalian element might reach Japan, Mr. Blakiston supposes, by the freezing over of the Tsugaru channel, which seems quite a reasonable idea. The fauna of the northern island Yesso thus stops abruptly at the channel which separates it from the rest of Japan ; and while many of the birds found on the mainland are peculiar to Japan, those found in Yesso are often identical with Siberio-Chinese species of the Asiatic continent.

As to the Human members of the fauna, there are two well-marked races—the Japanese proper and the Ainos in Yesso, of whom there are only some ten thousand surviving. The latter, in spite of a great deal of crude writing on the subject, cannot show any clear claim to be considered the aborigines, are not necessarily older in their occupancy than the Japanese themselves, and were never very numerous. There is no evidence that they were ever greatly different from what they are now, and it may be considered tolerably certain that they are an unimportant element in estimating the " pre-historic " traces of human life in Japan, which have a much closer relation to the present Japanese race. The Ainos have a language of their own, and are indeed in a sense anatomically distinct from the Japanese ; but of the so-called Ainos a large proportion, through inter-marriage probably, are almost undistinguishable from them, except by acquired language and' customs. Some of them are rather hairy.

As to the ethnological affinities of the Japanese, nothing is as yet very certain, and mere speculation is of no avail. They answer to that general conception most of us have formed of Mongoloi nations, but what a Mongol is exactly I do not pretend to know, and to call another race Mongoloid is only to deepen our ignorance immensely.

According to far-Eastern cosmography there are six points of the compass, the zenith and nadir very logically being added to those with which we are familiar. With charming completeness and symmetry science, aided by tradition, has provided a theory of original migration from each one of those six points ; viz., the Soil (Buddhist view); America ; China or Accadia ; Africa, or the Malayan peninsula, or the Southern Isles of the Pacific ; Saghalien or Kamtschatka ; the Celestial Regions of the Sun.

Practically there is now great apparent homogeneity of race—excluding the small gipsy-like tribe of Ainos—throughout the empire. I believe, however, that, as in Scotland, France, and Spain, there are faint traces of a long past fusion of once distinct ethnic types, which further study might yet clearly elucidate. The Japanese, in short, are a race of as yet unknown origin, comprising some thirty-seven millions speaking one language, of fair skinned, black-haired, pig-eyed, lithe, bright, good-humoured, revengeful, courteous, flighty, intensely pugnacious little people, who tell you they came originally from heaven, and I sincerely hope they will all get back again.

CHAPTER II.

First Impressions of Yokohama.

Tropical Fruits and Icy Decks—An Economical Lighthouse—Japanese Horror of Paint—Human Vultures—Yokohama and Its People—A Mushroom Settlement—Bird's-eye View—No Loafers—Human Hansoms—Building Stone—Straw Clothing—Tribute to " Tootsicums "— A Motley Crowd.

THE pale yellow bananas, so like a mixture of honey and mealy potatoes, and the pine apples with their bluish green leaves, covered with peachy bloom, and their golden, ruby-tipped juicy scales, of which we thirsty travellers had laid in such liberal stores at Singapore and Hong Kong—which had long hung under the awning in hospitable but fast diminishing festoons— have passed away as a sweet vision of the sunny tropics.

We have been steaming steadily now for a day or two, through a pale yellow sea, the colour of which, we are told, is due to the mud-laden waters of that euphonious stream, the Yang-tsze-keang ; the male passengers had given up their garments of white duck and were now—all but blue noses and red ears—encased in the thickest coats or cloaks they could fish out of their mouldy trunks ; for on these chill mornings in the end of February, when the daily scrubbing of the decks takes place, the salt water from the hose at once freezes hard on the clean planks, making a rather too slippery morning promenade. We are now in the latitude of Japan, and after two months'

tedious pilgrimage, a day or two more and our weary
journey will be at an end, and Japan, of which we have
longingly dreamed so often, will be once and forever a
genuine possession of our minds !

We have taken a **V** shaped course, whose angle almost
touches the equator, and in the short space of sixty days
have experienced, twice over, nearly all the changes the
thermometer can indicate to us.

On the third of March we passed on our starboard side
Iwoga shima *(shima* means island), an active volcano,
which was smòking away very vigorously from various
crevices that seamed its dark sides.   At night it forms an
inexpensive lighthouse of the first order.   Its chief peak
was said in the chart to be 2469 feet high, but it struck me
as being probably a good deal less in height, a statement
which, of course, in the case of an active volcano does not
in the least imply inaccuracy on the part of former
observers.

Faint through combined distance and haze hung in
the air on the landward side, dreamy visions of fawn-
tinted mountains patched with bright green, which we
knew to be at last the land of our aims and hopes.   As
we entered the great and busy Bay of Yedo, a thick haze
hung over all things, blending in one whitey grey sea and
land and sky.   We hailed the lighthouse which at once
gives a sign to the approaching visitor of an alert and
advancing civilisation ; got a pilot on board and were soon
steaming gently up into Yokohama harbour through fleets
of white-sailed junks and sanpans or small rowing-boats.
Unlike those of China, they are usually unpainted, and
we soon found this horror of paint to be almost a religious

principle with Japanese of the old school, of which more anon. The modern spirit, however, which in Japan is not always very "æsthetic," revels in *penki*, and can hardly get enough of it, either as to quantity or variety, laid on houses and furniture.

A Chinaman loves to have an ever unwinking eye painted on the prow of his sanpan, and his standard joke is to explain to the enquiring stranger, with combined simplicity and terseness, " no got eye, no can see," and in the progressive style of rhetoric dearly loved by Confucius and his followers, he adds, demurely—"no can see, no can go." Now, curiously enough, the Egyptians long ago had a similar eye—that of Horus—similarly placed on the prow of their galleys. In Japan, however, in place of an eye—which I have never seen there—a clever zoological compromise between an eel and a snake is painted in red, chiefly, at the bow, and this is usually the only trace of paint to be seen on the craft.

As we drew nearer our intended place of anchorage the boats seemed to be drawn towards us by something almost like magnetic attraction. We could see them hastening afar, with attendant splash and shout to share in the spoil, like vultures swooping down on a stranded whale.

The boatmen are exceedingly active, square-shouldered, squat little fellows with sinewy limbs ; as a rule, less tawny than I had expected to find them, although some of them were pretty dark-skinned. As their bodies were veiled with very little else than a damask-like pattern, in two or perhaps three colours, tattooed into their skin, one had a good opportunity of judging as to their degree of muscular development. The Japanese generally do not,

I think, like so many of the Eastern races, form good subjects for artistic representation. Neither men nor women have much of the subtle grace and impressive dignity of form and gait that in the Indian and Arab races impress the western imagination so powerfully. There are, of course, exceptions to this general fact, but after again seeing and studying other races this impression which I formed at first was greatly strengthened. Grotesque and humorous portrayal of the human form, and reflected likenesses of the same in animals was inevitably and naturally the direction in which Japanese art in relation to man had to assert itself, and in this line it has never been greatly surpassed.

Yokohama, where, of course, we arrived on a Sunday, is not a very striking place in itself—a low swamp, ditched all over at right angles with broad, shallow, tidal canals, filled with a concentrated essence of sub-tropical drainage which the sea does its humble best, twice a day, to assist the authorities in rendering tolerable ; and bridged over at very frequent intervals with unpainted wooden structures not of a very endurable character ; a town of rapid weedy growth ; choked up with closely built *hongs* or warehouses, some really fine and well-stored western shops, a good hotel or two, acres on acres of bonded and free stores, custom-houses, banks, shipping offices, poisoning grog shops, two well built churches, tiny shops of Chinese money-changers, tasteful bungalows with pretty gardens, riff-raff lodging-houses, a spacious railway station, an anchorage wide enough for all the fleets of all the nations, and above all, Fuji now gleaming in its snowy surplice like a solemn priest before the altar of God.

The foreign residences, quite home-like and tasteful, are built on the " bluff "—the sea-ward, wave-eaten margin of a gently undulating fertile plateau which marks the level of the ancient coast, and affords pleasant and tolerably healthy sites for numerous cottages and villas built when military protection was needed and afforded at the " treaty ports," and when foreign trade was much better and more hopeful than it is supposed to be now. The gardens are delightful to look at, and one sees here many plants growing openly which are quite rare in the British Isles. From the bluff you may get a good view of the native town, spread out on the reclaimed swamp of plain below, which we can also see to be bounded all round by the edge of the plateau which forms this same bluff.

We can see the busy harbour, dotted with ever-moving small craft, among which float several great ironclads of different flags, and many of the largest sized cargo, passenger steamers, and sailing vessels. Round the margin of the bay sweeps with firm geometric curve the Tokio railway and the centre of the channel is crowded with large white-winged junks, slowly making their way up with a favouring breeze to the great metropolis of the Mikado's Empire. Turning to the west, Fuji rises to a height of about 13,000 feet from behind a frowning mass of lofty dark hills which are sharply silhouetted against its dazzling snowy sides. They terminate a long rugged range which rises in the blue distance far north of Tokio.

Let us now, descending by an abrupt flight of stone

steps, or staggering down one of the steeply-graded roads
that connect the low-lying native town with the bluff, take
a peep at the streets and at the people who are moving so
actively about in them, for in Japan there are almost

no native loafers to be seen. Every
one has, or at least pretends to have,
some means of gaining a living by
industry. It is true, we shall not see
unsophisticated Japan as we might
have seen it, even here, a few years
before, but neither do we think can it
now be seen by living eye almost
anywhere in the empire, so great and
sudden and far-reaching has been the
influence of the once greatly dreaded

*Unloading a Rice Junk. By
a Japanese Artist.*

"black ships," and the lore and merchandise they brought
with them for good or ill.

Probably the first thing that strikes the new comer as
thoroughly Japanese is the *jinrikisha* or "man-power-
carriage." It is a kind of tiny hansom in which one or
two may ride, and is drawn by one man or by two,—tandem
fashion,—and not a bad means of locomotion it proves to
be if only the springs are good and the roads in tolerable
order. I have gone a continuous journey of about 500 miles
in this way, and at a most rapid rate. Those little "Pull-
man-cars," as they have been facetiously called, are used
by everybody, and are to be found everywhere throughout the country, and indeed even in some ports of
China and India. They were, however, unknown till the
"foreigners" came, and are usually said to have been
invented by an American in Yokohama. It is very

difficult to believe that an American ever did anything of the kind. Photographs may still be seen showing the first transition from the old familiar idea of the *mi-koshi* or sacred car to the more modern light carriage. It was certainly at first a vehicle of the clumsiest and most primitive kind, even when thus improved, and had no springs of any kind ; but perhaps the American "inventor" did not know about springs. They are often gaudily painted or lacquered and adorned with tragic subjects from Japanese mythology, tradition or the stage. In wet weather a hood made of a tough, almost untearable and evil-smelling oiled paper, without opening for light or ventilation, is drawn over the guest—as the hire is delicately called—while he is perhaps trundelled rapidly along in a direction quite opposite to that desired by him. Nobody, however, is supposed to lose temper on such occasions, and certainly the coolies themselves rarely do so, even when much time is lost.

On the way to the Tokio railway terminus—the word "station" is now almost Japanese—you pass a number of rather stately edifices, built generally of a soft, easily-carved pale green or marbled tuff, which has the double merit of always looking well without the meretricious adornment of paint, and of resisting fire for a long time— rarely long enough, alas! to resist the heat of those awful general conflagrations which are so common in the wooden built towns of old Japan. This lava stone also, I think, weathers much more slowly than its crumbly texture would seem to threaten, but there are many varieties. It is supposed to have been chiefly formed by the sub-marine deposit of masses of pumice stone from north-

ward flowing currents when the low-lying land was
submerged, as we know it to have once been.

When your biped in harness at last holds out with
well-feigned disgust the dirty little bit of government
paper, which is only twice his proper fare, and utters torrents of hopelessly unintelligible abuse, you look with im-
perturbable calmness over the hurrying crowds hastening
to take their railway tickets or their seats. If the day is
wet and cold, short cloth capes, often of fine broadcloth,
or little check woollen shawls are worn by the men,
while the humbler classes use tippets of plaited grass
with broad leaves, or of rushes with the pointed
ends turned out and downwards so as to shed the
rain, which it does pretty effectually. Strangely
enough, the same kind of grass coat is worn in the province of Minho, in Spain, but why this primitive-looking
garment should in Japan have long been called *mino* is a
fact which has not received any explanation.

Many of the passengers also are clad in oiled paper
waterproofs—black, dark green, or of the natural dirty-
brownish yellow colour ; while nearly all of them have
heavy clumsy paper umbrellas, gaily coloured, and often
with symbolic designs painted upon their covers. I think
they are pretty safe *curios* to send home to admiring country
cousins, but don't be too sure about anything when travelling. I bargained once for similar articles of great novelty
of appearance, while travelling in the valleys of British
Bhootan, but found that they had all been manufactured
in Glasgow, whither I was proposing to send them !

Men and women, boys and girls, all wear very short
indigo or white cotton socks hooked at the side like boots,

leaving the great toe apart from the rest in order to give hold to the latchet of the straw sandals which the peasants, artizans, and poor wear, or of the high-toothed wooden pattens which the better-off clumsily clatter about in. They are of various patterns, some resembling our clogs, others are lacquered and of rather elegant design. The noise of the wood-shod feet of passengers emerging from an arriving train reminds one of a regiment of cavalry passing. Other and sweeter associations seem to have been sometimes re-called. I remember reading a love song, in which the heart of a sighing swain is made to leap with tender joy as the dear little tootsicums of his adored one come " pit-a-pat, pit-a-pat!" down the alley. I think that poet had genuine imagination.

Rarely, very rarely now (1873), you may see a depressed and mournful *samurai*, or knight of the two-swords, with

basin - shaped hat, the prominent and richly-adorned hilt of his keen razor-like blade sticking out from his silken girdle, with which in better days he had ever been ready to maintain the honour of his lord ; and beside it, cross - wise, another little one almost like a stiletto, with which he was even now ready in a moment to defend his own, in the saddest and, to us westerns, strangest way. Few out of Japan have any idea of the distress that multitudes of those often unwise, but in many respects cultured, noble, and high-minded men have had to endure before they could bring themselves to part with a trusty weapon, which had been notched and bent in

A Samurai.

many a fray, to some cold *curio* hunter. Those
knights of the so recent feudal age of Japan are
fast falling into .other ways, hiring themselves out
as common servants, or going, often rashly, with
their slender savings into mean trade. What an un-
worked mine is here for the future Walter Scott of Japan ;
stores of living feudal romances in this prosaic nineteenth
century of ours !

The costumes of the people in this evidently transi-
tional period, are very amusing and suggestive. The
most original combinations of Eastern and Western
ideas occur in every few yards of our progress,
more notable usually than picturesque or pleasing.
You may thus see an intelligent young fellow, perhaps
a clerk in a merchant's office, with the newest style of felt
hat from Paris or London, an antique Japanese robe of
silk, wooden pattens of great height, and a common bath-
towel carefully wound around his neck for a comforter ;
if the gilded price ticket happens to remain on it, so much
the more ornamental ! It was not at the time of which I
speak at all unusual to see some important official going
to dine in full dress—that is, with European " claw-ham-
mer coat " and white kid gloves, while his feet were shod
with pattens ; or you might meet a thoroughly respectable citizen of weight and presence going along the principal streets on a hot day in New European " store-
clothes," with nether limbs enveloped only in a cool white
cotton garment, not usually made visible to the general
public. Varieties of dress tend to become badges indicative of business or profession, and it has been interesting
to watch the crystallising process going on here, the very

same one by which our English wigs of different periods are like fossils indicating, say, the chronological strata in which particular offices had their origin. The government officials of inferior grades delight in a cap of western shape, the marines dress like our British marines, the pupils of the Imperial College of Engineering wear Scotch bonnets, while the medical students in the University appear in those neat dark blue caps which adorn the crania of peripatetic German bands in our country.

The country people, farmers or rural shop-keepers, have the most characteristic appearance, and are most interesting to visitors. They struck me as being considerably less in stature than the denizens of the towns, an impression which their stoop and sandalled feet does not wholly account for. In rain and in sunshine the rustics, who are always a target for city witlings everywhere, wear odd-looking, palm-leaf hats a yard or thereabouts in diameter, and in wet weather they thatch themselves in the peculiar grass overcoat I have already mentioned, which makes them look like so many hedgehogs. The country women, never very remarkable for beauty, are not seen at their best when staring and grinning with widely-open mouths as the foreign barbarians pass, more especially when their teeth are duly blackened after marriage. They wear light blue figured cotton handkerchiefs, tied in a clumsy knot round their heads. The young girls delight in scarlet, or other bright-coloured underskirts.

I suppose there may be about twenty millions of those humble, good-natured toilers in the fields, and civilization is slowly but very surely reaching them too. It is curious to notice how those simple people bow profoundly to the gold-laced guard before they can presume to enter the car beside which he seems to stand sentry. Sometimes the unsophisticated traveller would leave his pattens outside on the platform, as he had been wont courteously to do on entering a house, expecting to find them lying there when he should arrive at his destination!

There is a fair sprinkling in the crowd of fat, prosperous Chinamen, who somehow contrive to handle most of the money which passes out from or into Japan, of English or American "mashers" of both sexes doing the tour round the world, and getting done pretty well themselves; and not a few smart-looking, elegantly dressed Japanese, with gold chains of rather extravagant dimensions, who have exhausted the resources of European civilization, mastered all philosophies, sciences, and religions, and now come back to their countrymen, perhaps to teach what they be-lieve—if they believe anything at all.

CHAPTER III.

A Run on the Tokio Railway.

Granny and the Engine—A Solid Road—Lady Smokers—Paddy Fields and Egrets—Fuji, the Peerless Mountain—A Clerical Cyclist—Quiet Resting Places—An Unpicturesque Metropolis—Silent Streets—Musical Groans.

 O we are at last to ride to Yedo in a railway train! While we are waiting on the platform a group of most diminutive country women, who have come from afar to witness the wonders of the treaty port, are gazing with mingled awe and admiration on a handsome little engine gleaming with burnished brass, which is engaged in making up the train for Tokio.   One of them, who is very old and garrulous, and who speaks with a quaint *patois*, calls it a *jokisen* (steam-ship), and whenever it approaches she runs off screaming and laughing alternately, like the simple old girl she is! *O baa san* (granny) has evidently just seen the railway train for the first time.   It is rather wonderful, however, to observe how stolidly the majority of the people seem to accept and appropriate the new ideas and appliances from the west as mere matters of course.   Still there remains in the steam engine for a long

time a great fascination for the Japanese mind. The toy-
shops are full of pictures in which a railway train is the
central object of attraction, and an intelligent medical
student from the country told me with great glee, that he
had secured lodgings from which he could see the trains
glide past every day.

The line is now a double one, and passenger trains of
some eight or ten carriages, first, second, and third classes,
leave either terminus every hour or so.

The traffic is not only considerable, but the return on
the mileage is said to be unusually good. The line, constructed by British engineers, is, on the testimony of a
distinguished American railway constructor, "as firm as a
rock"; the gauge is somewhat narrower than the usual
narrow British guage; the engines are of British build,
somewhat too light, perhaps, but effective and extremely
elegant in appearance, while the carriages, with the exception of those in the third class, have the seats arranged
lengthwise, like our tramway cars. The first class cars
are sub-divided into three small compartments, the central one opening into the other two. Entrance is made
as in American cars, from either end of the carriage, but
the platform is narrow. Semaphore signals are used on
the block system, somewhat imperfectly carried out, it
seemed to me. The intermediate stations are very well
planned and built, and iron foot-bridges cross the track,
which is fenced in all the way along. There have been
very few railway casualties of any kind—omitting, of
course, deliberate suicides, which are painfully common—
and hardly one of those accidents shows any special
tendency to carelessness or inefficiency on the part of

Japanese officials or workmen. Already the railways in the country have begun to work a social revolution, more strongly cementing the family already united so closely, bringing communities into closer and more frequent contact, developing pilgrimages to obscure shrines, and stimulating commerce in farm produce. Above all, railway precision is communicating a notion of the importance of the minuter divisions of time, especially in relation to business appointments, for not long ago the twelve periods of two hours into which the day was divided was the only diurnal division of time met with in daily life.

Little square green cushions are supplied for about a penny a run, which are a great convenience to third-class passengers not blessed with much adipose tissue.

After our arrival in Yokohama we lost little time in getting our luggage cleared by the custom-house authorities, whom we found stringent in their examination, but civil. We then made our way in a train of jinrikishas to the terminus of the railway for Tokio. The company of our fellow-travellers would have been much more agreeable without the odious and depressing stink of coarse and ill-flavoured tobacco which filled the compartment. The pipe-bowl is fortunately very small, but its employment is just all the more frequent. Handsomely dressed and, I believe, quite respectable young girls, leaving their pattens on the floor, tucked up their white-stockinged feet on the matted seats, and proceeded to puff away with great solemnity and sweetness. The conversation seemed to consist chiefly of ejaculations and puffs of smoke, and certainly to one who had only acquired certain phrases and a few useful vocabularies on the voyage out, could not possibly prove either intelligible or interesting. The first station on the way is Kanagawa. Commodore Perry, of the United States, made his treaty—the first one entered into with western foreigners in recent times after long centuries of seclusion—in 1854, at the then miserable little fishing village of Yokohama or Cross Strand. It was thought by the timid Japanese authorities to be safely separated by a wide and barren marine swamp from the metropolis at the head of the Bay of Yedo. In 1859, however, Sir Rutherford Alcock and the Hon. Townsend Harris, ministers of the United States, gained à concession in Kanagawa, across the swamp, and three miles nearer the Shogun's great city of Tokio, and here practically modern foreign relations with Japan may be said to have begun. For various reasons Yokohama regained its ground, and Kanagawa is now little but a low and populous suburb of Yokohama, although the official documents of the British Government still, somewhat strangely for so radical a country, continue to give Kanagawa its full dignity. Leaving it to its full but fruitless enjoyment, we dash through a cutting, past a series of beautifully wooded eminences, and are out into the open country.

It seems to be one vast fertile plain of moist paddy fields, laid out in small squares, like the map of the United States, through which a few snowy-plumed egrets may be seen stalking, and on our right, seen through a sombre fringe of dark green pines, lies, spread out, the grand Bay, through whose foam-flecked azure fleets of white-sailed junks are sawing their way.

Away beyond rich loamy fields of leeks and garlic, rise

steeply-sloping wooded bluffs of no great height, whose bosky sides are dotted with unpainted Shinto or vermillion-coloured Buddhist shrines, and stained with sweet patches of pale rose-coloured early plum blossom ; while far above these rise the dark masses of the Oyama range, crowned with the lofty truncated cone of Fuji, still white with the winter's snow, and matchless in the delicate grace of its almost flawless curves. There is a tradition, still widely believed in Japan, that it bursts from the solid earth in a single night, making by way of compensation a great gap in the land which became the magnificent fresh-water lake Biwa, of which we shall hear again. One cannot refrain from speaking and thinking of Fuji while living anywhere almost within sixty miles of it. It forces itself upon one's notice, and is always beautiful from any point of view and under almost any sky.

Two German scientists give its height,—Mr. Knipping at twelve thousand two hundred and thirty-four English feet, and Dr. Rein at twelve thousand two hundred and eighty-seven feet. My brother-in-law, Mr. R. Stewart, of the Imperial Japanese survey, found it by his measurement to be twelve thousand three hundred and sixty-five feet. Messrs. Satow and Hawes mention that the Japanese suppose that the sand brought down during the day by the pilgrims goes up again at night !

At Kawasaki the river is spanned by a fine iron viaduct of great length, and the plain which seems to have been formed as a delta (in the wider sense of the word) is some twelve or fourteen miles broad where the railway crosses. The lower part of it was a few years ago flooded over a very large area, with disastrous results.

There are numerous pretty little villages and quiet hamlets on the way to Tokio which seem to be mostly the abodes of fishermen, workers in straw, or shopkeepers dependent on the simple wants of an agricultural population. Here and there we get a glimpse through its bordering pine trees of a famous imperial road,—the Tokaido,—dusty and ill kept, as most roads in Japan are. You cannot read very much of a good old romance without finding yourself "located," as Yankees say, on some part of this great thoroughfare, or at least on one similar to it, where so much of the romantic life and knightly activity of the ancient empire found its expression. But much of its glory departed after the Shogun fell, and the railway has since arisen and shrieked its doom along with that of feudal Japan. It forms still a pleasant drive, and one esteemed clerical friend *cycles* it with great gusto even in the dustiest weather.

On the railway you pass several populous villages with well-managed stations, through the turnstiles of which crowds are all day coming and going, to worship at some famous or family shrine, or to do business of some kind ; priests of every Buddhist sect ; pilgrims clad in white, with tinkling bells; fussy western-dressed officials or foreign sportsmen with gun, bag, passport—and whisky flask. Sometimes a little rural graveyard, with grey stones, lichened o'er with creamy or orange, pale pink or dark brown growths, reminds us of quiet holy spots amidst the hills of dear old Scotland.

Peaceful farm steadings with steep-thatched roofs

are embosomed, even at this early season, in dense clumps of dark green foliage (of the previous summer), through which feathery sprays of the lighter-tinted bamboo rise with bold curve, and droop towards earth again in a graceful sweep. The deep rosy pink of the frequent plum tree gives a warm summer-like blush to the woods, and the vegetable gardens are even now by no means lacking in rich young verdure of the most varied forms and tints.

As we draw near the Mikado's capital, bluffs, similar to those we left behind us at Yokohama, draw in towards the shore, showing well the water-worn margin of the old upraised sea-coast which bounded the bay when much of the great plain still lay under its blue waters.

Near the point where the railway touches it again lies an old shell-heap which has excited a good deal of heated discussion as to its antiquity. Others are still in course of formation of a more modern type, a few miles nearer the city. After some fifty minutes run over a smooth road, we pass at length through a lofty and leaky cutting, alongside of the Tokaido (which here becomes a busy street, full of vivid pictures of Japanese life and manners), into Tokio. The line sweeps along the curve of the Bay on an embankment, from which you view the line of rude forts, built by the aid of French military engineers, but now superseded by one or two silent " krupps " which lurk among the trees somewhere about the mouth of the river. As we first approach the straggling group of mean buildings called Tokio, I must candidly confess my feeling was one of great surprise and disappointment.

Imagine a grey expanse of dirty sea-water, dotted with dirty-looking grey junks, and bounded by a grey wilderness of dirty shingle, covering dingy wooden houses, with nothing to relieve the eye, save here and there, at great. intervals, a bosky clump of trees rising from a fragment of the old higher coast-line I have already mentioned, and shading the lofty tent-like tiled roof of a colossal temple. This wide waste of wooden structures seems in the thin smoky haze to merge into the horizon, while the sky-line is broken by a straggling big chimney or two which honestly do their best, by intermittently belching forth funereal plumes of hideously black smoke, to impart to this stagnant capital a commercial appearance.

But is this quiet, sleepy-looking county town on a large scale Yedo, "the largest city in the world" of our infallible school geographies?   Certainly its 700,000 or so of in-habitants contrive to keep themselves wonderfully well out of observation.   The population has, indeed, been often stated at a much higher figure than I have just given, and an important Japanese official recently referred in public to the city as containing a million of inhabitants. Complete reliance, I am fully persuaded, cannot be given to the statistics on this point ; but even those pro-perly do not refer to the city itself as containing a million of people, but to the municipal district administered by the Tokio *fu*, which is much more extensive than the city and includes some islands far out at sea.

I think I have never been in any city—always excepting, of course, dear little St. Andrews—whose citizens made so little noise—a fact which can only be partly explained by the vastness of the area over which it is spread, and by the great network of broad canals connecting the moats of the castle with the bay itself, an arrangement which has to a large extent rendered cartage unnecessary. The two-wheeled carts in use are very primitive in structure. They are usually drawn by two men, in slight attire, aided by other two or more pushing behind. They move very rapidly along, as you will find if you try to keep pace with them, in long swinging steps, to the accompaniment of a shrill "hoich! how!" which, in every variety of tone and key, breaks the almost painful stillness of the thoroughfares. In the suburbs chiefly may be also seen great trains of bullock carts and of heavy-laden pack-horses, which are chiefly used for far inland and mountain traffic.

Near the station, which is well built, there is a fine Japanese bank built of variegated volcanic stone, a stone arched bridge, rows of stores, and stretching away through the centre of the city lies the Tori or chief boulevard, built of stucco covered brick.

Light tramway cars now run from one end of the city to the other at very moderate fares, and are largely patronised, especially by artizans and shopkeepers, who seem all to be after business of some kind. This once fine street is, however, losing its characteristic regularity ; a wretched pavement of common red bricks trips up the pedestrian clattering along in his wooden pattens.

When we arrived in the spring of 1874, its double row of pines, acacias, and plum trees—which latter were in full bloom—formed a sight of rare and touching beauty in the very heart of so large and populous a city.

CHAPTER IV.

Street Scenes.

Shadow Pictures—Street Names—Æsthetic Mud-pies—Kite Flying—A Hint for Arctic Explorers—Fishy Conduct of an English Professor—The Queen's English—A Japanese Crowd—A Baby Cook Shop.

A GREAT deal of Japanese life is passed in the streets, and can best be seen there. In the good times for which old-fashioned Japanese people sigh, much more of the domestic doings were visible to the public than would now be considered comely or proper; but at all events there is little of that morbid concealment of private life which is so marked a feature in other Eastern countries. The houses are open from floor to roof in warm weather, and concealment is nearly impossible; and at night, when the paper windows are drawn closely together, you may see many a painful tragedy or side-splitting comedy enacted in shadow by the unconscious inmates. Japanese caricaturists have, indeed, not been slow to seize and utilize this salient feature in the national life, and comic silhouettes or shadow-pictures are to be seen in any print-shop or bookseller's window.

The cities of Tokio and Osaka are intersected with canals, and the bridges which cross them are necessarily numerous. They are often named in a very grand and poetical style: the "Bridge of Eternal Life," the "Fairy Assembly Bridge," and so on. A blind alley is called a

" bag street." So great is the love of nature amongst the people of Japan, that it is said some two-thirds of the streets in Tokio are named after natural objects; a tendency which is amply illustrated by the whole decorative art of the country. Mr. Griffis has pointed out that great battlefields—and Japan has not been without them—are not commemorated in this way, nor do we find many names of heroes handed down to an admiring posterity in association with particular streets; although popular wrestlers and fencing masters, priests and nuns, and one famous English pilot (Will Adams), have been thus immortalised.

Passing along "Shipway Street" into "Lance and Arrow Street," let us see what we can find to interest, amuse, and instruct us.

As we go out by the garden-gate, our cook's little girl (we have all men cooks here), *O Tsuru*, or Miss Crane, as she is called, is busy making, not mud pies, but a pretty little artificial garden, with bits of rock arranged with sloping strata, as in nature; a rounded mountain, furrowed as if by centuries of rainfall, with tidy, tasteful walks, shaded by gnarled twigs of pine, and brightened with cleverly contrasted half-open buds of azaleas of various tints. A few blades of bamboo grass, curved by careful art, complete a very pleasing little landscape, which occupies just about one foot square! It is common to speak of such manifestations of art-feeling in Japan as instinctive. I am not sure that I know what is meant by the term. I can understand, however, that certain ancestral tendencies and habits may be repeated, and in favourable circumstances emphasized in the offspring.

In regard to Japan, this almost unerring art-sense is demonstrably of comparatively recent origin, and was due primarily to foreign teaching. Art education of a most effective but informal kind, through diffusion of cheap illustrated books, has since then helped to develop taste for natural beauty, which had, of course, some existence before it could be developed.

We are recalled from this digression by strange whirring sounds high up in the air, which remind us of the æolian harp. They are caused by "singing kites," which are of all shapes: such as a baby in Japanese long clothes, an eagle with pinions expanded and tail spread out, the hideous face of an ogre, or they may assume the form of a gaudy flower, or of a swallow-tailed butterfly. They are kept steady by two long tails, one at each of the lower corners; and the radiant juvenile who is the happy possessor of a good high-flyer, manages it deftly, sending it up as far as his store of cord will permit without moving more than a yard or two from his starting point. Great is the good nature shown by the *jinrikisha* men, as I have witnessed with ever-increasing wonder when on my professional rounds, if their faces are brought into sharp and sudden contact with kite-strings. Much dexterity is shown by passers-by in avoiding contact by a timely duck, and by the kite-flyers also in piloting the strings; but whenever an accident occurs, however annoying it would be to us, it seems rather rarely to evoke even a frown, far less an angry word, or *theological* recrimination.

It is reported that in ancient times large kites were used to aid spies in estimating the forces of the enemy, just as among ourselves balloons have been used in modern warfare. A law existed in Tokio which enacted that kites were not to be made larger than a certain moderate size, the fear being that the Shogun's castle might be inspected from the city by conspirators. One of the most pleasing contributions by a medical writer in Japan (alas! no more) to the *Japan Weekly Mail*, describes a blind boy flying a kite in Tokio :—"Who shall describe the sight—who adequately pourtray our blind boy, as he stands with body bent forward and quivering with delight, as the kite tugs and strains to get away—his poor lustreless eyes widely distended, his cheeks flushed, his lips parted and trembling with excitement, and every involuntary muscle of his hands in action, as his fingers play with the string, along which he has surely projected his whole soul to the toy amongst the clouds? 'Hi! Hi! Stand aside!' 'It is of no use, my friends with the *norimon* (sedan-chair), you address yourselves to a mere outline of a boy ; the substance is far away above you at the end of that string, and cannot hear, call you never so loudly.'"

On a certain day in the year, many huge, brightly-coloured objects may be seen floating, or rather wobbling over the city. They represent enormous carp-fish, are made of thin painted cloth, and are hollow, so that the wind fills them and gives them a very lively appearance. They usually indicate the happy arrival during the preceding year of a male child, but are displayed where a family contains boys, though none of them may be recently born.

A learned English professor in Tokio somewhat

scandalised his portentously dignified colleagues in the
university precincts, by displaying over his door a very
large specimen in commemoration of his first-born. It
defied the breezes of Japan, and the more potent sneers of
his less fortunate fellows, for an unusually long period.

Woman Dyeing. (Japanese Sketch.)

In many quiet by-
streets you may see
women staining or
dyeing cloth in the
open air. It is a very
simple process, and
no attempt is made
to produce "fast"
colours. Chemicals
are used also to ex-
tract the colour in
patterns.

It is interesting to
peep into the various
shops as we pass along the busy thoroughfare. The
floors are covered with a fine kind of grass matting,
padded underneath, and you have to take off your shoes
respectfully, or apologize for not doing so, which latter
form has come to be painfully common amongst "barbarians" from the West. There are all kinds of European
nick-nacks for sale, or more frequently clever imitations
of them ; ready-made clothes of latest Parisian fashion,
fire-engines, patent medicines, scientific apparatus, great
numbers of a curious new stove invented by a Japanese,
made of a frothy kind of glassy lava, the iron door
of which is very appropriately fitted with a common

wooden knob! Paisley shawls and Brussels carpets; Bass's beer and Epps's cocoa; ancient suits of armour; decanonised Buddhist saints, and rusty American sewing machines.

The Japanese merchant is not above taking lessons from the despised "hairy foreigner," and there are some rare specimens of the Queen's English to be found now and again in this realm of literature. Here is a veritable one, not at all improved for the sake of effect :—

NOTICE.
SHOE MANUFACTURER.
DESIGN AT ANY CHOICE.

The undersigned being engaged long and succeeded with their capacity at shoe factory of Isekats, in Tokio; it is now established in my liability at undermentioned lot all furnishment will be attended in moderate term with good quality.

An order is acceptable, in receive a post, being called upon the measure and it will be forwarded in furnish.

U. INOYA,
No. 206, 5th St. Motomachi.

When the foreigner, who is a new arrival, stands for a little at a shop window, he is sure to be immediately surrounded by a rather big crowd, eager to hear his blunders in the language, and to observe how skilfully the wily vendor of *curios* eases him of his paper money. I have often thought what a boon it might be to the ethnologist were he able by some invisible and instantaneous process to secure facial types by multi-photographs like those with which Mr. Dalton has recently so interested the scientific world. Well, after all, is that not just what caricaturists like Leech and Du Maurier, Caldecott and Ralston have done for us in regard to the types of English society? No limited number of photographs could give us a better idea cf Tommy Atkins than Ralston's few strokes convey. And so too one might with skill and true artistic intuition ideally combine the untutored conceptions of their race left by native artists.

Look around at the calm unsmiling and stolidly attentive faces which compose the crowd. First there is a row of little girls, each with a very uninteresting baby, carried pick-a-back, and fastened by a kind of girdle used specially for that purpose. The wretched little urchin is toasted in the sun all day, and when asleep, as it usually is, its poor little noddle hangs over just like a drooping poppy bud, and is jerked helplessly about with every motion of the playful nurse. Japanese children are not usually weaned till about four years of age, and very often not then. The youngest children have their heads carefully shaved all over, while those a little older have tassel-like portions hanging down at the " four corners," or have a monk-like fringe left all round the shaven pate.

I long ago came to the conclusion that these various styles of hair-cutting are clearly survivals from the castes of Hinduism, the notion of which symbolism Buddhism, however improbable it may appear at first sight, brought over from India to the Far East. There are numerous examples of a similar kind which cannot be appropriately brought forward in this chapter.

Close beside us there is a group of very slovenly infantry soldiers, with coal-scuttle shakoes, unbrushed clothes, and badly made foreign shoes, trodden down at the heels. Their faces are flushed with wine ; they seem disposed to be rude, and carry side arms which they are not at all unwilling to use readily when crossed in any way. At a short distance, a pair of gentlemanly and substantial-looking *gens d'armes*, with revolvers and sabres, are keeping calm eyes on the soldiers. A pair of enormous black spectacles, accompanying a squat little policeman in dark blue, with naval cap adorned with white cotton sun-shade, and what looks like a window roller under his arm, are glaring fiercely at the crowd, and giving emphasis to the frequent gruff command in Japanese to " move on there !"

We obey the order meekly, to the shopkeeper's disgust, and turn our eyes to the street again, which is crowded with jinrikishas, cavalry, ricketty 'busses of the most primitive construction ; neat and well-appointed tramway cars ; a rare *kago* or sedan chair, with a yellow flag carried in front, denoting that a case of cholera or small-pox is

Japanese Waterman.

being conveyed to the hospital ; watermen with buckets of water, "full of holes," like Paddy's stocking, which divide the misery of dormant dust into one of flying dust, *plus* mud. These men carry their load by means of a pole laid across the shoulder.

To each end of the pole a bucket is attached, but the
originality of the Japanese mode of distributing
the burden is this—a shorter pole is placed across
the other shoulder nearly at right angles to the long
pole, and one end of it is used to lever up the weight on
one side, the other end being grasped by the free hand. The
weight is thus thrown more evenly over both sides of the
body. Immense loads are carried in this way, and with
great agility, as a certain springiness which aids quick
walking, is thus imparted.

A little further along, at a point where the main street
forks, a great display of some kind is being made. A
newly-finished building is gaily decorated with flowers
and flags—not the uniform glare of turkey red with which
the British householder lavishly resolves to let the world
know he wishes to be thought happy on some festive
occasion, not that, but a really graceful design of great
simplicity. Below the gay streamers, green nodding
plumes of bamboo and dark pine branches brightened
with festoons of golden oranges, rises a stately pyramid of
brand new straw-covered tubs of rice-beer, which a thirsty
public are invited for the day to partake of freely to their
heart's content. It is a shop-opening, and in this way
luck and the good wishes of the community are hoped
for by the enterprising merchant. A good-humoured
crowd is elbowing its way across the pavement in two
streams ; one pale and rather solemn, yet eager-eyed with
some pleasures of hope beaming on their faces ; the other
flushed, facetious, and rather drowsy.

Here is something which, I think, is sure to interest a
new comer. It is a peripatetic cook-shop for children, and

consists of two long complicated lacquer-boxes, slung at the ends of a strong pole, and laid across the shoulders in the manner already described. The bearer of the beneficent burden stops at the corner where the crowd is, sets his little charcoal oven fire going in a trice, and very soon the clean copper plate which forms the oven is quite hot enough to begin business with. A large bowl of sweet paste, in a fluid state, forms the chief part of his stock. There is soon a group of hungry children—and in Japan, as elsewhere, children are always hungry—round the tiny stall, purchasing little saucers full of the enticing stuff. Each pours his purchase out on the heated copper, forming such shapes as his own taste or ingenuity may devise, and in an instant it is hard, crisp and brown, to be scraped off in due time by means of a little spoon with which the vendor supplies them. It is really a great treat to watch the children at this useful pastime ; the very youngest managing his or her property most expertly, and all doing their work quietly, courteously and very methodically, with amazingly little bumping, driving or brawling. These itinerant cooks are usually called letter-toasters *(mon ji yaki)*, because in old times they formed with their paste Chinese characters. The thirty odd thousand of those useful symbols of thought, did not however present sufficient variety for the juveniles of Japan.

A greater genius still has since stepped upon this mundane scene. But here I feel it would be almost profane to attempt to improve on a description by the late Dr. Purcell of the English Legation, which appeared many years ago in the columns of the *Japan Mail* :—" The *Ameya* combines painting and modelling together. He

carries about with him his studio and appliances, and is
prepared to execute any order, be it never so difficult.
He'll stick you a bit of his tenacious barley gluten on a
bamboo joint ; and puff—f—f—f—it's a white glistening
balloon—pinch it in at the middle, fashion off the mouth,
draw out a bit for a cord, wind it quickly twice round,
and back again, tie it into a bow knot, and you have as
well-shaped a gourd in a few moments as nature ever took
months to produce. 'Please, sir ! I want a couple of rats
nibbling a bag of barley.' Ah ! My chubby little master,
that'll surely puzzle him you think. Not a bit of it. He
does not even stop to consider how it is to be set about,
but takes in a twinkling out of drawer No. 2, a lump of
his plastic material of just the proper size. This he
kneads, and rolls up again, and when of the right consist-
ency dusts it with rice flower, to prevent it clinging to his
fingers, and then, giving it a pyramidal shape, pinches out
a bit at each side of the apex, snips out with scissors a
pair of ears, lengthens out the snout, pulls out a tail a-
piece, fashions the cone in the middle into a bag, a couple
of dots for the eyes of the rats, a streak of red paint
underneath them, a bar of blue below that again, a puff of
gold dust and—'Now my little boy, where's your coin?
Your rats are finished.'

"To try and puzzle the old artist by devising difficult
commissions for him to execute, is a favourite game with
the youngsters. He is equal to any call on his ingenuity,
however, whether he be required to fashion a monkey
swinging by one hand from a branch, whilst it encircles a
little one with its disengaged arm ; a pair of rats in deadly
combat with their tails as weapons ; or a frog on its hind

legs, daintily pointing his toes and shading himself from the sun under a mushroom which he uses as an umbrella : —no flight of imagination seems too high for him. The thought once conceived, his execution of it is marvellously rapid."

I have often watched artists of this kind, and the above description is very true to fact. Sometimes the *ameya* indulges in loftier flights by way of advertisement, and I saw one quickly fashion a bouquet of bright coloured flowers and golden cereals, of some artistic merit apart from the narrow limitations the vehicle imposed on his skill.

Another very modest class of artists may be seen seated on the curb - stones, offering to dash off fine sepia, indian ink or water colour drawings—often with much grace and felicity—for little more than the price of the paper ; while a third set are engaged in cutting out of boxwood private seals in the ancient Chinese characters just as we have our monograms. Great antiquarian interest is attached to those humble engravers, for we see there being repeated the veritable first step the Chinese took, long before the western world was yet awake, in the art of printing. The characters were first engraved singly, and the ink used in those old times was simply brick dust, mixed with water—rice water probably. Does this not carry us back to the engraved brick tablets of still earlier times? I think that possibly the discovery that one of these tablets when accidentally pressed upon left an imprint of reddish brick dust may have been the very first step in typography.

The barbers' shops are numerous in all the large towns.

D

The honest citizen loves to have a clean shave and the latest gossip, albeit the barbers recently received solemn official instructions to report to government all they might hear of an interesting nature—a regulation which gives a powerful stimulus to one's imagination regarding the capacity of government generally.   A clean shave in Japan is rather an extensive operation ; it includes a broad strip of the scalp over which is folded and knotted a column of stiffly glued hair, like a little door handle. The whole arrangement reminded me always of a Scotch curling stone.   The ears and nostrils, outside and in, are carefully scraped with the razor.   The children require a good deal of attention also, as I have already hinted, and many are the variations of style in hair dressing.   Many now adopt our western ideas as to hair cutting, and I have been consulted by a lofty official as to the best way to develope a pair of good " Dundreary " whiskers.   The usual barber's sign is our own plate and pole, but. Japanese ingenuity has far outstripped our sober knights of the scissors and razor.   The primary significance of the symbol which raises the art to the dignity of a branch of surgery has been ignored, and the pole has been looked upon simply as a vehicle for the display of gorgeous combinations of *penki* (oil paint).   In place of our simple band of tape used by the chirurgeon of old, to stanch bleeding after the proper number of ounces had been withdrawn from the patient's peccant veins, we have rings and other ornamental displays of colouring, while the flat rounded knob at the top, which the victim had to grasp may, in Japan, become a spike or even a star.

Such facts may seem too trivial to record, but to the

archæologist nothing is common which seems to throw light on the workings of the human mind as displayed in the evolution of symbolism.

From barber to beer-shop is an easy step. The national drink of Japan is a fermented decoction of rice called *sake*, of slightly intoxicating properties, and not very pleasant flavour. Wines, white and red, are now made from the juice of the grape, and English and German beer, not to mention the appropriate labels, are manufactured in Japan. Even in former days before brandy and other strong foreign drinks became naturalised a rather potent kind of spirit was distilled from rice. The wares are contained in bright clean tubs labelled with such titles as "The blooming flower ; " "Great goldfish," with suitable trade mark ; "The good luck-peony," or "The wine of three virtues," warming the skin, filling the belly, and soothing to sleep. Curiously enough, the ordinary Japanese wine-shop displays a bush (of *sugi*, a kind of cedar), as a sign, which recals our old saying, "good wine needs no bush." Whether the custom, like the use of the barber's pole, came over from the West long ago, no one can at present tell.

Here is a literally exact copy of a sign-board in the city which helps to indicate the rapid advance being made in civilization :—

A BRIEF ACCOUNT OF NINDOSHIU.

This is an intoxicating liquol made from alcohol mixed with other things and flavoured with honeysuckles flower. It has a very sweet taste and is somewhat strong, it resembles whiskey and is good for any one—It has an effect of exciting the mind and promoting the health of withered persons. In 1878 it has obtained a high reputation in the International Exhibition of Paris. Ladies and gentlemen we wish you would take a cup of it and know what we say is quite true."

Not being disposed to rank as "withered persons" just yet, we pass by to look for something else of interest. Many of the back lanes of this great city are alive with poultry. They are mostly of a small, rather elegant breed, the cocks having magnificent tail feathers, which curve gracefully. The best of them now fetch good prices from fanciers in Europe and America.

The stoats make inroads upon them at night, however, and indeed it is not unusual to meet one of these animals in a back lane, even at midday. Foxes also, from the sacredness of their claims, are allowed the run of the city, but are much more rarely seen abroad.

Here and there you find fish-shops, which add to the sale of more perishable stock, that of live gold and silver carp. Those may be seen partitioned of into separate troughs, according to price, etc., in all stages of g‚owth and development. Some may be surprised to hear that young gold-fish are almost all quite black. Many varieties have been cultivated by breeders through careful selection of promising types, and some of those varieties fetch fabulous sums—if they are only ugly enough!

I was consulted as to a disease which was spreading amongst the stock of a large salesman of carp. It had been caused by the voracity of a tiny parasite, the *Argulus foliaceus* which, almost contrary to the usual phenomena of parasitism, possesses a highly specialised and beautifully complex structure, transparent as crystal. It is one of the most beautiful objects I have ever seen in the microscope, and may be kept under observation for a long time. It has two powerful suckers by which it fastens itself to its victim, and then unsheathing a long, hollow, rapier-like probe of extreme sharpness, it drives it into the unhappy gold-fish, and thereby sucks no small advantage. It is also armed with a series of powerful hooks, and by means of its flat, fringed, oar-like limbs, it can propel itself at will from one feeding-ground to another.

The cleansing of the streets is greatly assisted by armies of large, raven-beaked crows *(Corvus japonensis, Bp.)*, and rather kingly-looking black-eared kites *(Milvus melanotis, F. & S.)* which may be seen in myriads, on a calm day, circling at a great height above the city. They have a curious guttural, tremulous cry, similar to that of the kites about Calcutta, to whose habits they very closely conform. A butcher in our vicinity used to amuse himself by throwing tit-bits to the kites, which caught them with great accuracy, although their movements were often tumultuous and clumsy. Sometimes they are caught by means of a piece of meat placed in the centre of a running loop, which is drawn tight when the bird alights. I saw one of them trapped in this way by a boy. After it had taken to flight and had gone the full length of its tether, it fell suddenly to the ground like a stone, its pinions remaining all the time fully outstretched, and its tail expanded. It remained in the same position, looking at the group that surrounded it with unabashed dignity—fallen, but as proud as Lucifer.

CHAPTER V.

Life in Tokio.

New Friends—Sir Harry Parkes—Mine Inn and its Master—A Hyper-
Calvinistic Parrot—Plague of Frogs and Students—New Mode of
"Running a Restaurant"—The "Great Workman" and his Little
Ways—Charm against Leaks—Pic-nic and Fireworks—A New Mode of
Signalling—Charm for Finding Drowned Bodies—A Japanese Tower
of Siloam—Christmas in the Far East.

N arriving in the city we were not long in
making acquaintances, our first call being
on Bishop Williams of the American Epis-
copal Church, who received us very kindly.
The Bishop—a model of scholarly Christian
modesty—is now the oldest missionary in
Japan, having arrived in 1859, at the opening
of the treaty ports.   We had an introduction, amongst
others, to Mr. Henry Dyer, Principal of the Imperial
College of Engineering, whose hospitality we enjoyed for
some time.   The college was just getting into excellent
working order, and the energetic and far-seeing Principal
was still busy carrying out schemes of enlargement, and
establishing practical workshops of all kinds affiliated to
the central institution—a plan which was afterwards extended to embrace a very large portion of the circle of
artistic and scientific industry.

Indeed, Japan had very thoroughly wakened up to her
dire need of light and leading in all such departments of

practical usefulness, and hence it became possible for able men who knew their own minds to carry out great plans for education and other things, almost by a stroke of the pen. Now, however, there are many efficient and even distinguished native young engineers in Japan, who have literally nothing to do. Time will mend this condition, perhaps ; but much capital is needed to carry out the improvements—the roads, railways, and harbours of which the government know very well the importance. Since Mr. Dyer's return to this country the college has been under the genial guidance of a distinguished scientist, Dr. Divers, and is nobly sustaining its reputation for original and genuine work.

As a loyal subject of the Queen, I paid my respects to His Excellency Sir Harry S. Parkes, whom I found very accessible, as he takes considerable interest in the philanthropic efforts of his countrymen. No one would ever suppose that Sir Harry is one of the oldest foreign residents in the Far East.

He is a fair auburn-haired, fine-looking, unmistakeably *English*, man, not very tall, just in his prime, and reminded me of George Eliot's description of Grandcourt's appearance. He has, of course, the clever little diplomatic stutter which belongs to official Englishmen generally, and knows exactly when to leave a sentence unfinished, or to wind it off in a rapid series of little inarticulate coughs, which may be interpreted in any one of half-a-dozen ways, and usually wrongly. Sir Harry, in spite of one or two errors, has been of vast service to the young Empire of New Japan, while no one has suspected him of being inattentive to the commercial interests of his own countrymen.　He is capable of taking a broad cosmopolitan view of affairs, but is essentially and typically a British minister ; and we could not have in China—where he now is—at the present crisis in her history, an officer more thoroughly alive and intelligent towards our owr interests, or more likely to serve in a broad and lasting manner the higher interests of that vast and, I believe, most friendly empire.

We soon took up our quarters in the *apology* for a hotel which then existed in the " foreign concession." *
The owner—peace be to his once rubicund visage —was an Irish-American, whom evil-tongued rumour credited with having suddenly left Shanghai, after some one had died of a dose of lead improperly administered. Apart from the absurdity of leaving such a port as Shanghai hastily, under such circumstances, as an extenuation, at least, I may be allowed honestly to testify that he was never able to hit any of the neighbours' dogs, even at short range, during my period of observation, and he used to practise pretty often—before dinner time. When he was fairly asleep, which he generally was about midday, it is fair to state that he seemed disposed to live quietly and peaceably with his guests and neighbours.　The same, however, could hardly be said of a parrot of hyper-calvinistic tendencies which he possessed, and which never seemed to sleep at all, and whose conversation on Saturday night and early on Sunday morning, when billiards and beer were in great request, was rather loud

---

* The very limited territory attached to each treaty port on which foreigners may build is so called.

than edifying. Its frequent and vigorous condemnation of the company in the strongest of pulpit language, was usually greeted with hoarse roars of drunken laughter sufficient to drive away any possibility of associating the holy day with rest and peace.

By-and-bye we succeeded in securing at an exorbitant rent a little barrack-like wooden building, erected, I think, for some French soldiers, the chief objection to which was a plague of frogs. They were " fat and full of sap," and seemed never to be happy unless when getting under one's feet. At night they kept the sour reedy swamp which was honoured with the title of " compound," vocal with their hoarse pæans. Here some doctors' apprentices, thirsting for Western lore, scented me out from afar, and would patiently appear at break of day, tapping gently at our bed-room door, or, peering in at the open front and back windows, would salute us with a very deferential *ohayo* (good morning). This ought no doubt to have been very pleasant from a social point of view, but it takes a little while to acclimatize one's self to new phases of manners. Patients soon followed in daily growing numbers, and for a long time, till my medical work had been fully organised in suitable premises, neither my wife nor I knew what privacy was. The surroundings soon told on us both pretty severely.

After several unsuccessful efforts had been made, the foreign consuls agreed to ask the Japanese government to allow a sale of the land assigned for the purpose by treaty, and we got a promise from them to do so in the following year. Meanwhile, through a Japanese Christian, we had already been able to rent the buildings of the extinct

" Cosmopolitan Restaurant," a rather pretentious edifice
seated on the bank of a romantic artificial lake.   It had to
be taken down and rebuilt on another site with many
alterations.   It is an amusing thing to hear of one in Japan
buying an eligible family residence with fine wooded
policies, and to see the stately mansion tottering along on
a platform resting on barrows, to the inspiring groans of
a body of half-naked but tattoed carpenters, while it is
followed, perhaps, by a nodding grove of solemn cypress
or gloomy pine trees ; but something like this you may
often see in Tokio.   And yet many things that seem
strange to us in Japan may have been quite familiar to
our ancestors.   In Henry II.'s time it was decreed that
the house of the individual who harbours a heretic shall
be carried out of the town and burned.

Still more remarkable is the resemblance which the
framework of an ordinary Japanese house bears to that
of an English one of the olden times.   According to the
History of the Preston Guild, English houses, like those in
Japan, were formed of a wooden framework, the interstices
of which were formed of clay mixed with straw.
Each piece of wood in the framework was usually
tenoned, fitted into a mortice, and fixed by a wooden
peg.   The framework was put together by the builder
before it was taken to the site.   The corresponding
parts were also numbered, just as we find them in Japan
at the present day, and the rest of the description fits almost
word for word.   Sir Rutherford Alcock, in his *Art and
Art Industries of Japan* (p. 16), ascribes the want of
architecture in Japan to the instability of the soil.   But
earthquakes here are not, so far as I can find, so much

more common or more severe than in Italy, where architecture, on the contrary, has always attained a very high state of development. Still, the frequency of earthquakes and their pretty general distribution over the country, may well be supposed to have had some deterrent effect, as hybrid Buddhism has in other countries reared grand edifices of a solid and abiding character.

The *daiku*, or carpenter (literally "great workman"), is usually dressed in tight pants of blue cotton, a short blouse, a girdle, blue cotton socks, and straw sandals. One is reminded here, too, of our own past, and the costume is exceedingly like that worn by what, I suppose, were Anglo-Saxon workmen about the time of the Norman conquest. The latter, as ancient tapestries illustrative of the period show, seem also to have gone about their work in a somewhat similar way to the Japanese carpenter of to-day, who uses his feet to steady the plank he is sawing, and sits down deliberately to his work. As the great toe is free, a " finger "—if the term be allowable —being made for it in the sock, a certain firmness of grasp is maintained. The *daiku* also cuts with the saw on the pull stroke, and so the blade does not buckle. This method, I believe, gives good results with fine " keyhole " and other thin and narrow saws, but for common work the weight of the body is necessary, and it is also said to be easier to saw to line by our own method.

The carpenters are reputed to be afraid of the god of metal. Certainly, they use his products rather badly. We could never, for instance, get them to put in a screwnail by any other process than driving it in by main force with a hammer It was of no use to apply the counsel the butcher gave to good Tom Pinch—"Meat must be humoured, not druv," and so right smash went the biggest screw-nail into the finest piece of wood-work.

It was amusing to see those nimble workmen, whom I had daily to superintend, running up the light scaffold-ings which are of pine, or sometimes even of flexible bam-boo. They were almost as agile as monkeys, and seemed to me to grasp with the whole foot, as hard-shoed races cannot do. Very seldom do they fall, and judging from my own experience as a surgeon, they do not often hurt themselves severely, even when falling from a consider-able height. Indeed, their great temperance—as com-pared with our own workmen—is largely the cause of their comparative immunity from severe injuries, along with the fact that few buildings are made of stone, and none are lofty except "pagodas" and temples. Their superior nimbleness, however, is, I am sure, one element in the case.

At the ends of the ridge-tiles a tinted plaster ornament, like the conventional curly foam-crested waves of Japanese art, was wrought to form a charm against the entrance of water. So the tilers said, at all events; but I formed a suspicion that perhaps the motive might be read the other way, as the roof always leaked dreadfully just about that very spot.

The 20th of July being the great festival of the *Kawa-biraki*, or "opening of the river," and a general holiday in the city, we made a pic-nic party, including some very prettily-dressed Japanese girls attending a mission-school, and sailed to the festive scene in the gondola of Japan— a miniature unpainted copy of Noah's ark, clean and generally very compact, as the cramp in your unaccustomed legs will soon enable you to testify. The boatman sculls from the side while standing upright. The broad and rather dingy river was quite lively with similar crafts similarly laden, and the tinkle of the inevitable *samisen*— a kind of guitar—was "sounding sounding" everywhere.

On holiday and festive occasions such as this, young maidens dress in loose, prettily-figured robes, with great wide necks. The folds are always made studiously graceful, as even our own artists have learned, and books are sold showing the folds and attitudes, considered to be æsthetic and fashionable.

The outer robe is fastened with a stiff, plain silk or, it may be, richly brocaded girdle tied in a careful and prominent bow behind. The robe opens at the bosom, disclosing the well-powdered neck, and the parallel edges of a series of pale-coloured vests made of the most delicate crape silks, and with skilfully contrasted hues. A medical man has opportunities of discovering many little secrets about dress; and just as the lofty man about town, when knocked over by a plebeian cab, has been found by his horrified medical attendant to indulge in "dickies," so I may be allowed here to whisper that those costly strata of silk garments which are the wonder and admiration of the unsophisticated foreigner, are, in modern times, simply very narrow folds of the required material laid together so as to produce a fictitious appearance of great expenditure with the minimum of outlay.

During the day fireworks are let off, which form cloudy patterns high up in the air and give forth paper prizes of curious shapes, in pursuit of which crowds of city urchins

may be seen rushing frantically with their loins girded.
Those smoke-clouds are often tinted beautifully, and
assume fantastic shapes. The substance used to produce
the effect is the dried dung of the she wolf—for wolves still
abound in the northern parts of the empire. The powder

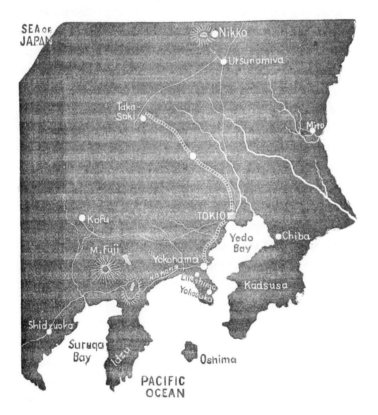

is said to cause a dense white smoke which hangs together
for an unusual time. I have thought that a similar kind
of fireworks might be used for military or other signalling
through the day, and might often also give valuable
indications as to the direction of currents of air in

balooning, or for general meteorological purposes. I have
seen them break high above low-lying fleecy clouds in the
city, and to take a different course from the latter, thus
clearly indicating two currents of wind.

After the "river-opening," which was first celebrated in
Kioto the capital of the country, and still is with more
meaning than in Tokio, summer comes in apace, and
during the twenty-one days following, the people used to
leave the hot and dusty city for the cool breezy banks of
the Sumida, which, in the upper reaches, are lined with
tea-houses, looking into the river, their verandahs almost
overhanging the once limpid and wholesome stream.
When passing along any of the narrow streets in a neighbourhood where the population is dense, every room
seemed to be filled with perspiring citizens, nearly naked,
and lying outstretched, fanning themselves or trying to
persuade themselves that they were asleep. At night,
during the extremely hot season, the people seem to keep
walking in little parties about the streets, which are kept
moist and as cool as may be by the stagnant water from
the gutters being sprinkled about from time to time. I
am not sure that the effect is at all unhealthy. The
samisens are kept also going all night to tremulous vocal
accompaniments.

This period might perhaps be called the dog-days,
but I have never known a single case of a mad dog
in Japan, although I have had to treat numberless
cases of bites from angry dogs. Turkey is said also
to enjoy a like immunity, and this has been ascribed to
the prevalence of a certain tick which greatly infests the
dogs there. Strangely enough, a similar parasite is one

of the greatest afflictions to dog-fanciers in Japan, but I am not prepared to give any opinion on the relation of the two facts. Our housefactor's children got bitten by white mice, about this time, and the sorrowing relatives told me that in Japan this was always fatal. I did what I could for them, but my advice was not closely followed. One child quickly died ; the other suffered for more than a year, but seemed to be recovering when last under my observation. The disease, which was thought to be allied to hydrophobia, seemed to be well known in Japan, but I never saw another case of the same kind.

The canals near us were usually lively in the hot days with schoolboys bathing, and frequently there would be a shout and a sudden rush of people ; an hour or so afterwards a pale little limp and lifeless corpse would be dragged out, still clutching firmly a tuft of *chara* or other water-weed, under the cruel coils of which the swiftly out-rushing tide had dragged the poor child. Often with sore heart I tried to get something done to prevent those pitiful accidents, as people called them, but almost in vain. On one occasion the body could not at all be found. The bystanders, though not for lack of advice, were at their wits' ends, when I heard some solemn old wiseacre propose that the excellent old charm of placing a cock on a raft and setting it afloat should get a trial. Of course the cock must needs crow when it came to the spot. Some men waded into the canal, pushing the raft about in all directions, and at last baffled in their project, let it go. By-and-by it got aground, and master chanticleer, in contemptuous silence, leaped nimbly ashore amidst the loud voltairean laughter of the crowd. The wise propounder of the scheme had meanwhile quietly slipped away. I must candidly add that the raft had never been pushed across the spot where the body was afterwards found lying, in fact nearly opposite the place where the raft had stuck fast.

On many of those hot days happily there blew a strong cooling breeze from the sea, which made life tolerable. The air was laden with fine salt spray, and at night great indigo-coloured banks of cloud regularly massed themselves over the hills to the north-west of Tokio. Sheets of silent violet lightning would keep flitting over them till a very late hour,—the forked lightning being invisible behind the outer stratum of vapour, and the distance being too great for the thunder to be heard. This never ceased to be a very impressive phenomenon in spite of its regularity. Sometimes violent thunderstorms burst near us, and once, while at dinner, a terrible crash led me to look out to the river, where I saw that the tall mast of a junk, the most prominent in the bay as the storm swept towards Tokio, had been split right down from top to heel. I got a little boat and pulled off to see if medical help were needed. No one had been hurt, but in the hold the grim old skipper was bowing his head solemnly, while with clasped hands he muttered some prayers or incantations. He seemed greatly annoyed to find his vessel the object of so much sudden curiosity, for crowds of idle gazers had put off from shore, and many were commenting pleasantly on the probable wickedness of those on board, just as they would have done in a good Jewish or Christian country, a matter which furnished me with a theme for some wholesome and, I trust, edifying remarks.

E

Tokio was not without its gaieties, and the visit of some prince or ex-president, now and then, found the sombre capital ready to indulge in a great feast of lanterns—and champagne. The preparations for General Grant's reception were on an unusually lavish scale. The shop-keepers told us gravely that they had received strict orders from the government not to part with any soap or tooth-brushes meanwhile, lest those useful articles should be required for official purposes during the work of festivities. The outlay at last became so extravagant that a serious remonstrance was sent in anonymously to government on the subject. Indeed the feeling was generally entertained by respectable citizens that the irresponsible expenditure of money raised by taxation must henceforth be carefully watched. I believe this little episode, which did not attract very much attention, has been felt to mark an important stage in the history of Japanese political progress. Whether the soap was all used or not remains doubtful, but it was whispered that some official hands remained pretty dirty after all! What I have to say of Japanese amusements will be said farther on.

Christmas was a great time for hugging memories of the lands we came from. The amount of home feeling which so many " Anglo-Saxon " children claiming origin from both sides the " mill-pond," excited in the hearts of case-hardened old residents, was very touching and beautiful, and, I am sure, altogether purifying in its influence. While might we sigh with the laureate—

> " We live within the stranger's land,
> And strangely falls our Christmas eve "—

the season itself was usually cold, clear, and bracing—

often a bright blue sky above us, while the hard ground rung beneath our feet, and under the shade of green bamboos skaters might be seen gliding on good ice merrily. On a wet day the rows of hooded *jinrikishas*, grouped in some lantern-lit compound shadowed with sub-tropical foliage, did not suggest an English Christmas at all till the little fair-haired ones emerged from the dingy oil-paper covers of their vehicles in gay evening-dresses, as an accomplished lady friend once remarked—"just like so many butterflies from the chrysalis."

CHAPTER VI.

A Consultation in the Hills.

A Rembrandtesque Scene—Novel Style of Drag—Daybreak on the Plains—A Remorseful Knight—Wayside Tea-houses—A Formidable Ferry—Buddha in Bronze—Presbyterian Church in the Hills—Dining in Public—A Doctor of the Old School—Scotch Service amongst Silk —Utility of Yawning.

ONE day, in the summer of 1879, having had a sudden call to go into the interior to see an aged silk grower in consultation with his native doctor, I found myself at midnight, after a hard day's work, drowsily contemplating a scene which might have sprung to life from Rembrandt's canvas. A quaint, old-fashioned Japanese hostelry, outside of which lay, as if they were never to move again, a dusty, dingy, beggarly array of much bepainted and bepatched vehicles, on which had accumulated the dust and mud of every journey they had made since first they issued in coats of bright scarlet some time after the dawn of civilization from the builder's yard. I soon noticed that there were others like myself, with strong faith and small bundles, ready to commit their precious souls to those frail tenements of clay. A fat old woman, with strong Tory tendencies, much local knowledge of routes, coaches, and hours—one never speaks of minutes in travelling by coach in Japan, and only of hours as a figure of speech—and a formidable array of square dark green bandboxes of split bamboo, for the care and

transit of which roads, drivers, and waiters, seemed to
have been specially called into existence ; a wizened'
irresolute looking old man, with a "guid gaun" law suit
in the city, who was always nervously preparing for a
smoke, but had perhaps run out of tobacco ; a group
of portly people in "silk," whose talk was too pro-
fessionally technical to be well understood by a foreigner ;
a few morbidly well-behaved, nicely-dressed, and unemo-
tional children ; a rather merry, red-faced old boy,
with a foreign hat on, who had many hospitable city
friends to say *sayonara* (good-bye) to him ; and a quiet,
important, clean-shaved man (a local dignitary) with a
piping voice ;—such was the group of intending travellers
that seemed to gravitate around one frail vehicle—crankier
than any of the others it seemed to me—by the solemnising influence of one common destiny.   At last 12.30, our
hour for leaving, was indicated by my infallible pocket-
chronometer ; but silence—broken only by the abortive
attempts of the old man to start his pipe—reigned around.
Now and again a nonchalant stable-boy, with dark blue
skin-tights, would appear with a paper lantern that sent
gross caricatures of us all dancing like fiends on a background of ruddy fire, while the varied features of each
face were emphasised with such deep shadows that you
felt some great tragedy was in preparation.   At length
there was a decided stir in the courtyard, the clatter of
hoofs and the sweet accents of irate grooms broke upon
our grateful ears, while the erst silent streets began to
echo the hoarse bray of approaching bugles, in clumsy
juvenile and tentative strains that would have driven mad
an English guard of the good old coaching days.   Two

raw-backed and bare-ribbed ponies were yoked to the crazy vehicle, one of whose wheels was really not quite circular, and dispensed with the need for springs, of which however there were home-made substitutes. The climax, however, was reached in the drag. My object in this work is to pourtray Japan as it is * and not to invent amusing things. Well, it consisted simply of an old Wellington boot of tough texture, which had probably seen much previous service, pressed against the wheel by means of a wooden pin, round which, with the boot, a rope was twisted. Like Captain Cuttle's watch, it had the disadvantage of requiring somewhat frequent adjustment, but thus aided it did its work marvellously well. The vehicle in front of us, going so far the same way, came to grief outside of the city, and we had to give the good-natured occupants some help. There was no grumbling and no blame cast on any one. After hours of hard galloping—our horses being changed every seven miles or so—and rough, painful jolting through sleeping suburban hamlets and gloomy woods, we began at last to have faint glimpses of the landscape, over which the soft grey dawn was now shedding a cold silvery radiance, that seemed to owe nothing to the sun. We were dashing along a vast and fertile plain through which roll several broad branches of the grand river which pours itself into the bay of Yedo, at the city which used to bear that name.

This great flat, loamy, garden-like expanse, was gleaming with golden patches of the *sesamum orientale*—very

---

* The railway, since the period above mentioned, has been carried along the route herein described.

like the mustard plant—which filled the air with a somewhat heavy but agreeable odour not unlike honey.
Sometimes a bright purple flush of wild clover broke in
strikingly through the monotonous check-tartan of green
and yellow ; or a pool of still water, dotted with broad
lotus leaves, or quivering with frogs, flashed its glory
through broad blades of blooming iris. Everywhere the
poor, hard-wrought peasants, in preposterous umbrella-
like hats, and literally thatched with straw which made
them look when stooping exactly like porcupines, were
damming up runnels of water for their rice fields, or trying
to urge sluggish and most unpicturesque oxen to drag a
wooden plough through the stiff clods. It was curious to
observe that this most primitive-looking engine was
exactly like the ancient *pekton* of the Greeks, yet telegraph-
posts were near enough for the wearied oxen to rub themselves on, while not many miles away you might see the
steam plough at work. Such is modern Japan !

Here and there a snowy egret, in sharp and dazzling
contrast to the dark ooze of the paddy-fields, might be
seen poking its long greenish yellow beak into the
mud, through which the first green promise of harvest
was timidly peeping. The whole atmosphere, and even
the damp dewy ground itself, seemed to vibrate with the
cheerful *crek-kek-kek-kex* of the frogs—an old and heart-
inspiring music, which has never wanted admirers.

As the purple hills seemed to rise and draw nearer to
us, we came at last to the end of this part of our journey ;
for the carriage road ended, for us at least, at a notable
little place called Kumagai, where a fair was being held
when we arrived. The town is named after a famous

warrior of ancient times who, by the rules of warfare, had to behead a tender young captive who had shown great gallantry. In bitter remorse, and with an utter disgust towards his profession, the grim old soldier afterwards shaved his head and became a priest, famous for learning and sanctity. The festival which we witnessed was held in his memory. After a very short pause here we were off again, this time in the now world-famed *jinrikisha,*—rattling along narrow horse paths, between rigged fields of tender green buckwheat or Indian corn ; resting now and then for a minute or two at one of the houses by the wayside. These were always musical with the soft tinkling of glass ornaments which convey most grateful suggestions of rest and coolness to the ears of the wearied, hot, and dust-stained traveller. There is usually a wooden bench placed under a spreading vine or cucumber tree. At one of them I got a little tea-girl to warm up a bottle of cold soup, which thoughtful hands had stowed away for me. It was put into a very fishy, but otherwise clean copper, which always gives a nice metallic flavour to Western dishes, and I dined sumptuously—the sweets coming first, then soup, fish being served last of all.

Off again, now through drizzling and depressing rain, which increased at last into a thunderous downpour, making the roads anything but pleasant or easy to travel over. Two rivers, now terribly swollen by the rain, had to be crossed, and this was done by means of flat and frail boats, worked by pole-oars of strong, but alarmingly flexible bamboo. A rope of rudely twisted straw was stretched between the banks—some parts of which had been recently washed away—and was used by the boatman to propel his scow by grasping it hand over hand. At one point the risk seemed terrible ; but after a hard and painful struggle, we landed safely on the other side. One of those torrents is lined by huge ruddy-purple boulders from the famous volcano called Asama Yama, whose cloud-wrapped peak, from which the whitish yellow smoke of continual burning rises in slow curling wreaths, is an object of most impressive grandeur.

A short walk through field-paths, embanked with homely stone " dykes," and crossed by a thousand streams fretted by tiny water-wheels and shaded by brakes of the slim and tapering bamboo,—over which the magnificent *wistaria* hung its pale lavender festoons of drooping blossoms—brought us to the mountain town of Kiriu, where my patient lived. It is a solid comfortable-looking place, with a well-made street sloping mountainwards, and claims as its "parish church" a dignified old temple, in the wide court of which the calm-faced image of Buddha rears in bronze its majestic height, from a granite pedestal, resting on finely chiselled lotus leaves. In the background there is an extensive grave-yard, filled with costly and richly carved stones, lichen-stained and moss-grown, shaded from the sun by many lofty trees of long growth. One of those trees is fully six feet in diameter, and must, I suppose, have put forth its first tiny rootlets about the time of our Cromwell.

The people in Kiriu seemed all to be engaged in the silk trade in one way or another, and had a wonderfully well-to-do appearance. I at once called on the pastor of the Presbyterian (native) Church, and was happy to find that he was an old Tokio friend of mine. After some talk we went through mud and rain to see the patient. His house was on the hillside, and was approached through two broad high-walled courts, with large outer buildings, in which spinning, weaving, and the various other operations of silk culture might be seen busily going on. Many tiresome but most courteous preliminaries having been gone through, I was taken to see the poor old sufferer, across a broad court-yard lying in deep water, for the rain still fell in torrents. After prescribing, I had a long and interesting talk with him ; and then, tired and hungry, laid myself down on the clean soft straw-matted floor of a quaint little room which was assigned to me.

A Japanese meal is quite a curiosity even to the accustomed foreigner, because you never know what may be served up. Sometimes the sweetest-looking crape paper napkins are given to you. They are, of course, only used once, and a custom so pleasant might well be imitated at home. They are far from costly. I have never enjoyed stewed *monkey* yet, but it was a favourite dish in Japan a few years ago. Recent Darwinian teaching has, perhaps, led to a recoil from such cannibalism ! I don't know how others feel in such circumstances, but hungry as I was, it was difficult to enjoy food under the alert and inquiring eyes of a polite crowd of Japanese. My prehensile operations with knife and fork began to appear, to myself at least, unbearably vulgar and absurd. While I was finishing with some chocolate, in came the old family physician, who, since the new *régime*, no longer wears his sword, which was intended, I suppose, to convey the idea of professional dignity and destructiveness.

The old gentleman did not seem quite pleased to find his preserves poached upon, and we had a little fencing in which he came off well, having read Western books with some care. His conceit was thoroughly national, but had not a very solid foundation. A suitable opportunity occurring, I quickly but firmly told him aloud, with the publicity he had courted, what had best be done, and prescribed some well known remedies. He had not heard of them evidently, but tried to put a good face on the matter. The crowd saw fun brewing, and " chaffed " the poor old gentleman rather sorely. He asserted that he had on his shelves all that the Government professors in Tokio hospitals prescribed, implying perhaps that my notions were a little antiquated. A pawky-looking old Christian servant of the silk grower finally silenced him, by saying dryly that he could not of course be expected to know about such remedies if he had never heard of them before, at which the crowd grinned, and the old doctor filled his pipe very quietly.

I had been asked to address the Christians, and had begun to wonder when my chance to do so would come. I found that the old doctor was a difficulty. To hold such meetings might at that time have been thought illegal ; indeed, Christianity itself is still formally under ban, although

the highly civilised central Government is disposed
formally to adopt liberal views. Beginning to suspect what
the difficulty was, and perceiving that the doctor was a
hard old nut to crack, and not very favourable to religion
of any kind, I told the pastor that it would be better to
invite unbelievers to hear what was to be said. We then
moved into a large room, into which three others with
sliding partitions opened. At one end a somewhat im-
posing pulpit, composed of boxes covered with red cloth,
had been erected. The large hall—for such it seemed—
was dimly lit by candles placed on tall candlesticks, and
I could see that the sick man had been able to "take up
his bed," which he had spread on the floor, and was looking up with earnest and wistful face. The audience was,
to my surprise, very large. I conducted a simple service,
such as we have in Scotland, and preached on the first
commandment. No preacher ever had a more attentive
and eager audience. I was glad to see, listening with
sharp and critical attention, the old doctor and his son,
the latter being a polite and pleasant youth, with long
black locks falling like a thick veil over his bashful face,
which he shook back with a jerk every now and again.
After bringing the service to a close, I had a good deal of
conversation with the people on the subject of the one true
God, idolatry, etc., and was glad to see that they had an
intelligent grasp of our teaching. No difficulties were
urged, but *suspense* was alleged by them as the most becoming attitude meanwhile. How thoroughly Eastern
this is. One would enjoy hard fighting better.

After sundry hints, I again got to the little room I was
to occupy, a large part of the congregation accompanying

me to light their tiny pipes at the charcoal brazier placed in the middle of the company, and continue the conversation. I was really ready for a meal now, and had to share my slender store of cocoa with those who were curious to taste the foreign stuff.

It was now late, or rather early, but no signs of my being able to retire to rest were apparent. After long forbearance, and one or two polite hints which were as politely and dexterously fended, I ventured on a highly original course not provided for in Japanese etiquette, and which I would modestly recommend to travellers in the Far East similarly placed. I stretched myself, and gave one most unmistakeable yawn, which a deaf man in the next house might easily have heard. A bomb-shell bursting in the apartment could not have more quickly dispelled its tenants.

In a couple of minutes one of the domestics appeared with a pile of silk-covered cotton quilts for bedding, and in a few minutes more, in spite of the picturesque *cirri* and *cumuli* of coarse tobacco that floated over my quiet couch, I was sleeping the sleep of the just.

CHAPTER VII.

A Consultation in the Hills (Continued).

A Charming Bedroom—Landscape Gardening in Miniature—Duck's Eggs and Duty—Some World-forgotten Ones—Doctors *sometimes* differ—A Hint for Pious Busy-bodies—Religious Radishes—Tincture of Snake—Rays of Buddha—Midnight in a Forest—" Resources of Civilization " —A Suspicious Case—Toddy *versus* Timidity—Loving the Darkness.

Y bedroom opened on two sides into adjoining and much larger apartments by partitions of open woodwork, like windows with panes of tissue paper instead of glass, a system which allows of a good deal of wholesome ventilation, especially in cold weather. One side of the room was plastered very smoothly and evenly with a warm iron grey cement, while trunks of young spruce firs, stripped of their bark and leaving a glossy clean surface like silk, did duty as posts. As such posts are always carefully selected with a view to ornament they gave the room an elegant air of primitive simplicity idealised, which I think is a chief and very subtle charm in a well planned Japanese house. The floors were of course covered with the usual thick, finely woven, and in this case, scrupulously clean straw mats bordered with coloured tape. My room opened into one of those marvellous little courts of some three or four yards square, containing a most effective suggestion of the margin of an impenetrable forest from which there projects into a pebbly lake teeming with gold fish, a most geologically correct cape, down which rushes a foaming cascade, and on whose sunny banks bask some metallic blue-tailed lizards and a sluggish turtle. You might cross to the island of well-cropped turf and find there an ancient stone lantern, stained by the grandest of colourists—Time —with every richest hue of velvetty moss and slow crawling lichen.

After the clattering of sliding shutters had subsided, I had a hearty breakfast of duck's eggs—hard boiled—rice, biscuits, and the inevitable straw-coloured tea, and then passed on to the pitifully monotonous little group of blear-eyed, crippled, and occasionally leprous humanity that dogs the steps of a medical missionary. It is curious how hopeless sufferers are dragged, as if by some strange selective magnet, from their retreats in dim sombre valleys, untrodden by the ordinary visitor, dark hovels and lonely garrets, all forgotten of the great busy world whom they can no longer serve. Here was the old doctor again, clean shaven and hair newly trimmed, grinning as sardonically as ever but vastly more polite in speech, looming in the background generally, perhaps alert enough as to what was doing, but in a most elaborately disengaged manner tapping with ever varying gesture on the edge of the brazier with that everlasting pipe of his. His distress was so apparent that I was compelled to comfort the good old man by drawing him out publicly—for by this time we were the centre of a considerable crowd—by finding what he did know, and we parted pleasantly, both of us with the happy feeling that we had taught as well as learned.

After visiting a few sick folk in the neighbourhood who were bedridden, accompanied by my former guide I started on my return journey through fields of mulberry, the people in the crowded court-yard ducking a wave of compliments like a patch of sedges under a strong gale. Then we got into our carriage and pair (of men) and were away through narrow pathways cut through golden sweetly scented acres of *sesamum*, past sloppy rice fields into the mud of which men and boys were treading cut grass and weeds for manure ; then rattling across rough wooden culverts, or splashing through gleaming pools which the rains had formed.

Our way lay past an interesting cave naturally formed, I think, in a very hard rock which scratched glass, and not far from it we saw a famous temple, Me-no-ma Shoden. In the spacious grounds were numerous stalls adorned with toys, ornaments for rustic belles, and sweetmeats. The whole neighbourhood was gay with a festive display of flowers and paper lanterns. What struck me most was a very ample preaching hall, open at the sides and adorned—not with the commandments of Buddha or the precepts of Confucius, but with pictured advertisements of the trades to which the pious patrons were severally devoted. The idea seemed a singularly happy one, and I venture to offer the suggestion to some of those good people who give their energies to church bazaars. In Japan it is usual, by the way, to give credit for larger subscriptions than are actually received. At the gate there was a curious carved stone pillar, round which a horribly grinning elf was slyly peeping at the passing devotee—truly a clever

piece of rural work. The crest on all the temple adorn-
ments was forked radishes rampant with limbs entwined.
The temple, I was told, belonged to a corrupt Shinto
cult, tainted with Buddhism. The posts were lacquered
red like those of Buddhist temples, while within was displayed the mirror, of which I have said something in
another chapter. I have a manuscript copy of the engravings in a famous old work, the *Butsu-zo-dzui*, which
contains a Buddhist figure like the Hindu Ganesa, with
an elephant's head. He holds in one hand a trident, and
in the other a forked radish-like plant.

As I struck off from the main road by a mountain path,
a fine large snake of a species I had not previously captured, became a victim, and I soon had it comfortably
settled in a bottle of alcohol which I secured in an oil
shop, under the somewhat veiled form of *arukohoru*, as the
letter *l* is awanting in the copious alphabet of Japan.
I was generally credited by an inquisitive public with the
manufacture of medicine.

At Kumagai we found the last coach to Tokio had left
hours ago, and the hotel-keepers drew doleful pictures of
the state of the road, which, truly enough, was at that time
infested with gangs of murderous brigands. I could not
afford to delay, and after lavish inducement had been
offered, prevailed on two brawny coolies to contract to take
me into the city by daybreak. After a hurried supper, I
parted with my kind guide who, as I have said, was an old
servant of the patient I had been asked to visit. It was
clear to me that there was some concern for my safety,
and that the two men who drew me were not without some
apprehensions. However, I felt that I must go, and that

F

the risk might after all be very slight.   By-and-by the
shadows on the hills deepened—

> " The sun's rim dips ; the stars rush out :
> At one stride comes the dark "—

lowering summer thunder-clouds gather about the hills
we had come from, and they throb with pale purple
sheet lightning.   The *rayons du crépuscle*, too, which some
suppose to be due to a lofty stratum of suspended ice-
particles, stretch their long bows of indigo, alternating
with rose, across the zenith from west to east.   They are
often in the east called the " rays of Buddha."

We stopped for a long time at the entrance to a dreaded
forest which stretched in one almost unbroken expanse to
near the city.   Close by the little tea-house where the
men were refreshing themselves, was a wood-cutter's hut,
from whose dimly-lighted room came a hard, soul-piercing
cough, which sounded to a trained ear like a funeral knell.
The crescent moon was bending down through a strip of
lemon-coloured sky to the western horizon, when I again
took my seat, the men warning me that now came the
place of danger.   As a mild precaution, having no armour,
I buckled up a large, very knobby stone into my handker-
chief, placed it " convanient," and began to admire the
grand woodland scenery, dimly lit by stars and a setting
moon.   It was highly fascinating, and the sense of
lurking danger kept me awake and served to give
a certain piquancy, but it at last grew monotonous.
By-and-by I glided quietly from the sombre forest with
its impenetrable shadows, into a trim railway station, and
was off at express speed through gas-lit villages merry

with the whirr of giant factories, across magnificent viaducts
which spanned lordly rivers crowded with great vessels ;
over points with many a bump and crash, and at last with
a sudden bang—into a magnificent terminus, with palatial
hotel and crowds of welcoming friends ?—no ; but after I
had rubbed my eyes very well for a minute or so—off the
main road altogether, and into the forest itself, the shafts
of my vehicle on the ground, and my trusty varlets standing a little apart from me, and indulging in vehement
whispers. I clutched my formidable *ballista*, assumed a
dramatic attitude, and prepared, in the solemnising language of public bodies, "to take such steps as the circumstances might seem to call for." I at once saw that in
the first place, at least, I had to deal with allies—not foes.
They had quenched their paper lanterns, and besought
me to remain silent, while they crouched with hands at
ears listening intently. There was a faint sound from
along the road, which soon resolved itself into a vehicle
of some kind, drawn by two horses, galloping madly in
our rear I was still in great doubt as to what the whole
thing meant, when the vehicle swept up, and the two men
who were with me leaped into the road with a sudden shout.
The driver pulled up in fear at first, friendly salutations
ensued, and anon a sleepy man tumbled out. At this
precise moment I candidly admit that I believed myself
to have fallen into a fatal trap, stood with my back against
a thick trunk, and took a much cooler last glance (as I
really thought) at mother earth than I had supposed at
all possible for anybody to do in the circumstances. In
a moment I recognised in the drowsy man my recent
guide, who lost no time in telling me that he could not

sleep after his usual " wee drap " of rice-whisky for thinking of me lying murdered in this wood, after I had been
committed to his care.

The faithful old fellow had got out of bed, communi-
cated his superstitious dread, or rather toddy nightmare,
to the townfolks, and had, at considerable expense to his
wealthy master, engaged the vehicle which my coolies
only recognised when close to us.   That his dread was
not quite imaginary I fully comprehended, when I read a
few days afterwards in a native newspaper a vivid and
trustworthy account of the stoppage of two coaches near
that very spot, in daylight, by armed bands of robbers,
who wounded the driver and guards and made the
passengers stand and deliver.   At the post-town close by,
and at the same time, the banker and several well-to-do
people had their throats cut by robbers.

I rewarded my two men liberally, took my seat
in the little car, and was soon jolting along
merrily, to the accompaniment of some lively tales
of murder and robbery by the old man, who waxed
garrulous.   I arrived in Tokio just before daybreak.   The streets were deserted, dark, and silent ; but
here and there might be seen a broken-down old rascal,
with a broken-down and very dirty jinrikisha, doing night
work.   I engaged one for my bag, and found that his
story was a commoner one than many old residents may
suppose.   He had taken to drink, could no longer get
respectable day-work, and so busied himself dragging
slowly along, with legs trembling as much from disease as
old age, red-faced old Japanese gentlemen who had been
"dining out," or spending a day at the theatre, and on

whom blind fortune had smiled a little more favourably than on himself. So ended my consultation visit to Kiriu.

CHAPTER VIII.

Mitake San—The Sacred Mount of the Three Peaks.

Bad Roads and Better Language—Spiders and Beetles—A Japanese Scarecrow—Night Storm in a Forest—A Dispirited Coolie—Sunday Quiet
and Questioning—Buddhist Teaching and Modern Science—Passports
and Preaching—A Picturesque School—Sick Cicadas—Art and Nature
—Brambles and Barefeet.

AFTER a hard day and night's work we got off one
morning in the hot season long before daybreak with
our pale sick-worn little ones. We were quickly hurried
through dark miry streets, by mossy walled moats, and
through weary long drawn suburban rows of wooden
dwellings, the inhabitants of which were just stirring up
into activity. Now and again our perspiring jinrikisha
men would stop to have a thimble-like cup of pale tea,
a tiny pipeful of tobacco, and a spasmodic colloquy,
chiefly composed of very significant but to Western
ears mild ejaculations about the quality of the roads
which, according to the profession, must be under-
going very steady deterioration. Poor fellows! I
wonder when some Japanese Thomas Chalmers will be
able to solve the problems which they suggest to one.
Soon the sun rose laughingly, and then hospital cares, and
the raw, clammy mist seemed to vanish together. The
children began to be amused with the flowery hedge rows,
the patient oxen, and the noisy village festivals in which
the Japanese are always commemorating, with gay lan-

terns and merry processions, some old dead emperor or
the birth-day of his great grand uncle !

By-and-by we stopped to give our men a meal and
rest.   Some kind farm people in the neighbourhood
brought sweets and tempting fruits and vegetables, with
now and then some gay flowers, and the children got out
to wander amongst the luxuriant vegetation of the garden-
like fields through which our road passed.   It was wonderful to see how their eyes opened with a new delight
when they discovered a great gaudy spider, which began
clumsily to vibrate her curious zig-zag netted web to avert
attention, or when they happened to uncover a bevy of
copper-brown beetles cropping the tender vine leaves.   At
last with ruddier cheeks and brighter eyes than we had seen
for a long time, they came running to announce an as-
tounding discovery.   It was a curiosity of the quaintest
kind—a real Japanese scarecrow, which of all the—but I
fear a description would hardly be suitable for these grave
pages.

We are soon off again with greater speed.   One coolie
has sold out his contract, and a new man joins our company, with strange, guttural " slangy " Japanese which
none of us can understand very well.   After some hours
we stopped for dinner at a pretty little wayside tea-house,
with big, fat gold-fish and a grand Scotch " burn " foaming and tearing through mossy boulders.   I distributed
here a good number of books to the villagers who flocked
to see us.   Off again ! for miles along a very broad and
leafy avenue, with a ditch running through its centre, on
and on till we all began to nod, and awoke to find ourselves being heavily dragged at night through a dreary

wood, with rain pouring upon us in violent torrents, and
even our poor coolies invisible in the gloom, save when a
flash of lightning lit up the murky scene.   Our men all
began to be afraid, and it required all my available wits
to keep them up, and to keep them together.   Sometimes
we had to stop and halloo for five or ten minutes on the
others, as we could not find any definite path, and one
of the coolies fairly broke down in spirits.   He never
entirely recovered his cheerful disposition, and I think
had been overcome by superstitious dread chiefly.   We
had two hours of this work in the dark wet forest, but at
last arrived at a cheery place of human voices and flitting
shadows.

There are worse places than a clean Japanese inn after
such a dismal night, and we all fully appreciated its com-
forts.   We had intended to reach the hills that Saturday
night, but I was not sorry to find so comfortable a
Sabbath resting-place on the way.   I arranged, with some
caution on account of certain regulations, to have a meeting, and went out to see about me.   Ome is a large and
very pretty market town with an avenue of trees then in
full bloom, gnarled pine and cherry, with some plum trees
and crape myrtles, running up its main street.   It lies at the
base of the hills, which are grandly wooded just where
the sparkling river which supplies Tokio with water breaks
from its enclosing valleys and runs joyfully down to the
plains.   The town lies on one of the boulder-strewn terraces left by the ancient river.   There are no clear
evidences of glaciation.   It boasts of a fine temple to
which you climb by a very lofty and dangerously steep
flight of stairs.   The people seemed to be better built and

rather healthier than those of the plain around Tokio, and their oxen were notably large and sleek.

We went to the temple, and there found a great many children playing about the shrines, with whom we con‐ 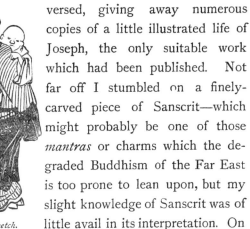 versed, giving away numerous copies of a little illustrated life of Joseph, the only suitable work which had been published. Not far off I stumbled on a finely‐ carved piece of Sanscrit—which might probably be one of those *mantras* or charms which the de‐ graded Buddhism of the Far East is too prone to lean upon, but my slight knowledge of Sanscrit was of little avail in its interpretation. On

From a Native Sketch.

coming down to the town again, a kind, hearty old woman, seeing that our little ones were thirsty, asked us into her clean little hut, and presented each of us very gracefully with a cup of deliciously cool spring water, such as the wealth of Tokio could not buy in that city. Gracious old heathen woman, may thy kind and gentle deed be remembered to thee on that Great Day !

In the evening I had prepared to address a good audience, and at the hour appointed came down to a large room of the tea-house opening into the street, which had been kindly offered to me. I was amused to witness the discomfiture of my old cook when we looked round on an array of empty mats, for I am sure he had puffed the proceedings very thoroughly and conscientiously. I tried to assure him that the audience would be all right, and

that we should have a full house. I got the children to
the door and began to talk to them playfully in English.
It was irresistible. Respectable people, with small bank
accounts even, who were lounging about as if waiting appointments, of course quite unconscious of any proposed meeting,
would condescend to pause in passing and laugh for a
little at the gibberish, so we bagged them all. We began
with about thirty people, and before I had read a portion
of Scripture the room was quite full. Some noisy young
Japanese lads—from the city probably—began audibly to
criticise in not very polite terms the doctrine of the cross;
but they were soon stabbed into silence by a polite but
oblique thrust which the audience appreciated heartily,
and some of them sneaked in to join us. By-and-by the
head official, with a small party, peeped in *as he was passing,* and stood patronisingly to look on from above the
rest who were seated. Curiously enough I proceeded just
then to speak of our holy religion requiring proper respect
to be paid to those in authority, and was glad to see that
he waited till the end. For fully two hours I had
as closely attentive an audience as any one could wish
for.

   I told the main facts of the life of Christ, just as we may
suppose them to have occurred in the view of a heathen
observer ; of how claims of divinity had roused the hatred
of the Jews against Him, of His peculiar trial by mixed
judicial forms acquitting Him of moral guilt, but condemn-
ing Him for calling Himself God ; of His strange and
terrible death, burial, and reported resurrection. I went
on to examine the evidence of the latter, and told how the
civilised races of the West had soon been compelled to

accept it as a glorious fact, full of hope for all men. When
I spoke of the resurrection, they did not laugh as others
did of old, but a very fine-looking, pale old woman with
silvery hair, sitting beside her fat, prosperous, jolly-faced
husband, and drinking in all that was said with great
eagerness—stopped me in the most courteous Japanese
manner to say, that although I was a foreigner she had
understood very well what I had been saying, but that she
could not quite understand my meaning when I spoke of
Jesus rising from the dead after having been laid in His
grave !

I had all my books cleared off very quickly, and could
have disposed of many more. Questions about them
were freely asked. Long after I had retired for the night
I could hear murmurs of conversation on the subject of
the religion of *Yasu*, which was till recently a synonym
for every kind of horrible sorcery. Before leaving I was
asked to send some one to teach them more about our
religion ; but when Mr. Miura, a very able native preacher,
went out, he does not seem to have got very much
encouragement in fact, and speedily returned. I did
not quite agree with him as to this course, as no actual
opposition had been offered, and such would now, I am
happy to say, be illegal in Japan, where all peaceful
religions are tolerated. It is right to add, that this place
is in the diocese of a Buddhist bishop, who holds that the
earth is flat, and who has been mobbed, it appears, in
Yokohama by lads of modern tendencies for teaching
such an absurd doctrine. In my first address and before
knowing anything about this, I laid down very dogmatic-
ally, contrary opinions, and appealed to scientific text-

books to support my statements, although I am not quiet clear yet as to the immediate connection of that subject with Christianity. However, I have faith in the truth of these things ultimately helping us, and the people are beginning to find that we are more accurate and trustworthy in ordinary matters than their own teachers are.

It is as yet very difficult to organize regular evangelistic work in the interior, not on account of any bigoted intolerance of our teaching, but simply from the fact that passports are needed for foreigners, and the only objects which have been legitimised are " scientific research " and " health." I have never gone out except on *bona fide* errands of the one class or the other. I am sure, however, that it was not the intention of the Japanese government to restrict us in propagating Christianity by this regulation, but simply to prevent large mercantile transactions being imposed on simple country folks outside of the treaty ports. There can therefore be nothing wrong or illegal, as some who are uninformed have supposed, in seizing passing opportunities to proclaim the gospel of Christ. The legality of this course is not now questioned by the authorities at all. I trust, however, that such a modification of the existing treaties may soon be made as shall permit, not only the unfettered use of our tongues in the interior, but the organization of regular tours for the purpose of pleading our cause. The Japanese government have shown a very excellent spirit, and are largely tolerant. It remains for our press and high officials on their part to show a somewhat more sympathetic and conciliatory disposition than has sometimes prevailed.

We left the pretty town of Ome early, and had a delightful journey past peach orchards and through the rising valleys till we came under the solemn shadow of those "great protuberances" which, in spite of Dr. Samuel Johnson, will always awe and cheer the heart of any genuine warm-blooded Scotchman. The river here was seen through tangled bamboo brake and fresh scented pines to run far below us, through great white plains of pebbles luminous in the sun. It was studded too with clumsily picturesque water-mills, built on huge boats which are strongly moored to the banks, but are ready to be let slip if need be, when the rain floods raise them. Numerous rafts of roughly cut wood are floated down from the mountain forests to the populous plain. The road, for a rural mountain road, is very good, and is built up with huge water-worn stones of great geological variety. At one place far from any large village, a very spacious school has been built in the new foreign style, but with Swiss-like and romantic modifications—just such a place as one's boyish memories must cling to with love. I have visited several of those new schools which are spread all over the country, and have been quite pleased to witness the marked efficiency of some of them. What is needed more than anything now is fresh and good text-books suited to the changed times and new life of the country. The Japanese have adopted many translations of our own best text-books, but not a few of them are quite unnatural grafts upon Japanese civilization. Now as mission schools are being opened all over the country to which we have access, something of this kind might very soon be attempted, with reasonable prospects of success. It may

surprise and please many to hear that in Japan there is
not only now an official Sabbath-day of rest, which is
spreading its influence wider and wider, but that the
government text-books also are often theistic, and might
even on account of an obscurity in the language be thought
monotheistic. Some may think that this is rather, however,
an example of the shallow eclecticism that has so largely
characterized the recent progress of Japan. But neither
theism nor monotheism are quite fresh and foreign to the
Far East.

My wife and
the children
were packed
tightly into *kagos*
—the old sedan
chairs of Japan
—which are still
found useful in
mountainous
districts, where
wheeled vehicles

From a Native Sketch.

cannot go.

As we toiled up the shaded paths which lead to the quiet
little hamlet and temple which crown the misty summit,
we were constantly cheered by the tinkle of many a cool
and pellucid rill, the sound of the wood-cutter's axe, or
the shrill but not unpleasing note of the cicada, which
may be heard at an almost incredible distance. Once or
twice while listening to its metallic *skirl*, which, like the
sweet old bagpipes, derives some enchantment from distance, the painted singer suddenly ceased its song and

fell dead at our feet. Though its three central eyes still gleamed with their own ruby-like lustre, and its outward form and colour were quite fair to see, within it was a mere mass of dust and rottenness, for a deadly fungus had rapidly consumed all its vital organisation, leaving a sweet voice and nothing more. Many insects die in this way, and it has been proposed to cultivate and sow the special parasitic germs which are hostile to any given species, where they can be readily infected. So the much-abused germs of disease may yet come to render friendly services to man.

There is a great variety of timber in the mountains of this range, and the forestry department is becoming alive, not a day too soon, to the economical wants of modern Japan in this respect. Very neat books are published by the Educational Department, which contain thin sections' of all the woods which are grown. Deforestation had been going on very rapidly in the "good old" feudal times, but when the cry of alarm was raised, efficient measures were taken to remedy the evil in the future. Many are the advantages which the country seems to be about to reap from its intercourse with the scientific activity of the West, and benevolent forethought for posterity is certainly not the least of the virtues which are being derived from contact with our Christian civilisation. They have planted many new trees here, such as the Eucalyptus, or Australian blue gum tree, of whose universal virtues rather wildly exaggerated notions seem to prevail here as in Europe.

When we got up into the rarer atmosphere we found it delightfully cool, and the forest paths were gloomy with an almost raw mist, which seemed at once to brace up one for almost any undertaking. Buckle is partly right, although he was late in the field. This influence of the mountain air was disappointingly transient however, and I think we were still under a great malarious fog-blanket which spreads over this part of Japan and of which I could sometimes define the outline very well. Other ranges are more free from it, and I find many medical facts to support this observation.

We visited the temple more than once, and, along with a missionary brother of another denomination, had some interesting talks with the old rector. He showed me a fine old native work on archæology, consisting of about a hundred thin volumes magnificently illustrated. I was fortunate in picking up a complete copy a few years afterwards in a back lane in Tokio, and found the figures relating to Buddhism very valuable. The priests all seem to foresee the decay of Buddhism in Japan; and some of them also see pretty clearly that even now the battle amongst educated Japanese is between scientific agnosticism and Christianity. The Roman and Greek systems have been very well considered by the Japanese, and will always have " converts " so long as their funds hold out. The " Greeks " use our books largely, and the Bible is read by them. I trust that many of them have got the essence of the faith in them.

One misty day we went to visit a very wild and impressive glen, through whose mossy boulders a foaming stream tears with thunderous uproar, forming some small but very romantic cataracts. In the midst of the glen there rise up from the thick foliage two rocky and precipitous peaks, bare of soil, but mossy and lichen-stained with many a rich hue. In a cleft on each peak a very skilfully wrought elf in fine bronze, has been erected. The two figures, which are nearly life-size, are different conceptions. Anything more weirdly *gruesome* and unhuman I have never seen, even in childhood's dreams. They are really high works of art, and characteristically Japanese. Those who placed them there must have had a keen sense of their harmony with the wild scene which surrounds them.

I had other plans to carry out ; but before anything could be done, and while sitting at a lamp one midnight catching moths which were numerous and very beautiful, a Government messenger appeared with a telegram from Tokio, requiring my immediate presence there. After a short nap, I left my sick children, and at daybreak started with my friend, to whom I have alluded, taking unfortunately a short cut down the mountain. Of course we lost our way, and just after the sun had fairly warmed to his work, we had to climb again the long and exposed spur we had come down. I lay down at last faint, sick, and thirsty, and was glad to lick any drops of dew which remained on the leaves. My friend had to return after we got into the track. Soon my shoes, cut up by the sharp stones, fairly gave out, and I threw them away. The flinty bed of a dry stream, which served for a road, kept me in active employment for more than half-an-hour, and then, when I thought my troubles were at an end, an interminable brambly footpath spread its charming vista before me. With torn and dirty clothes, shoeless, lame, and with bleeding feet,

I got to my halting place just in time to carry out my plan. My appearance was not calculated to promote respect, and I got an exceedingly rude reception and welcome refreshment at a little dirty tea-house in an out-of-the-way village at the foot of the mountains. A benevolent jinrikisha-man was induced to take me on a bit for double the usual fare, and I got a pair of Japanese socks and sandals, but found that I had been mischievously supplied with women's. However, they were very clean and comfortable, although they *did* receive more notice from travellers than was pleasant.

I got two fresh men, and dashed at a rapid rate over hill and dale, through brake and stream, till at last the large and picturesque town of Hachoji, with its clear cool river, and its great sacred cars, now bright with paint and varnish, began to draw near. There, after a hearty meal with chop sticks, sitting cross-legged on the mats, I caught an antiquarian oddity of a 'bus, which held together tolerably well till we got to Tokio, which was, as usual, red with the glare of a great conflagration.

CHAPTER IX.

Pilgrimage to Fuji the Peerless.

A Village Festival—Butterflies and Cicadas—A Noisy Inn—River Scene—
Silk—Dining on Hot Water—Mimicry in Spiders—A Mountain Pass—
Tea and Tattle—A Tragic Pool—Dissolving Views—Spindle Whorl—
An Exciting and Ludicrous Scene—Limbs of the Law—Curious
Bridge—Pious Parishioners and a Prudent Rector.

NE who wishes to admire a great
mountain must remain below. The
very worst possible use you can put it
to is to climb it. I have never climbed
Fuji, and don't mean ever to do so. I
believe what people say as to its
height to be pretty nearly correct,
and can quite understand that it must
be intolerably cold up there, and that the fleas in the
rest-houses, on the way up, are found unusually stimulating ; but I don't know that the simple repetition of other
people's monotonous experiences in this way would add
much to my own knowledge or enjoyment. Besides, if it
must be said, I am getting middle-aged and somewhat
short of breath, and to go up Fuji on a man's back, as a
friend once gravely proposed to me, would be simple
profanity.

I left Tokio one afternoon late in July, under a dull
sky, in a jinrikisha, with tandem ; was spun rapidly
across the lotus-covered moats, past the ruined castle of

the Shogun now mantled with ivy and bowered in sweet-
scented honey-suckle, through a lordly avenue of hoary
pines, past the trim barracks of the Life Guards and the
red brick walls of the English Legation—away out through
the wooded plains after the setting sun.   As we reached
the outskirts of the city, a village festival was going on ;
white-robed Shinto priests in a wooden cage were per-
forming some rites ; prettily-dressed girls, be-flowered
and be-powdered, their lips reddened with carmine and
their faces whitened, were ringing the prayer-bell, while
there was a prolific display of *gohei* or white paper symbols,
and piles of unleavened show-bread.   A crowd of worshippers was busily engaged in making huge pasteboard
standards for the impending procession.   There are always in the suburbs great trains of bullock-carts, pack-
horses, and slow-thinking bumpkins in charge of them.
I was greatly struck with the lush verdure of the country,
which is a great plain of lava-sand and loamy alluvium,
with which worms have had something to do ; but sub-
aerial deposit of dust has evidently here, as elsewhere,
played some part in the original formation of soil.   The
hedge-rows—not at all like ours—abounded in tiger-
lilies and a tall, white-flowered plant, something like honey-
suckle, which emits a yellow juice.

A great many green or golden-red dragon-flies, and
most magnificent butterflies, were fluttering about in
shady lanes,—large " swallow-tails," black or spotted with
sapphire tints, and a smaller jet-black butterfly, which appeared in the evening ; others bore a close resemblance
to dead leaves, and the more closely they were examined,
the greater seemed to be the likeness.   When they

alighted amongst old wood chips or decayed leaves, they kept jerking themselves about with their wings elevated. I saw also what seemed to be humming-bird hawk-moths fluttering in and out of large leafy trees. As there are no humming-birds in Japan, we must either believe that the humming-bird once mimicked such moths—and I have often seen them in other parts of Japan—or suppose, with the great naturalist, Mr. Bates, that similarity of habits has determined similarity of structure.

The houses on the wayside are all thatched with great skill and neatness, and wild-flowers often adorn them. As evening closed in, great log fires blazing up for the preparation of the evening meal on glazed black stove-like erections not often seen in Tokio, cast a ruddy glow on the smoky interiors and roused inspiring memories of happy winter evenings in the old country. Those fire-places, which were new to me, resembled in appearance those used by Russian peasants, and were made of clay, blackened and glazed like an American stove. The country through which we were passing was thickly wooded, and care seemed to have been taken to prevent deforestation. Some of the trees were apparently about two centuries old, and were immensely tall. The tree grass-hoppers and the cicadas made the woods resound with their strident notes as with the roar of a cataract. The cicada beats a pair of drums situated under its belly. The tree grass-hopper plays a kind of fiddle by means of the serrated margin of its wing sheath and the roughened edge of its thigh, and plays indeed often with such sweetness of tone that the Japanese imprison them in tiny cages, and feed them as we do canaries. Sometimes, however, the screech of those musical tree insects is almost like that of a locomotive whistle competition, and becomes quite painful to listen to.

There are in Japan a few grand main roads or imperial highways along which almost all that is important in history seems to have clustered, and they have been determined in early times by physiographical conditions. That on which we are now travelling is called the Kôfu-kaido, from Kôfu, an important silk and grape growing town to which it tends. Wood, at all events, is plentiful on the way, and we met many an old man tottering along under his load of lichened faggots.

At last the landscape grew grey and then dark, and we began wearily to ask the distance from the first stage. It seemed a long time before the welcome cheery gleam of a lantern-lit town began to show itself through the masses of cypress and bamboo. It was Fuchiu where we were to pass the night, and a gay and festive scene was that on which we entered. The hotels were quite crowded with strangers, but we got accommodation at last. For supper we had *ai* fish and yams, tea, and that never-to-be-forgotten semi-putrid " bean " sauce concerning which there are dark rumours that the makers of certain well-advertised English sauces import large quantities from China and Japan. I got under an immense green mosquito net with my paper lantern, as the insects were troublesome, and began to make the foregoing notes. A fine gold and green *buprestis* got in and fluttered about the lamp, while I prepared to compose myself for reading a chapter or two of Bates on the Amazon. The coolies, like pigmies refreshed after supper and a hot bath, came in ducking most vigorously and beseeching me in the most winsome tones to give them a small advance towards my contract, as there was extraordinary and irresistible jollification going on in the hotel. Certainly the halls were filled all night with the sound of revelry, the smell of *sake* (rice-beer), and the fumes of coarse tobacco. Sleep was impossible, and I found myself to have been the victim of a horrid nightmare, in which the Amazon swallowed up the Tamagawa and Pera merged into the purlieus of Yokohama,—but whether I had been dreaming that I was Mr. Bates, or Mr. Bates that he had been me, I could not for the poor life of me tell. At length the impatient cock duly crowed in that pert and mathematically proper style peculiar to such an unimaginative bird, and the shrill scream of sliding shutters soon drowned its impertinent and fussy voice. The swallows, who had their nests under the eaves, were twittering in and out of the house, seeming to be specially fond of the telegraph wires and hardly ever alighting anywhere else. The usual washing appliances in a Japanese hotel are a piece of fossilised soap, a blue cotton and malodorous coarse miniature table-napkin for a towel, and a wooden comb like a garden rake, common to all comers, as in the trite story told of the American passenger and the "ship's tooth brush." A small saucer full of dirty salt completes the set, as no Japanese is supposed ever to desire to look at himself in a mirror. The ladies of course have polished metallic ones, and like those of ancient Egypt, alas! see only therein faces of brass! Well, I am afraid my lack of sleep had spoiled my temper a bit.

After rice and cocoa (I shall not be tempted here

to advertise the maker) we left about six o'clock, the day promising to be a hot one. The country a little beyond this opens up pleasingly, and our way now lay through fields of buckwheat, groves of persimmon trees now in fruit, and yams with great handsome leaves like lilies of the Nile. We had a glimpse of the river Tama-gawa, running between its reedy and gravelled banks, and which for the time had shrunk to small dimensions. Under the overhanging roots of an old tree on the edge of the bank I got hold of a magnificent large fungus, which I brought home with me. While crossing the ferry we found the water to be delightfully cool and clear. It supplies the city of Tokio through wooden mains twenty-seven miles long. Looking up the stream steep wooded banks appeared which had in some parts suffered from landslips, and the raw wounds showed through their bosky sides in whitish strata, looking in the distance like pipe clay. The banks were level atop on both sides at a similar height, showing the old alluvial plateau of the river's bed. In the far distance bluish toned mountains sweetly closed in the scene from the north.

The land was now one great garden of mulberry plants, the dark green leaves of which form the food of the silk worm. On the highest of the old river terraces is an old temple built on a platform of large stones, and surrounded by a grove of trees some of which seemed to be nearly two centuries old. Passing by some reedy marshes teeming with interesting microscopic life as I afterwards found, we rattled into the busy little town of Hachoji, which has a population of about 8000. Along the centre of a long sloping street stood rows of patient pack-horses, with trappings of burnished brass and long flapping fringes of red and brown leather paper to keep off the flies. They were as usual shod with straw slippers, and had each an extra couple of pairs slung to its harness. Through the middle of the street a stream of clear sparkling water rushes with pleasing gurgle, filling the frequent wells and turning little toy water wheels which children were watching with interest. Silk is the dominating idea of society in Hachoji. The country is green with mulberry for the silk worms ; the shops are filled with baskets and other apparatus required in the rearing of the worms or winding of the cocoons, and every one seems to be engaged in some part of the various processes of silk manufacture. And yet one is not prepared to hear that Japan after all produces a very small proportion of the silk consumed in the world. More energy, more science, more economy, and better means of transport are all needed.

Before entering the pass there is a small village— Kawara-no-hiku, where were some very fine cocoons and some beautiful floss silk. The roadside was adorned with many tall, straight and slim orange lilies growing wild. I examined them carefully but could not in this species detect any trace of those curious contrivances for insect fertilization of which so much is now written. At the bottom of each calyx lay a considerable quantity of clear fluid. They were quite smooth inside. Many of them were also growing on the grass ridge of the thatched cottages, where they produced a very striking and original effect. Large humming-bird hawk-moths were fluttering in and out of tall tree tops like birds, and I saw some lively specimens of *cicindela* or tiger beetles about the mulberry bushes as we brushed past them.   When we stopped to rest an old woman in a dirty little tea-house offered to prepare me some refreshment.   I shall not readily forget her astonishment when I told her to prepare a simple dinner of clean hot water for me.   She had never seen chocolate before, and ventured timidly to taste the "foreign clay"—and it seemed to please her very much.

I got a fine nest of a *Polistes* hanging under the eaves —rather a queer situation for a wasp's nest, was it not ? While I was sitting at my simple repast, a splendid butterfly, having pale, dingy green swallow-tail wings, with dark spots of great size, was fluttering constantly about a piece of dung on the road opposite the tea-house.

Common *plantago* was growing in great profusion. Here and there the steep hillsides have been terraced with the aid of boulders to yield rice, buckwheat, yams, etc., but the mulberry plant prevails over all this district of Japan.   Our way now lay up the toilsome Kobotoke pass. The road is singularly beautiful as it winds up through shady rocks and across boulder-strewn mountain torrents, whose cool white foam made one, panting under a hot sun, distractingly thirsty.   The heat was really intense, and here jinrikiskas were of no avail.   When resting from time to time on the mossy trunk of a fallen tree I saw many curious spiders, and captured a few interesting specimens which illustrated the principle of protective— or in this case rather destructive—mimicry in zoology. Those spiders bear a strong resemblance both in colour and form to fresh, unexpanded leaf-buds, and the sly wretch places himself just where a similar bud usually occurs. Others I found which closely resembled grass seeds, or withered spikes of larch. Those latter are very expert in hiding themselves, and cling closely to the side of the twig on which they hunt, generally changing their position quickly if you watch them so as to have the stem between themselves and you.

After some hours' hard climbing by zig-zag paths I arrived at a delightfully situated tea-house on the mountain's brow. It was propped up partly by a huge tree, and hung from the edge of a rock on a platform of half-rotten pines over a great abyss. Pilgrims with their tinkling bells, pedlars and farmers were constantly arriving and departing, after having bought about a half-penny worth of tea. A refreshing breeze played over my heated forehead, and but for the day's rapid advance I could have remained much longer. The garrulous old landlady, who had something to say to everybody in a hearty piping voice, told me they never had any earthquakes there. Now this appeared to me a little striking, as one very notable earthquake apparently traversed the lofty range which this pass crosses, and was distinctly observed at Kôfu, many miles beyond, as well as at Tokio, Yokohama, and other places on the other side. The rocks in the vicinity are very interesting, and some good sections are visible. In Japan seismology has been prosecuted by native scholars as well as by foreign professors, with much originality and enthusiasm, and it is to be hoped that clearer ideas will soon emerge.

On the way down we met further trains of pilgrims panting up the pass. I overheard two very amusing old fellows discussing in pathetic and most philosophic style the peculiar effect of gravity in making an uphill road so painfully exhausting to human beings. It was clear that, had the universe been left to them to amend this grave error in its constitution would soon have been put right.

A series of short climbs, alternating with rapid and rocky descents, in one of which I sprained my foot severely, soon brought us to the river Baniu, which is navigable up to this point for small sailing boats. As my foot was beginning to get red and swollen, I sat down and laved it in the cold clear water for a long time. The scenery was very pleasing, and almost Swiss-like, an impression which was greatly aided by the white semi-Italian tower of a modern court-house rising above the shingled roofs of a village on the mountain's side.

There was a pretty little fountain playing in the court of a tea-house where we stopped. It was supplied from a spring by bamboos, the thin partitions at the nodes of which are driven out by a long iron rod. Bamboo is often very useful in this way, but unfortunately it requires too frequent renewal. They told me, in answer to inquiries, that earthquakes were felt occasionally there, but they were usually very slight. There are some very remarkable river-terraces of natural formation at Futase-goye. After crossing the river here, our path lay along a broad plain of glaring water-worn pebbles, which tried my still tender foot very greatly. Again we had to climb in order to regain the plateau of the old terrace on the opposite bank. There were sections of great cliffs exposed which were built up of loosely stratified water-worn stones of variable size, and which had been deposited when the climatal conditions of Japan were probably very different from those that now prevail. In some parts the way was rather dangerous, and as night began to draw on, we passed a dreadful pool on a little lonely moor, surrounded by tragic red shafted pines. Soon the moon rose, solemn and clear, and, all alone, I trudged on amidst awful stillness.

The valleys were filled most of the time with soft fleecy clouds. Sometimes, ere it got dark, the great green plain of Yedo, with its meandering rivers and tangled maze of dusty gray roads hanging almost perpendicularly from the sky like a vast panoramic map, would break forth quietly for a little, soon to fade dreamily away again like a dissolving view on a white curtain of mist. The whole scene was to me like a dream. I spent a very happy, peaceful Sunday in the midst of those calm, quiet hills near Yose, with a most home-like Japanese family, the members of which did everything they could to make me comfortable in mind and body.

On the morning of the following day my host was sweeping the floor, and happening to require something, I spoke to him *en deshabille*. He answered me in humble language like a domestic. By-and-by, robed with dignity as master of the house, he came in to give me my morning salute, as if he had never seen me before. This seems a strange kind of hypocrisy, and yet one feels it to be essentially good-breeding on the whole. The morning air was delightfully clear and invigorating, and I started early, passing down hill through a very fine valley. At one quaint little hamlet I got a glimpse of primitive life which gladdened me very much. Some women and girls were busy spinning lengths of yarn by means of old-

fashioned spindle-whorls. I have never seen stone ones
used anywhere, however, in Japan. That which was
being used was a vertical pin of iron with a horizontal
whorl of heavy wood. It was sent spinning round
rapidly, the yarn being fastened to it and so receiving the
proper twist. The lines were supported as in our rope-
spinning yards, and several lines of thread were being
twisted at the same time, each, of course, having its own
spindle attached. The same instrument was used in
Tokio by a previous generation. As we continued to
descend various kinds of rock appeared in succession—
some of them recent, and of volcanic origin. Springs
were very frequent too, and the water was pleasant and
cool—a real treat to any one coming from Tokio, where
the water supply, though originally almost perfect, is con-
taminated to an alarming extent by sewage and other im-
purities. The roofs of the houses were mostly covered
with shingles held in their places as in most mountainous countries against high winds by boulders placed atop.
Rich balsams were growing in the stone walls from
crevices ; the gardens were very trim, the roads wonderfully well kept, and everything when I passed seemed as
neat and clean as if the Mikado himself had been expected to make an imperial progress in a day or so. I
had got two coolies to carry me along, but they had been
drinking heavily, and when we came to a sloping and
sinuous road, which let you look sheer down over the jinrikisha into a leafy segment of infinite space, they nudged
each other, and commenced a series of very amusing
attempts, regardless of my helpless efforts to get out and
stop them, to run me along with one wheel just on the

verge of the abyss. I have never used my fists to a Japanese in any circumstances whatever, but on this occasion as I was really in danger, I at last stood up waving a corpulent umbrella over their wine-flushed pates like an excited American stump orator, and "felt like" applying it pretty vigorously. As a matter of course, we suddenly came in sight of a little police station, with its inevitable pair of goggle-eyed preservers of the peace, who rushed out with severe inquiry and menace on their stern visages —but the cause of my offence was too obvious to be mistaken, and my impetuous steeds were reproved with great severity.

This place was Koma-hashi, on the river Katsura, which dashes in white foam over great boulders, hollowing out a gulley through hard stratified rock. You cross by a high bridge into a busy market town. This bridge is called Saru-hashi or the monkey's bridge, and is built on something like the modern cantilever principle. Messrs. Satow and Hawes thus describe, it :—" It rests on the ends of a series of horizontal beams planted deep in the soil which covers the rock, laid in tiers, each tier projecting beyond and above the other, with cross beams laid in between, and a little roof over the extremities to protect them from the effects of the weather."

A little further on and to the right there was a massive dark basalt-like mass of rock, seemingly bare of trees, save two great pines near the flat summit, which only served to emphasize the general barrenness. Another prominent rocky spur rose up behind. We passed several water-falls and tributary brooks turning sluggish water-mills on their way, and then came to a halt for the day at Odzuki.

There is no good tea-house or hotel at this little village, but by aid of a friendly letter I found a quiet tidy little room, and soon scraped acquaintance with the neighbours, who seemed glad to have a chat with a foreigner. It was surprising to find how well they could understand an English large scale map of Japan (Brunton's) which I had opened out on the floor. The villagers in an English county town would by no means have been so well able to point out rivers and bays in Wales or Scotland on an English map. I am disposed to think that the system of military service and of religious pilgrimages have done very much not only to spread local geographical knowledge in Japan, but also to maintain comparative uniformity in the language.

By-and-by my religious function became known, and some amusement was caused when it leaked out that the Kan-nushi of the adjoining parish, who had been consecrating a new bridge, was to lodge there that night. I expressed great joy in the anticipation of a little friendly conversation before the company on the subject of the merits of our respective religions ; namely, Shinto, or the Way of the Spirits, and Christianity. The proposal was very heartily received by the pious parishioners who had assembled to do him honour ; but after many whispered communications it was made clear amidst much hearty laughter, that the worthy rector had found his duties call him to a hamlet a little further on. This gave me a quiet opportunity of laying down the truth in a non-controversial form. Some levy was made on my very small, and on this occasion, merely personal supply of drugs, and I disposed of my remaining stock of books.

CHAPTER X.

Pilgrimage to Fuji the Peerless.

Pretty Tree Frogs—Ancient Trees—Buddha-faced woman—Peep into a
Village School—*Ai* Fish—Sweet Scenery—Awe inspiring Walk—Lava
" Froth" and its Use—Mild Martyrdom—A Heavenly Vision—Moun-
tain Lake—Volcanic Prairie Flowers—An Æsthetic jinrikisha Man—
A Statuesque Stoat—Novel Tail-piece—Patriotic Bias—Fans *versus*
Flies.

THERE was no post office in the town, and as writing a letter would have been useless I took a stroll
to the river to look at the new bridge which was being
built.   There were some dark purple velvety-winged
dragon-flies hovering over the river and alighting on the
smooth boulders.   In a garden I saw a fine shapely
column of basalt, hollowed out as a water-basin on the
top, which confirmed a report I had heard of a beautiful
formation of that kind further down the river, but which
I could not reach.   An old lady with an immense crowd
of children about her was spinning, and looking now and
again with calm interest at the " hairy foreigner."

There are many venerable trees in this neighbourhood,
and I saw one stump which showed more than two hundred rings.   I am aware that now-a-days it is not supposed that a single ring invariably stands for a year ; but
I think that those trees were about two centuries old at
least.

In the evening I walked along to the temple.   The

H

moist rice-fields were swarming with beautiful little bright green gilded tree frogs—at least the tips of their toes were expanded into small cup-like discs exactly like those of tree frogs, of which there are many in Japan. The little animals were exceeding lovely in colour, form, and even in expression.

A curious water-worn stone is placed conspicuously by the wayside, its hollowed out cavity containing water. Close by is a wide court-yard containing a tree of great diameter, and what appeared to be an old temple. I saw no one there, but when I began to measure the girth of the trunk I became conscious of the wondering gaze of a kindly calm-looking matron, with the very expression Japanese artists so often give to their Buddhas, but which I had never seen in real life before. She was looking down on me from an adjoining two storey building of some dignity, from which the drowsy hum of many boyish voices rose. As I felt myself to be somewhat of a trespasser I explained that I had been attracted by this wonderful old tree, on which she asked me with great genuineness of manner to rest for a little, when her husband the schoolmaster would be glad to give me any information about the district I might desire. The good dominie soon joined us, some very intelligent lads, who had been busy at vulgar fractions as I could overhear, chiming into the conversation with much pleasant humour, good sense and useful information. There was soon put before us all the usual pale strong tea in tiny cups, without sugar or cream, and little tablets of peppermint sugar—a favourite sweetmeat. After this the children, who were mostly from about seven to ten years of age, were put through their exercises in reading and arithmetic very creditably. Indeed many of our own school inspectors would really have been able to appreciate their work, even in an unintelligible language. None of them knew a word of English, but it was clear that they were being taught efficiently to garner some of the best results of modern cosmopolitan civilization. They used the Arabic numerals as being more convenient, and had good maps and diagrams on the walls. The teacher himself was a new arrival, and had been educated in Tokio. He and his wife felt lonely in such a dreamy rustic neighbourhood, and he was longing for a sphere with greater stir and

Angler.

bustle. In a little the good lady hurried in with some fresh country eggs—a treat to any one who is accustomed to the fishy flavour of those produced on the seaboard The fowls were of unusual size and vigour.

The teacher had arranged a little excursion for next morning, so I was up at cockcrow, and found him along with a troupe of bright-faced merry big boys waiting for me when I arrived at the schoolroom. His kind spouse pressed some very eatable little dumplings on me, which were of good service before I

had gone far.   We crossed the rushing Katsura, here
famous for its fine *ai* which are caught with live bait, consisting often, as the teacher told me, of the young of the
same species, usage quite as bad as seething a kid in its
mother's milk, and certainly not what one would expect
in a Buddhist country.   But modern Buddhism does not
strictly forbid either fish or wine, though you may see on
any temple court-yard notices forbidding the carriage of
those popular commodities *through* the sacred precincts.
Evil-minded people whisper that they may be taken into
the enclosure, however, without any serious penalty being
incurred.   The *ai* is a large fish when full grown, and resembles salmon a little.   The object of our little expedi-
tion was to visit a great dark basaltic rock resembling that
on which Edinburgh Castle is so grandly perched.   Its
steep sides are thickly wooded, and we found it hard and
hot work to reach the ruins of the old castle of Sir
Oyamada Bichiu, belonging I think to the latter part of the
sixteenth century.   The boys leaped along the peaks of
basalt like goats, now yelling with delight when they unearthed an unfortunate snake, or with a somewhat different
emotion when they trod on a prickly shrub.   The stones
were very slippery, fallen trees presented good opportunities for gymnastics, and every spot was covered by long
rank grass which cut your hands like a badly set razor.   At
one secluded spot there was an old forgotten looking temple, the images in which were of a rather primitive type,
found in only a few parts of Japan.
   On our way down we called on a wealthy silk farmer,
whose mulberry groves flanked the mountain.   He gave
us a most kindly and hospitable reception to his large

and orderly establishment, and showed us his collection
of Japanese drawings and pottery. After my back had
been suppled with profound salutations to each member
of a large family, tea and a delicious kind of Turkish delight made in the district were laid before us, and we sat
on the clean straw mats discussing the latest news from
Tokio and the new doctrine of *Yasu*, till it was time to
return. On hearing I was a surgeon it was felt at once
that the "gods were gracious," as the good lady of the
house was suffering severely from an eye affection, for
which I was able to leave some useful medicine and directions. After a present had been given me of fresh grapes,
candied in a way for which the adjoining town is famous,
and many hearty parting salutations had been exchanged,
we hurried back amidst gathering shadows through the
river valley to Odzuki.

After crossing the Katsura again in a frail and trembling boat, which a silent Charon with face like a withered
apple, guided across the foaming torrent by aid of a rope
stretched from bank to bank, I engaged a pawky old fellow with great conversational powers, and a never failing
fund of humour, to carry my "traps." We set off briskly
on foot amidst a slight shower of rain for Kami Yoshida
—a great resort of pilgrims preparing to make a meritorious ascent of Fuji, or returning after having performed
that feat. The road was good, I was now in capital trim
for walking, and the scenery was very pleasing—hills soft
in outline and green with new verdure refreshed by the
shower, sometimes well wooded, but more usually terraced
visibly by the ancient carving power of the river, aided
somewhat by the art of man in fitting the soil for the cul-

ture of rice ; but the country was here richly diversified
with the varied products of a most economical and industrious husbandry. There seemed to be no room for weeds
anywhere. Melons, gourds, or cucumbers trailingly spread
their bright golden flowers and veiny leaves, so rich in form
and mellow shadow tints, over the cottages. Every flower
plot was brightened by rich balsams, scarlet,—crimson or
creamy white, delicately tinted with pink ; while close by
every gateway tiny streams of cool clear spring water
gurgled, and cascades were crashing on their way to turn
some lazy but picturesque moss-clad old mill-wheel which
were met with at almost every turn of the road. We passed
through many villages, the country seeming to be populous even for Japan, and the streets were crowded with
stolid, attentive, unamused children, of the type to be found
anywhere throughout the empire. Here the idols, or
"statues" as it is fashionable to call them, now presented
some unique features, but whether purely local or not I
have not found. For some distance our way lay between
great walls of rough ruddy grey lava, tumbled about in
great rocky masses, that gave an air of hideous ruin and
desolation to a moor-like expanse, on which the shades of
night were now closing, tempered by a broad bar of lurid
red in the western sky. I could not help picturing to
myself, as I picked my way over the lava, scenes of blood
and violence, such as might have supplied plots to any
number of "penny dreadfuls," and really, some of the
inky pools over which huge contorted demon like masses
of lava kept watch might have hid many a dreadful
secret.

My jinrikisha man gave the expressive name of *awa*

(froth) to the honey-combed slag-like lava. These curious bits of scoriæ are utilised in making rockeries, and many tons of the material are sent to Tokio and other large towns for this purpose. In some places great walls were built of the material, a slight growth of vegetation had covered the stone, filling the crevices with rich mosses and rare ferns, while here and there a gnarled pine tree had audaciously struck its roots into the stony soil. One could not help thinking of that fearful time recorded in Japanese history when the hot liquid stream ran down those now silent slopes, carrying terror, death, and desolation with it.

A cold dry wind began to set the fossil demons a-howling in the eeriest way, and right glad was I when the upward-sloping main street of Kami Yoshida at last stretched its pale dusty vista before me.

I have arrived late, footsore and soiled with dust, at many a Japanese town, but never before nor since have I had such a rough reception as I am about to relate, and which is very rare at the present time in the experience of foreigners.

At first I merely thought that our advent excited unusual interest, which puzzled me a little, as I knew that travellers from the West had often been there. By-and-by something like a crowd collected and dogged my weary footsteps, and once or twice I thought I overheard some not very complimentary epithets. Thereafter a few little pellets of mud came curving towards my devoted head, and in a trice I was conscious of being stoned by a large Japanese mob. The slightest loss of temper or lack of firmness, and my case might have become serious. I kept watch on the ringleaders and steered steadily for the inn which I had been advised to seek. I there planted myself firmly in the doorway, faced the mob—now becoming somewhat roused at prospect of losing their prey—and requested shelter for the night. It was refused, but on showing my passport and requesting the presence of the chief magistrate or head of police while I temporarily, at least, claimed shelter, the master of the house thought it wise to give me his countenance. I civilly asked the apparent leaders of the mob—young lads they were—to be reasonable, and to explain the offence which seemed to them to justify such an extraordinary reception of a quiet traveller who had come to admire the famed beauties of their district. I received no explanation, but the very mild and practically harmless stoning began to cease, and the more active lads whom I now fixed with my eye slunk off, when I warned them that their government would hardly thank them for embroiling the country again with foreign nations. The innkeeper, fearing trouble, arranged that I should go elsewhere, and at last by the efforts of my pawky old baggage-carrier, who kept aloof till all danger was over, I got into splendid quarters— the very best the town had to offer as compensation for the first rudeness of my reception. The old fellow, in short, I could hear dilating in the most eloquent terms on my many excellent qualities and on the considerateness which I had shown to himself and to others, as reported to him before starting with me. I need hardly say that his pleading was urged as a ground for fresh liberality when parting next morning.

My quarters for the night were in a large newly--

matted room, from the open verandah adjoining which I could see the base of Fuji, which rose steeply to the heavens, its summit buried in widespreading cottony *cumuli*. No food was forthcoming, and to all my requests the curt answer was, " There is none." I had seen potatoes growing in the garden and asked for some, offering to dig them up myself. This brought me a good meal at last. A lady who was, according to the simple manners of the country, to occupy a portion of my large room was joined by some intending pilgrims of both sexes, and the conversation, as a preliminary to sleep, at once turned upon the entrance of the " blue-eyed, red-haired devil." I am fortunately neither blue-eyed nor red-haired, but in Japan all Western foreigners *ought* to have the qualities those terms describe. Well, such had been the rhetorical effectiveness of my porter's defence, that the worthy lady—a model matron of Japan it must be admitted, appearances to the contrary notwith-standing—spoke to her numerous associates during the night in the most appreciative way of my manners, and admitted that externally nothing had been shown to reveal the depravity that belonged essentially to foreigners. The fact was, as I afterwards heard, the place had recently been visited by one or two French naval officers, and the worthy inhabitants of Kami Yoshida—not bad sort of people, I can assure you—had erroneously supposed that Englishmen were something like them, and hence the, in the circumstances, very justifiable stoning. *Verb. sap.*

Just before daybreak I arose refreshed, and went into the tiny courtyard to wash. The sky was grey and misty as on a raw winter morning in England, and nothing was to be seen in the grey dawn but a leafy patch of yams, bounded by a straggling forest of young cypress and pine trees. In a moment afterwards the mist had whitened and rolled away in torn masses like the rending of the temple veil. Then one of the most impressive and heavenly sights I have ever witnessed burst upon me with a strange surprise. The great tent-shaped mass of Fuji, then of a dark bluish purple, looking awful in its silent majesty so suddenly revealed, swept up in one perfect unbroken curve from where I stood, as if to the very throne of heaven, while its base—seeming to have become immeasurably broad—lay immersed in great billows of glistening silvery vapour which lay stratified in perspective. Above this gleaming veil of clouds rose, as if to meet her strong bridegroom the sun, the now blushing cone of Fuji. Such exquisite gradations of warm flesh tints ruddying into the deepest rose purple shaded with indigo grey, no mere pen and ink could be made to paint. Two bars of glistening snow flecked the summit, and when the remaining clouds fled as if affrighted before the rising majesty of the sun, dark woods still in the gloom of night shewed themselves as if crawling over the purple grey lava up the lofty slope. Exclamations of chastened surprise and joy rang from the lips of the now awakened pilgrims whom the hazy yesternight had bitterly disappointed, and even to me there seemed for the moment to be a sacred solemnity in this beautiful mountain which might almost justify the most ascetic pilgrimage—a feeling not a little deepened by the slow and sonorous boom of a large temple bell close by the inn.

After an early breakfast of tea, rice, and hard boiled

eggs, I set off in a jinrikisha, intending to join the main road again at Odawara which lies at the foot of the Hakone pass. The road lay for the most part through rough masses of lava, which seems to crumble down as you descend the slope leading to the sea shore till at last it is reduced to a fine dark sand and even into a loam like soil which is well cultivated. The watercourses there are a curious and interesting study for the physiographer, and seem to form a geological model of the earth in miniature, almost every style of mountain carving, river bed and lake, being richly illustrated. A great gloomy wold spreads itself out, between the sea and the southern base of Fuji, and as you rise above its level to cross the flank of the Oyama range the vast view becomes deeply impressive. On the one side sleeps a quiet lake in whose glassy bosom was mirrored a range of partly wooded, deeply furrowed hills that reminded me of the shadowy Ochil range near Stirling.

On the other side the lofty Hakone range—of volcanic origin—hid its ever cool forehead under a thunderous canopy of dark clouds. All around near where I stood lay stretched a great prairie of lava sand, as it were emblazoned with the richest and most varied display of wild flowers I have ever seen. A rich flora is said to be common enough at the base of such extinct volcanic cones, and while the chemical constituents of the soil may partly account for it, the high temperature of such a region is long retained, while there is also much moisture. The Japanese are passionately fond not only of beautiful scenery, but of flowers ; and I was not quite surprised when the sober-looking coolie laid down the shafts of his

rickety " hansom," and rushed amid the tall flowers with
open arms like a school-boy. After his fit of enthusiasm
had somewhat subsided, he returned with an armful of
bright yellow and white compositæ, orange lilies, and
some graceful sprays, on which shone numbers of beautiful large crimson scarlet brambles, or rather raspberries,
with which he adorned his vehicle. They tasted, however, very much like hot cinders, or rather water in
which red-hot iron has been cooled, and recalled to one's
mind the famous apples of Sodom.

Thanks to the æsthetic culture of my drawer, we lost
our way twice on this lava plain.

At one point the river beds, which are cut through the
lava sand, were quite dry, and although a thunderstorm
could be heard muttering in our rear, I waited patiently
under a broiling sun to see the effect of a spate, and was
not entirely disappointed. When the rain at last fell, the
foam-edged water would come rushing for a few yards
further, and then sink into the deep sand, as if it were so
much blotting paper. Another wave, and a new channel
would be opened up for a moment, again to dry up as
suddenly. At last passers-by warned us that the soil
under our feet might become soaked, and carry us away
Indeed, there was genuine cause for alarm, as at last we
began to feel and perceive, and we lost no time in gaining
a distant ridge which wound towards the path we sought.

Here I had some muddy and insipid tea, dismissed my
charioteer, and engaged the humbler services of a pack-
horse for the mountain pass, while I trudged along on
foot with the aid of a stout stick. The ditches were overhung with the coarse webs of enormous greenish and

yellow spotted spiders, which had a lace-like zig-zag net-
work to strengthen one segment, and on this part the
host sat disguising his presence from inexperienced insects
then just emerging from their pupal state, by rapid vibrations which rendered him nearly invisible. Beautiful large
swallow-tailed butterflies, of dark blue velvety texture,
seemed to be sipping the puddles on the shaded roadway.

At one point, where a quaint mossy bridge crossed a
mill stream, I stopped to rest, and, looking down, I saw a
kind of stoat, I think, emerge from between the stones of
the piers. Our eyes met, and silently and motionlessly I
watched him till he seemed to become mesmerised, as he
stood arrested quite in a statuesque position lifting a fore-
paw. At last I moved, and he disappeared amidst a
bunch of ferns like a flash from a pistol. As the pathway
emerged from under the grateful shadow of pine trees it
became hard work panting up thirstily amidst the dust
raised by a train of pack-horses, and under a fierce sub-
tropical sun blazing in a now almost cloudless sky. I
was fain at last to take hold of my pack-horse's tail, and
in this undignified fashion did I toil up many hundreds of
feet. By-and-by we came to a welcome spring bubbling
through lichened boulders and graceful ferns. I sat down
on a mossy rock and turned round to admire the scene
through which we had been passing. Away above me
and out of sight I heard a voice shouting, and soon
there came plunging down the rock-strewn footpath an
eccentric form in foreign clothes, which I took to be that
of a native of the country. He turned out to be an
Italian silk dealer. He was in a state of wild enthusiasm,
and said the scenery beat anything he had witnessed even

in Italy.   I politely expressed my regret that he had
not seen Scotland, but really even the "patriotic bias"
could not restrain me from joining warmly in his praises
of the landscape.

Nothing in Japan is absolutely without its uses.   Here
I came across a scene which set me laughing, all alone as
I was, very heartily.   A small "sweetie" shop, as it
would be called in Scotland, was planted beside a tiny
cascade, which, besides giving romance to the scene and
cooling the air around the bench on which customers
might regale themselves, supplied water to the interior
through a hollow bamboo.   Now, flies are fond of sugar,
raw or manufactured, and in a hot country and warm season
they are apt to multiply at a more rapid rate than their
natural foes can keep pace with.   Well, the worthy old
couple who owned the shop had devised a complex net-
work of cord moved by a little water-wheel, and in turn
giving wild and impetuous movement to a set of fans which
were made to wave in an absurdly jerky, angry, human-
like fashion over the precious wares.   My laughter brought
the smiling, ruddy-faced old confectioner out with apolo-
getic bows—" Really they were very ignorant and clumsy
people, but those nasty flies were so troublesome and
greedy!"   I cannot yet get rid of the ludicrous impression
made by the frantically impatient movements of the fans
and the rhythmic dance of the irrepressible flies, in and
out of what they no doubt considered their lawful
preserves.

I soon arrived at the gay and bustling town of
Odawara, at the foot of the pass, once a military post of
great importance when East and West in Japan were like

two kingdoms. Its castled moat, over which now ivy crawls and water weeds thickly grow, speaks of a vanished age of war and romance and practical misery. Next morning I was dashing along the Tokaido, or great main road to Tokio, behind two nearly naked jinrikisha men, through a piny avenue and in view of the stately march to solemn music of foam-crowned rollers from the Pacific, rushing up the tawny beach at last like a charge of plumed cavalry ; and in the evening I was clasping in my paternal arms sweeter flowers than ever bloomed out of lava dust.

CHAPTER XI.

In a Cottage by the Sea.

A Fair Breeze and Holiday Aspirations—Voyage of Discovery—Crabs and
Canal Banks—A Marine Tunnel-borer—Snakes and Frogs—Stone Net-
sinkers—*Tai* Fish—A Lovely Marvel of the Sea—A Dying Cuttle-fish.

FOR many hot, breezeless days the river had been
choked up with idle junks waiting for a fair wind
to carry them to distant ports. At last, just as the tide
was turning to go out, a favouring breeze sprang up, and
there was a sudden commotion ; the strange, prolonged
tones of shipmates on shore for boats, and of shipmates
on board for help ; the creaking, rasping, and groaning
everywhere of primitive capstans, followed by the rattling
and flapping of great whitey-grey square sails ; and in
almost less time than I have taken to tell it, a countless
fleet of junks, as like each other as peas, was curving out
in well-kept line through the dingy brown mixture of
brackish mud and city sewage which forms the head of
the bay, past the lemon-yellow buildings of the U.S.
Legation ; along by the noble pine-bordered gardens
of " The Palace by the Strand," through the silent weed-
crowned forts built by the French for the defence of
Tokio, and away out at last to where the sea became
blue and the haze veiled them at last from sight, leaving
us to dream of imaginary beauties of scenery in places far
away. I had been following with longing eyes those

white sails gleaming in the mellow sunset, and, tired, hot, and stupid with many a hard summer-day's work in a crowded dispensary, thought I should like to make a little voyage of discovery in a Japanese junk.

My wish had not long been expressed when its fulfilment was secured. Two seafaring country fellows thought of making a venture for cargo to a village just in the vicinity of the place I wanted to reach, and they offered to take myself and family, including our *lares and penates*, for the usual unnameable " mere trifle," to Tomioka, a pretty quiet little place on the sea-shore, where is an hospitable Buddhist temple and rectory, and a few native houses which can be had during the hot season for the sea-bathing. We had the usual fate of running aground several times in the shallow bay, which did not, however, seem to modify our rate of progress very much. By-and-by we passed through an artificial canal, cut through high rocks for a considerable distance, and thus we saved a long detour. The worthy boatmen duly dined on a great bucketful of very grey-coloured rice, flavoured with raw fish as a relish, and frequent cups of pale green tea. We toasted our share of fish on the charcoal embers on the brazier, and enjoyed some boiled yams, the unwonted fresh scent of the sea giving me an appetite I had not enjoyed for months. As we gently glided along it was amusing to watch the stealthy scuttling away of myriads of crabs into their holes on the canal bank. They destroy those banks very greatly, but no remedy has been proposed. Is it they who drag in the straws of which the ends are to be seen protruding in many places, and, if so, what can be their purpose in doing so? Those burrowing

I

crabs, which are to be seen in hundreds, are large, dingy grey, with reddish-coloured markings, and are roundish in shape. Further along is the deep cutting just referred to. It has been made through beds of a rock that looks as if composed of stratified pumice formed by submarine deposit. As the boat cleaves its way through the glassy water, we could see down into depths of verdant forests, consisting of a kind of *chara* and other water plants. On the surface with heads up out of the water and tails down, there were generally three or four frightened pipe fish, of more than a foot long, wriggling out of the way, and leaving long wavy angles in their wake.

The cliffs at Tomioka are of a soft blue sandy tuff, which is somewhat tenacious like clay. They are bored through in all possible directions by a little crustacean about the size of a horse-bean and like a rock slater (*Ligia*) in appearance. Their work has been ascribed by a good scientific observer to *Pholades*. I have seen the empty shell of a *pholas* now and again in the vicinity, but never have I seen a living animal of the species, although I daresay they may sometimes be found. Wherever I have met with the characteristic borings in the rocks about the shores of the bay, I have always found this slater-like animal at work not far from the spot, and have carefully watched their operations while supplying them now and again with salt water, fresh from the sea. A fragment of cliff bored by them often presents the appearance of a bit of sponge, although the tunnel made by each animal is as a rule almost perfectly straight and cylindrical. The little creature rolls itself up into a ball like an armadillo when you meddle with it, and is slow to unrol itself again.

When at work they scuffle the water out from below the abdomen with, great rapidity, and in a continual stream. I made a careful microscopic examination of them, but am not quite satisfied yet as to the meaning of what I have seen and drawn. In order to work they must be constantly supplied with fresh sea water. They spring in the water in a very peculiar way, and they seemed to me to study well the bearings of a particular spot before they began boring operations. Some of them tried to climb up the glass side of the vessel in which they were confined, but they invariably slipped down again. The little ones often began to bore from the sides of a tunnel made by the larger ones, and in course of time the rock for a few inches about water mark is thus quite riddled with tiny tunnels, so that portions become readily undermined and give way by the action of the waves. In one place further down the bay, there is an exposed section of the rock already mentioned, having one regularly waved central layer lying evenly disposed between an upper and a lower horizontal layer. It seemed to be somewhat like the result of expansion by molecular rearrangement. The appearance presented was like this, ~~~~~~~~~

"Our cottage" was a very pleasant little residence indeed. We could step from our rooms almost right into the tepid waves of a good beach, and from its open verandah, one could watch a great American packet churning the entrance to the Pacific with its huge paddles, and now and again a British gunboat, under its pious symbol of the triple cross, plodding on to Yokohama. I found much to interest me in the insects of the little garden amidst the foliage of which our youngsters discovered with much joyful emotion, many tiny green tree frogs seeking an honest livelihood. The frogs at Tomioka are varied and numerous, and include an edible variety, whose nutritious qualities however we did not venture to test. Close beside our modest cot, we once saw a large snake attempting to swallow a larger frog. I saved master froggy, whose lower extremities were already engulfed, and sacrificed the snake, as the worthy villagers believed (so I was afterwards told,) to the shrine of Æsculapius, which seemed to them a highly rational proceeding.

Nothing occurred of special interest, except that after we were all asleep a loud banging of antediluvian muskets of preposterous length, roused us with the idea that a revolution was taking place in the village. It turned out to have been a robbery. An old couple living not far off, had been bound and robbed, but succeeded at length in giving an alarm, and we all turned out very courageously, I must say, to help the noise.

Next morning after a refreshing struggle with the briny surf, I wandered along the beach, and had a chat with the

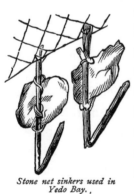

Stone net sinkers used in Yedo Bay.,

fisher laddies who were helping to lay out the nets. I have not found many examples of the modern use of stone in Japan, but here, sure enough, were stone sinkers of a kind quite primitive enough to satisfy any archæologist. A pair of dark grey, almost bluish-black, martins were circling about our heads in swift pursuit after in-

sects. They had a nest, the boys said, in a cliff, behind

a temple by the shore. On the morning, I heard sweet notes which a friend compared to those of a wood-lark, but which our host said were those of the martins. They called them *Iwa tsumu*, which sounded very much like a local contraction of *Iwa-maki tsubame*, the "Black-chinned Martin" (*Chelidon Blakistoni*). A pair of rooks also, they told me, had built their nest on a tree on the cliff, close by the same temple, for three successive years.

Out at sea, some black-tailed gulls, (*Larus crassirostris, Vieill.*), were disporting themselves merrily. The boys called them " sea-cats," a name which their mew-like cry might readily enough suggest.

Near the chief landing place, at a height of about ten feet above the level of high tide, there are layers of recent shells naturally embedded in the soft slate-grey coloured rock. They have been chemically softened, and some of them were partly, I think, altered in shape by the pressure to which they had been subjected. I have often seen the effects of such pressure on early fossils, but I have not observed any reference to the fact of similar changes going on at the present time. There is also a small artificial shell heap of recent origin quite near the same spot. At another point on the same beach, I found similar layers of recent shells, at a height of about forty feet above the present level of the sea.

A day or two was spent in exploring many woodland footpaths, which so wind around little semi-cultivated knolls, water-worn vestiges of the old upraised shore— that you are apt to return to the very spot you started from, without intending it. On one occasion, we had spoken to a ruddy cheeked old woman who was hoeing

yams near the shore. By-and-by, after working steadily
inland as we supposed, we came upon her again, and gave
her a fresh salutation. She laughed a good deal at this,
which opened our eyes to the fact that we had been
making a grand circle and were near home again. On
the way we gathered some rather insipid yellow raspberries, and a kind of prickly walnut (?), of which I made
a rough sketch.

After exhausting the novelties of the neighbourhood,
we set sail on a glorious morning for Nojima, which is a
few hours further down the bay. Winding through
wooded islands and shallow channels, we at last landed
on a wide shell-strewn shore, over a part of which extended many acres of shallow troughs where sea water,
caught at high tide, was being evaporated by a powerful
sun for manufacture into salt.

There were many sandy-coloured, prawn-like creatures moving about in the concentrated brine, but I could not examine them very closely. Sea-birds, of which gulls formed the major part, wagtails, and numerous little long-legged shore birds were poking about the wet beach, from which the tide was fast receding. Myriads of tiny crabs, some of a pretty pale violet colour, were hurrying after the receding waves, and hosts of soft-tailed hermit crabs, in all stages of growth, were hiding snugly in shells which their lawful owners had vacated.

We stopped to dine at a tea-house near the landing place. As we sipped the refreshing beverage of Japan, we sat overlooking a deep clear pool fed directly with water fresh from the sea. It was lined with large rough-hewn stones, loosely built up so as to leave numerous spaces from which sea-weeds hung in radiant clusters, giving variety of colour to the lucid green depths.

Koi Fish. (From a Japanese Sketch.)

One or two elegant *koi* fish were curving about play-fully. They are among the finest table fish in Japan, and are of two varieties—rosy scarlet and black.

A single specimen of a very striking fish called *hobo*, and

which, I suppose, is a variety of gurnard, arrested my attention.   It was apparently a little more than a foot long,
nearly cylindrical in shape, but flattened a little from side
to side.   Its pectoral fins were exceedingly large, and
spread out like fans.   The body was of a light greyish
colour, and had several cross stripes each about half-an-
inch broad, dark on the back, and fading quite away on
the belly.   Its spiny wing-like pectorals were of a bluish
grey, brightening greatly towards their margins so as to
form a broad edge of lovely sapphire blue.   The *hobo*
seemed to rest on a series of barbel-like structures spring-
ing from below the mouth near the pectorals, and these
bent under its weight so as to make them seem like the
jointed legs of a great insect.   Indeed, when it gently
opened and closed its sapphire vans while crawling along
the rocky lining of the pond, it assumed a very startling
resemblance to some large and gaudy tropical butterfly
basking in the air.   The likeness was even intensified
when, without other apparent aid than its leg-like appen-
dages, it crawled perpendicularly up the stone wall and
hung (under water, of course,) almost upside down.   I have
seen few sights more fascinating than this one was, and I
tried, but in vain, to secure the strange and beautiful
creature.

A large cuttlefish was lying in a pail of salt water, and
as it was still alive, although in the agonies of death, I
had an opportunity which was quite fresh to me, of
observing minutely the strange mysterious flushes of
varying colour that swept over the surface of the dying
animal.   It would pass from a pallor that, to our emo-
tional nature, appeared deadly, to an angry flush of dull

scarlet changing to fiery orange, and then suddenly to a warm indescribable shade of chocolate—like mother-of-pearl mixed with golden bronze. On looking into the skin more closely, it could be seen that it was all speckled over with minute points of orange colour, which never faded entirely away. The sepia spots, on the other hand, were often very large and distinct—each being usually about the size of a sago grain, from which size they would quickly contract to an almost invisible pin point. Very often they assumed an oval form, or again they would change into that of a ring of pigment surrounding the original coloured point, but the ring would not remain of equal breadth throughout, and at some points might become so narrow as finally to disappear before the unassisted vision. When you looked at one of those little dilated points of pigment from the side so as to view its depth, the skin was seen to be quite transparent, and the fluid underlying colouring matter could be seen, but I could not detect any visible rush of pigment from below when dilatation took place. The point of colour seemed rather to spread out flat like drops of grease on the surface of hot soup, and yet I could not say from observation that the depth of colour was diminished by actual loss of density. Rather it seemed as if there were an outrush of colouring matter from some unseen reservoir below. The process, however painful to the poor cephalopod, was intensely interesting to me, and singularly beautiful as a display of changing colour.

The Japanese revel in cuttle-fish, fresh or salted, and they are to be seen in great numbers for sale in a dried state all throughout the Empire. Fresh specimens occur in the fish-market almost rivalling the famous monster depicted by Victor Hugo, and did not my exhausted space forbid, I could tell many a strange and startling tale of their doings from the lips of fishermen and others who have coped with them in Japanese waters.

One of the most touching I have heard was of a hard-working mother, who had to leave her infant by the sea-shore while reaping a little croft. She heard faint screams, and, looking up, was horrified to find her little one encircled by the strong stinging arms of an appalling monster of this kind, which had just been cast on the rocky beach. The brave woman sent her mingled mother's love and hate thrilling through the curved blade of her reaping hook with such strength and skill, that the great ugly brute soon lay writhing in pieces near her unharmed darling.

CHAPTER XII.

Trip to the Tomb of Iyeyasu.

Unpromising Start—Bridge of Japan—Suburbs of Tokio—An Amorous
Ascetic—Flowering Palm Trees—A Brazen Serpent—Hotel Gossip and
Pagan Devotions—Wonderful Avenue—Primitive Ploughs—Weeping
Cherry Tree—A Quiet Priest and his Garden—Shrines and Saints—
Uncountable Buddhas and Nature's Cynicism.

ONDAY, 19th May, 1877, was a bright day in
my calendar of routine experience, but a par-
ticularly dull one in Tokio so far as the
terrestrial sky was concerned. I had been
completely knocked up with trying dispensary
and other work, and it had dawned upon me
that I must at once get a week's rest in
bracing mountain air, or give in altogether when the
grilling dog-days came. What with one sudden call after
another to professional duty, my well-laid plans for the
day's journey were spoiled, and the afternoon was
far advanced before I took my seat in the jinrikisha,
after a display of voluble guttural eloquence on the
subject of pay. Out of a crowd of tight-limbed coolies,
each secretly ambitious to be liberally paid in hard cash
for a meritorious pilgrimage to Nikko's sacred shrines and
groves, followed by a quiet rest of three days on the hills,
I selected two whose running and staying powers I had
often tested and could rely upon. They were in high
spirits, lifted the shafts with a too hearty jerk, and were

off with me like a stone from a sling, amidst the mortified
felicitations of their comrades and adieus of my little
household.   My steeds—heavy *chargers* I might have
called them—carried on a brisk colloquy, eager with
anticipation of the wonders of a region which fills the
popular imagination more than any other in the realm
with ideas of dreamy grandeur and almost super-mundane
sanctity.

The grey, wooden streets and lanes of Tokio seem interminable on such a dull drizzling day as this was.   I had
soon to draw down the mal-odorous oiled paper hood, leaving no room for my pith helmet which is a necessary protection in hot weather, and there was but a narrow opening
before which a depressing panorama of the world, as it
must have appeared at the opening of the deluge, flitted
past.   All distances in Japan are estimated, as a rule,
from Nipon bridge—the London bridge of the country,
a crowded but common-looking structure close by which
the imperial edicts and other official announcements are
posted up.   From the summit of its " hog back "—now
improved away fortunately—you see a great bustling fish-
market, the Central Post Office built in western style, and
miles of great solidly constructed stores, white plastered
or black lacquered, and quaintly marked with crests and
Chinese characters.   The moat, which here widens into a
great river is covered with acre upon acre of closely packed
junks, as like each other as peas, which are discharging
rice, evil smelling dried bonito, cuttle-fish, *sake* or rice-
beer, and other enticing commodities, for the consumption
of some 700,000 hungry and thirsty Japs.

Taking a short cut through narrow lanes, we were

soon careering over slushy suburban roads, anon dashing along the wooded banks of the noble river, whose whitey-brown was fretted now and again by clumsy little old fashioned steamers, screaming frantically with their hoarse whistles whenever any object appeared within a quarter of a mile of them.

The Sumida at this point of its course, reminds one somewhat of the upper reaches of the Thames, between Chelsea and Mortlake. When about four or five miles out of town you pass Senji, the old execution ground and the chief crematory, (*not* the place where ice-creams are prepared, as the cockney young lady supposed) whose germ-destroying fires burn almost nightly. There is nothing offensive about the place to sight or smell. Senji consists to a great extent of one long main street lined on both sides with large rather dignified-looking edifices, through the open portals of which may be discerned as we glide past them, cleanly matted rooms looking down into court-yards, green with choicest foliage, cool on the hottest days and richly adorned with old stone lanterns or fantastic bits of rock work shaded with ferns. The merry tinkle of guitars and strident falsetto notes that pain refined western ears now and again waken the silent echoes, followed sometimes by hoarse winey laughter and coarse masculine jests. By the dignified doorways are hung in massive lacquered frames, coloured photographs of gaudily dressed girls with powdered faces and reddened lips, richly bejewelled as to the stiffly glued hair. Their names, which almost remind one of those the fairies bear in *The Midsummer Night's Dream,* are written beneath, as wares might be ticketed in a shop window, and at night amidst a blaze of light the frail creatures themselves, more modestly dressed, the Japanese say, than our model Christian matrons at evening parties, are seated at the glassless windows fanning themselves coquettishly and carrying on conversation I dare not listen to with every passing message boy or government clerk. My esteem for the Japanese people has almost compelled me to pass by this subject, but I am not without hope that public morality is still strong enough to aid those who are trying to impress on their countrymen the need of social as well as of political reform.

The most beautiful and highly accomplished daughters of respectable parents, as things go in Japan, take temporarily to this degrading life almost as those of similar rank and circumstances in our country go to become governesses. Nor does it involve final disgrace. It is recorded in a daily native paper, for example, as a heroic act of wifely and maternal devotion that the mother of several children thus sold herself for a term of years, in order to rescue her husband from debt. The wives of many influential citizens and officials in Tokio have had such a history, and it is but simple justice to state that when duly married, they often lead blameless lives.

Looking at the whole question broadly one can only sigh,—God help and pity the state which almost systematically selects its fairest women for a life of sterile and sinful bondage, and makes wives of them only when disease has done its retributive work in stamping a great people, whom every other circumstance favours, with marked physical decay !

Not far from this spot there is the statue of a Buddhist priest with a hammer and gong, who used to toll mourn-

ful requiems day by day and night by night for the re-
pose of those who had fallen hard by, by the headsman's
swift stroke. The pious peasants, hurrying past at night,
used to dread the eerie sound and quicken their footsteps.
The story goes that the lonely ascetic was beguiled to
give his heart to an accomplished and beautiful woman,
who loved him in return. The sacrilegious lovers could
not brave public opinion, so, in Japanese fashion, they
filled their wide sleeves with stones, and locked in each
other's arms cast themselves into the dark river. By-and-
by they made a Buddhist saint of the poor weak man.

The country here is almost like a great cultivated fen,
and the croaking of frogs accompanied us for many miles.
After the town is fairly left behind, the hedges in front of
private houses or well-to-do farms are trimmed with the
greatest care, all withered leaves and dead branches being
removed. They are generally of privet, holly, or camellia,
and sometimes rise to the height of fifteen or even twenty
feet, dense and square as stone walls, and giving most
grateful shade, except at noon in summer; in winter they
afford shelter from chill winds. All the way to the foot
of the hills, I saw with delight for the first time a palm-
tree (the *Chamœrops fortunei*, I think), laden with pale
golden clusters of tiny granular seeds, drooping like great
bunches of grapes, and forming a bright contrast to the
dark green of the leaves.

At the gateway of a village temple on the way, there is
a very striking carved stone image of a serpentine dragon
twining around a straight two-edged sword of primitive
pattern. Soon after seeing this, I found a similar figure
of a Buddhist object of reverence from India, in a manu-

script copy of a rare old work, the original of which is one of the temple treasures of Tokio.

The whole subject of the connection between the *naja*, or cobra cult of the Indo-Malayan region and of ancient Egypt on the one hand, and the dragon or vapour-force of China, is very interesting. I think the transition might almost be shown stage by stage, and the last one was very recent. The figure, as it first struck me, instinctively recalled the brazen serpent which Moses used in the religious instruction of a body of slaves escaping from Egypt, and it is in close analogy to the ordinary classic symbolism of the healing art. It is a very common thing on country roads in Japan to find a dead snake hung across a forked branch, which is stuck upright in the ground in a prominent position. It is intended for the convenience of any wayfarer who may desire to use it as medicine.

We passed at Sōka a busy cotton cloth factory and print-work. Close by was a shrine, guarded by large, strongly-carved lions of grotesque and mythical type, and shaded by a grove of very tall and stately pine trees, amid the withered needles of which large velvety black butter-flies were fluttering. Those strange lions with grinning visages, strong teeth, and fantastic curls over all their joints, are perhaps as sacred and solemn in the association they present to good Buddhists, as the spotless lamb is to the sincere Christian. Like the Lion of the tribe of Judah, the Buddha is spoken of in their scriptures as strong to conquer and crush his spiritual foes, while the curls are amongst the marks of his true Buddhaship.

My resting-place for the night was to be Kasukabe, a

well-built, clean-looking, quiet little village. The principal production of the bare tea-house garden seemed to be green moss and liverworts, which were in subtle harmony, as art critics would say, with the raw drizzling mist which hung over the whole prospect. This lovely Eden, which needed no Adam to water it, was bounded by a dull vermilion wall, the upper part of which was a pink, which made my head ache badly. While I waited in eager expectancy for a Japanese dinner—in which there always lurks a large element of the unpredictable—I could find no other amusement than to stare at the vermilion till my eyes got hot, and then to rest them again on the cool, damp moss, listening meanwhile to an invisible orchestra of great bull frogs, which quacked like ducks. This became rather monotonous after a lengthened trial, so I got my muddy boots on again and sallied forth to look for the lions of the place—Buddhist or otherwise. The first one I met was bellowing very lustily down the lanes and up the by-lanes something sounding remarkably like " the last speech and dying confession of that 'orrid and hinfamous murderer Bill Sykes " of our innocent and joyous boyhood, when halfpenny newspapers were unknown ; but the damp and dirty little chap-books turned out to be the lives of the classic virtuous women—a popular work in quiet country places. Two withered old cronies were intently discussing with a cooper some absorbing question about renewing the wooden lining of a well, while some boys were playing under a shed— rather sheepishly in the presence of their sedate seniors. I might have been an invisible ghost so far as any evidence of my presence being perceived could be detected.

K

Finding nothing to entice me any further from my prospective dinner, I returned, not, alas! to my mutton, the rarest delicacy in Japan, but to sticky boiled rice, sweet yams, bean sauce, Japanese sardines, and delightful mushrooms, followed by the inevitable thimblefuls of pale tea.

Ere the clean rush-matted floor groaned under the smoking viands, I overheard an amusing discussion in the distance as to the nature of foreigners. A kindly, forbearing old gentleman, travelling on business and resting here for the night, and who was always addressed as *sensei* (rabbi), seemed to have the impression that we were a peculiar kind of animal for which enlightened people must see to provide the proper kind of food, however absurd it might seem, and diffidently made some rather impracticable suggestions to the energetic landlady. He chuckled very pleasantly, however, when a report entirely favourable to the Japanese things was brought, and seemed specially to approve of my asking with emphasis for another pot of the special tea of the district, in which I suspect he was interested. The girl who waited table—or, to be quite accurate, floor—had a large lacquered band-box kind of arrangement in which to hold the boiled rice, which is always administered *ad libitum* like potatoes, and I suppose for combined security and comfort she always, after administering a dose, closed the box and sat down firmly on the lid thereof. As the band-box was weak and the fair waitress unusually heavy, I ate my repast amidst constant fears of an appalling catastrophe, never having had any professional experience of hot rice poultices applied on so extensive a scale. A soft-eyed, bright, intelligent

little girl, just learning the fine art of making and presenting tea, entered on a modest little chat with me, and was
quite anxious to hear about the strange countries I had
visited on my way from *Igirisu* (England). She was quite
as much surprised as I expected her to be when I told
her I had once lived on the Himalayas, for this sounded as
mysterious and supernatural in her ears as a narrative of
a visit in the flesh to the Heavenly Jerusalem would seem
in those of a little Christian maiden in this land. She
told me in return that she had heard of a great prince
who had left her own province to visit India, and had
passed through four seas—one being indigo, another
yellow, a third white, and the fourth—I forget of what
colour. This peculiar, almost tabular, use of numbers is
a very common feature in traditions derived from
Buddhism. I am disposed to think that it simply arose
from experience of its mnemonic utility when Buddhist
literature was merely in the stage of oral tradition, and so
a false habit became fixed.

While the good-natured, kindly old scholar was pouring
forth in loud but not pharisaic tones his prayers of
thanksgiving, I, too, knelt down beside my paper-cased
rushlight, and raised silent prayers to the Father of all
lights and Giver of all good, and the tender Saviour of
mankind, before whom race and rank are as nothing, and
who enlighteneth every man coming into the world.

The mornings come round very quickly when you are
travelling in Japan. After a hurried but hearty breakfast,
we set off in real earnest, hoping to make up for the
delays of the previous day. One cannot control the
weather, however, and we had rain and mud great part of

the way. In place of nobly riding, I had humbly to push, the wheels of our vehicle being up to the axles in mud, and often we found it much easier to abandon the king's highway and take to the fields ! The old roads in Japan are nearly all bad in foul weather, but where the over-hanging trees cut them up with rain-drops their condition is indescribable.

Surely every one now must have heard of the great avenue which gives romantic beauty to some fifty miles of the road leading to the shrine of Iyeyasu, the combined Moses and Cromwell of Japan.

Furzy plains blushing with pink and crimson or blaz-ing with scarlet azaleas, lay on either side of the way, which was arched over with tall pines on the plain, and with the *Cryptomeria japonica*, a kind of cedar, further up the hills. It would be degrading to speak of those grand fluted shafts as like the columns of any temple made by human hands. They often lean over gracefully breaking the rigid lines of the view with interlacing branches. Sometimes, and more frequently, they rise straight as masts to a height of thirty or forty feet, with never a twig nor leaf. Some few of those stately old giants had been blown down by a recent *taifun*, and when I passed, were being cut up into logs, sending a grateful odour all around.

Near the shrine the road is often greatly eaten away by the rain, leaving bare the gnarled and twisted roots of the great cedars, which here are taller than elsewhere, and their colossal shafts are joined in many places so as sometimes even to form an impassable wall for short dis-tances. Even where the stiff, straight cedars predominate, the ruddy branches of a great pine will assert its individuality, its fleshy tints contrasting very wonderfully in the subdued light which plays under the greenwood, with their own dark foliage and the gleams of sapphire sky which luminously fill up infrequent gaps.

I have since walked on foot over every inch of this wonderful road, and have learned to love it. On a recent occasion I passed along there in the month of April. The air was quite musical with the sweet though familiar song of the lark, while ploughs of the usual primitive kind were at work in all directions. There are many raised and interweaving footpaths outside of the two great hedgerows of trees, and beyond these a broad strip of leafy, uncultivated scrub wood or *hara*, amidst which beautiful wild azaleas flaunt their gay rosy pink, pale or deep lavender, crimson or scarlet petals. The latter variety, when in full blossom and of a flame colour, is a favourite garden plant, and used to be called " the burning bush" amongst foreigners, not a leaf being visible in the glory of floral flame. When the soil was not covered with rank, saw-edged grass it had a thin skin of damp liverworts, with here and there on a shady bank a sweet little home-like patch of violets. At noon, dead stillness and a cemetery-like calm reigned around, and you might look along the shadowy vista fading into gloom at either end, like an immense tunnel, and see no living thing in motion. I rested frequently on the trunk of a fallen cedar, avoiding prostrate pine trees on account of their tendency to form too strong an attachment to one's snowy inexpressibles. At one lovely spot there was a *weeping* cherry tree in full bloom, over whose honied blossoms hung a loud booming cloud of bees and a bevy of large-winged butterflies.

Among the snaky roots of the great pines myriads of ant-lions had formed their smooth funnel-shaped pits and were vigorously showering the dry soil upon their luckless guests. A tawny red fox passed by quite close, looking at me askance the while in a sneering and quietly contemptuous way as an evident unbeliever in his pretensions to sanctity as an incarnation of Inari, the august protector of rice fields. In spite of the intense simmering heat the air felt wonderfully crisp and bracing as compared with that of the muggy plains about Tokio. The white piled-up cumuli and the underlying shadowed mountains showed sharp clear outlines free from haze—a happy state of things for invalids suffering from malaria, but unfortunately rather rare in Japan.

Near Nikko, sparklingly clear and delightfully cool streams course along both sides of the way with musical murmur, and little valleys with boulders hewn into tomb-stones or memorial tablets with chiselled Chinese inscriptions, are a frequent feature in the landscape. Most of the Buddhist images here are of a peculiar type—the head reclining pathetically on the palm of one hand, the elbow being grasped by the other. The country houses are much larger than any I have seen elsewhere in the east and have immense neatly thatched roofs. Frequently a clear stream rushes through the "crown of the causeway," with many openings in its pavement covering by which the villagers may draw water. About the roots of the cryptomeria trees the soil is of a remarkably pale brick-red colour, as if mixed with iron, while under the roots it

is white and dry and very like touchwood in appearance.
I saw, in passing through Utsunomiya, that this material
was liberally applied to the roots of some flowering cherry
trees which adorn the main streets.

Well, the westering sun had sunk to rest behind a wall
of forest clad mountains ere we entered Nikko, or rather
Hachi-ishi, pushing our way through a laughing, tea-
sipping crowd, clustered around a sober, quick-eyed story-
teller, who was constantly waving in his hand a most
eloquent fan. The shops are chiefly devoted to the sale
of various nicknacks as mementos of the pilgrimage,—
photographs of glens, temples, and waterfalls, and an
ecstatic kind of " Turkish delight," which is one of the
specialties of the district.

Pilgrims Buying Souvenirs. (From a Japanese sketch.)

What can I say of the beauties of Nikko, natural or
artistic, that has not already been better said? To me,

however, the shrines and temples were disappointing. Great wealth, lavish expenditure of skilful workmanship excellent carving; there was plenty of all that, and, in addition, red paint enough even to have pleased the infallible British workman demonstrating on the franchise. My first impression was that the august and mysterious Wombwell of our school days had set up his menagerie in the midst of those silent eastern hills, an impression which the brightly painted monkeys, tapirs, tigers, elephants, wild boars, and cranes cleverly carved on the panels and eaves of the wooden temples did not rapidly tend to dissipate. In spite of the lack of religious solemnity, and the artistic incoherence of the whole, added to the sense of veneer and paint everywhere, I yet finally came away feeling the wonderful sublimity and pathos nature itself has contrived to throw around the whole scene. Over every chiselled stone she has so lovingly hung a rich drapery of drooping mosses, or stained deep into its texture gory hues breaking into patches of almost fiery red, or deepening into velvety maroon, and overlapped, perchance, by scales of deep green liverworts or rich orange and creamy toned lichens. And then over and through all this there is the sweet grand murmur, sometimes very gentle but never quite unheard, of fresh mountain air sifted through the million leaves of great solemn forests of memorial pines and cedars.

I cannot here attempt to write in detail of the shrines and temples at Nikko, already so faithfully and fully described by Messrs. Satow and Hawes.

In one court I idly plucked a strange looking leaf from a tree which grows not in Japan, and was told that it had sprung from a shoot of the Bo tree under which Gautama attained the peace of Nirvana fully two thousand years ago. There is in another court a carved stone trough from which flows all around a smooth, perfectly flawless sheet of clear water—a marvel of exact workmanship. In another there is a memorial lantern all hacked with sword-cuts ; but I have not space to tell of the magnificent gifts of bronze, of the great bronze candelabrum which is in style somewhat like the figure of that shown on the arch of Titus, which once glittered in the temple of Jerusalem ; of the great pagoda within which hangs like a colossal pendulum to steady it against earthquakes, one of the tallest of tree trunks; of the mellow deep-toned bell whose sound floats down from the hills like a voice from another world ; of the wind-swept heights ; of the rushing torrents and the roaring cataracts, on which eye and ear might feed unsatiated for weeks.

Walking on the free hills was intensely enjoyable after being cooped up for five years in the midst of Tokio's grim urban acres. I went off to see one of the famous waterfalls, literally enough—

> " A pillar of white light upon the wall
> Of purple cliffs, aloof descried,"

and brought home an armful of rare ferns, lichens, mosses, and orchids. While returning I found a wasp's nest which her ladyship was busy adjusting under the surface of an overhanging cliff. High up in the air a woodcock was " tilting " in the curious eccentric manner recently described by a writer in the *Zoologist*.

I found that I had to cross a very wonderful little

garden belonging to an old priest. He was much interested in my rather amateurish botanical collection, and showed me many rare plants he had collected. His garden was a perfect model of fine culture and rich variety, and had cost him the earnest labour of a long lifetime. He was anxious to hear of the latest phases of the Eastern Question, and weighed the influence of European statesmen and sovereigns with a good deal of insight. I have the pleasantest memories of the hospitable cup of tea and profitable chat I had with this gentle, genial old priest.

My last walk was up along a leafy glen through which tore in angry foam over glossy bluish boulders and through dripping ferns a mountain torrent called the Daiya. Along the mossy footpath were arranged some hundreds of stone Buddhas, mostly of heroic size, which it is said no man can number. The reason is perhaps very simple,—the rank is so irregular, some having fallen, others being overgrown with long grass or hid in bamboo brake, so that although I along with several others essayed to count them we could in no wise agree as to the number. The Buddhists in Ceylon believe that the steps to Adam's Peak are uncountable, and so it used to be said in their neighbourhood that the stones of Stonehenge in England can never be correctly enumerated.

All the oft-told glory and magnificence of Nikko did not impress me so strongly as this long row of Amida Buddhas, their faces—portraits of old monks I think they must surely have been—leprosied over with lichens of every tone and colour so as to give one strange impressions as of frozen grimaces of pain or sardonic laughter

stereotyped into a changeless calm.   One felt, indeed, as
if the frenzied living world with all its intensity of sweetness and beauty were but fleeting vanity, and that in
death alone could the eternal truth of things begin to be
fitly seen.

CHAPTER XIII.

Nagasaki and the Inland Sea.

Yedo Bay—Matsuwa's Sacrifice—Rapid Currents—Fair Islands—Atmo s-
pheric Effects—A Tight Fit—Shimonoseki—The Resources of Christian
Civilization—A Big Indemnity—Grand Sea Scene and *Mal de Mer*—
Nagasaki Harbour—Papenberg—Story of the Martyrs—Chinese
Money Changers—Tortoise-shell Work—Schools and Missions.

I T was on an evening late in October that the donkey-
engine on the P. & O. S.S. "Sumatra" ceased its
continuous braying, and we glided out of the harbour of
Yokohama, past the glooming bluff through which a few
ruddy lights gleamed and twinkled, shining, we wot, on
familiar faces, threaded our way through grey junks,
showing their lights as civilized ships ought to do, cleav-
ing a smooth obsidian sea till we were past the lighthouse.
At the entrance to the Bay of Yedo white phosphorescent
wavelets began to gleam, the good steamship to rock, and
I climbed rather hastily to my humble hammock.

The morning dawned—without any sun having taken
the trouble to rise—on an angry heaving sea of monot-
onously dark indigo, through whose white capped waves
great bonitos were leaping joyously alongside of us like a
crowd of schoolboys racing beside a mail coach. Great
numbers of those giant mackerels are brought to the
Tokio market, and bring good prices. The Tokio people
are even proverbial through the Empire for their absurd
love of a fish that can hardly be eaten fresh, it decomposes.

so rapidly. It is therefore sold when alarmingly "high," and the market is not very pleasant to pass through in hot weather when the supply is a little more plentiful than the demand.

We were soon off the beautiful, but wild and rugged Kii coast, which lay north-east of us. The valleys are said to be well populated, but no signs of habitation could be discerned. The mountains were thickly wooded, and not much cultivated land was to be seen. The people, indeed, are chiefly engaged in wood cutting and fishing. Not to speak of the Great Sea-serpent which once turned up somewhere thereabouts, and was well authenticated— for such an animal—whales are hunted for in a peculiar way. Many boats go out in pairs with long loose nets, which are woven around the monster one by one, some- what in the manner in which I have seen a spider fasten an unwelcome wasp, till he is fairly worn out with worry and ineffective attempts to free himself from his tormentors, and becomes an easy prey to their weapons.

There is a fine revolving light of the second order at Cape Kashi, which is visible for eighteen miles ; and at Shiwomi Cape there is a fixed one of the first order, while an inferior one is situated on an island, so that a difficult passage has now, I believe, been rendered quite practicable at all hours.

The route from this point to Nagasaki is one diversified panorama of striking beauty, although I cannot say that it is altogether unequalled, except, perhaps, in mere extent. Hiogo is the western terminus of the projected grand trunk line which is to connect that port with Tokio and the north, and with its modern foreign suburb Kobe, it forms one of the most important seaports in Japan. The railway has already been completed for a good many miles past Kioto, the old inland capital, and passes through what in times not very old was the greatest commercial city in Japan—Osaka, where there are still fully a quarter of a million of busy people residing. Its many named river might easily be deepened, I think, and then poor old Osaka would quickly renew its once vigorous youth.

Beside Hiogo there is another river overhung with tall pines, which had its course artificially diverted many centuries ago. On its now neatly laid out banks a bloody battle, disastrous to the Mikado's army, was fought in 1336 by the first Shogun of the Ashikaga line. There is, as mentioned by Messrs. Satow and Hawes, an artificial island called Tsuki-jima. As the narrative related by them in connection with the island is one of the most remarkable occurrences—supposing the original story to be genuine—in the religious history of Japan, I transcribe it closely.

STORY OF MATSUWO'S SACRIFICE.

" Tradition says that this island was twice constructed, and after each occasion demolished by the waves. A great scholar named Abe no Yasu-uji, being asked to find out the cause of this repeated catastrophe, discovered by his art of divination that the sea in this part was the abode of a dragon, who could not endure that it should become dry land, and to appease him it would be necessary to bury in the sea thirty ' human pillars,' upon which should be placed stones engraved with Sanskrit texts. This being done, the construction of the island would be allowed to proceed without further opposition. Acting on their advice, Kiyomori beset the high road by Ikuta wood with a guard of soldiers, and made up the required number of victims from travellers who passed that way ; but the people of the neighbourhood protested so strongly, that all belonging to Hiogo were let go. This gave rise to the saying, ' Spare him, he is a Hiogo man.' The number was afterwards made up again, but the friends and relations of the intended victims made such an uproar that the ceremony of sinking them in the sea was postponed by Kiyomori, and in the meantime a youth named Matsuwo Kōtei came and begged that the thirty might be released, saying that he would allow himself to be buried in their stead, and that the dragon would doubtless appreciate his intention, and accept his life fcr theirs. This magnanimous offer was accepted, and Matsuwo being accordingly placed in a stone coffin, was sunk in the sea, to the entire satisfaction of the dragon, and the island was completed without any further difficulty."

I think there can be little doubt that the Kiyomori mentioned in the narrative is a historical personage. A monument may be seen which is said to have been erected in A.D. 1286—a century after his death. Possibly, however, the existing memorial simply represents the one just mentioned.

It must be remembered that Buddhism was then widely professed all over Japan. Long before this the idea of substituting images for living persons had been adopted, and the act here recorded is very like a sudden reversion to an old and forgotten rite. The history of Taouism in Japan has not yet been written, but it is not unlikely, from the mention of the use of Sanskrit mantras or charms,

that the Taouists, who are little more than heretics from
Buddhism, had some influence there.   The adherents of
at least one of the chief Buddhist sects in Japan are little
else than Taouists, and they are now very poor sort of
creatures indeed. The number thirty is somewhat remarkable, and is not very common in Buddhist symbolism.

I do not feel that it would be possible for me to do
justice to the romantic, changeful beauty of the Inland
Sea, of which Japan is justly proud, and so no pictorial
description need be looked for here.   Few of the islands
we passed near enough to see distinctly were of marked
geological individuality, or such as to demand special notice.
In another respect also the view was perhaps to some
little extent disappointing,—I refer to the general lack,
here as in Japan generally, of soft mellow effects of golden
light and warm, half luminous shadows which give so
much subtle sweetness to our home landscapes.   I missed
also those shifting shadows of well-defined clouds in a
clear sky which are almost constantly to be seen amongst
the western isles of Scotland, unless when the hills are
half-veiled in a tenuous mist.   Indeed I must frankly say
that I have rarely been impressed with the beauty of
atmospheric effects in Japan, and in nine years' attentive
observation can only recall five or six such sunsets as are
to be witnessed very frequently in places so widely removed as Ceylon and the West of Scotland. The sunrises
may perhaps be what Japan lays herself out for specially,
but for reasons which I need not enter upon, this department of nature has received less of my attention.

I cannot name any special reason why the scenery is
felt to be so charming as it is.   Truly—

. . . " The earth and ocean seem
To sleep in one another's arms, and dream."

The width of the channel varies very greatly, and the isles and islets are very irregularly distributed, so that as the panorama unrolls itself there is a constant sense of change and movement, of wild expectation and pleasing surprise. There is one feeling perhaps always lurking obscurely in a practical mind, too, and weaving threads of interest around each fairy scene,—the sea is studded with trading junks ; the larger of those fertile bosky islands are well inhabited by a rising race of most industrious, orderly, and friendly people ; and one cannot but believe that in a short time this great navigable inland channel with which Providence has so richly blessed Japan will yet be fretted by the fleets of all nations, bent on the peaceful errands of commerce to great towns and harbours which as yet exist only in day-dreams.

I do not know anything of the natural history of the Inland Sea, which would, I am sure, prove very interesting. Mr. Griffis mentions that a " mollusc " is actively engaged in those waters, perforating timber and doing much destruction. I have already referred to the similar action of a *Ligia* in Tokio Bay, but there are many marine borers of a destructive kind in Japanese waters, and they would seem to demand the careful attention of the Government.

The afternoon was advancing into evening, when our large steamer, steered with great caution, passed through the rushing current of a narrow crooked passage. We were before the old batteries of Shimonoseki—the Gibraltar of the Japanese Mediterranean.

Here, in 1864, the grim "resources of a civilization"

calling itself Christian were brought to bear on the
recalcitrant prince of Nagato, whose forts and ships had
fired on the U.S. Pembroke and other vessels.   Finally,
one hundred British guns and another hundred or so
of French, Dutch, and American drew much blood
from the Japanese, and an indemnity of three million
dollars, which sum was divided equally amongst the
avenging nations.   America, after some discussion,
has restored her share to Japan, without interest and
minus the amount claimed for actual trifling losses
sustained.   It is to be hoped, therefore, that Britain
which is not yet on the eve of bankruptcy, may find it a
pleasure to restore the sum, which was really never expected to be paid.   The policy pursued, as a piece of
sharp diplomatic practice in an urgent crisis, may not
have been without a certain influence from which good
came ; but we have nothing to lose and everything to
gain now by soothing an old sore which has ever since
remained open, and which irritates to a degree few out of
Japan can quite appreciate.

We were soon out in an open rough sea, from the
seething current-tossed waters of which stood out boldly
in the pale light of a youngish moon, strange fantastically
carved columns of black rock.

Next morning we awoke at the sound of a sudden
salute, to find ourselves dropping anchor in the lovely
lake-like harbour of Nagasaki, close beside a large well-
manned British ironclad.   After selecting from a fleet of
small boats one which seemed tolerably safe and sweet,
we made for the landing-place, and found the usual rows
of radiant jinrikisha-men making ducks—decoy ducks ?—

to secure our favour ; scaly crowds of fish hawkers, jolly

Fish Hawkers. (Japanese Sketch.)

tars of every flag, a Loochooan or two, crowds of Chinamen, and a few phlegmatic Dutchmen. There is now a
splendid graving dock in the harbour, and, on the whole,
Nagasaki did not look to me as if it were quite on its
last legs.

As we steamed out in the evening, we passed on the
right a steep wooded cliff, on the brink of which once
stood crowds of Roman Catholic Christians—pallid with
torture perhaps, but not from fear—waiting to be hurled
down the face of the cliff and perish in the deep, unless
they should trample on the cross and disown their faith.

It is not supposed by the heathen that any significant
number of them shrank from this awful test of their faith,
and so it came to pass that the infallible historians could
for once record that persecution had blotted out a Church.
It was not really so, however, and thousands claim Christian
and blood descent from those who then gained the
martyr's crown. The Dutch Calvinists, who seem always

to have had some of that delightfully Christian spirit the
Boers manifest in Africa, humorously called the ever
sacred spot where so many Christians meekly met a
pitiful death—the Papenberg ; and so the name lives,
though not the sneer.

CHAPTER XIV.

Ten Days on the Tokaido.

On the Osaka Railway—Cold Water Cure for Sin—A Kaleidoscopic Cook—
Hints for Travellers—Glimpses of Kioto, the Old Capital—Buddhists
and their Bells—A Lantern-lit City and a Star-lit Hedge—Salamanders
and Singing Frogs—Snake-baskets and River-banks—On the Tokaido—
Hakone Pass—A Volcanic Cup and some of its Contents.

AMONGST the many overlapping geographical
divisions that distract travellers and students,
none perhaps has been so permanently popular as that
which is connected with the great old highways of Japan.
Suppose we were daily accustomed to divide England
into great districts or circuits according to our railway
systems, as the Midland, the Great Northern, and so forth,
we should then have some idea of this peculiar arrangement. The Tokaido, or "East-sea-way," is the road
inclusive of the bordering country which runs close by the
southern shore of the Hondo or Chief island from Kioto,
the old capital, eastward on to Tokio.

Along with an American professor I had arrived in
Kobe by steamer through a rather tempestuous sea, sick,
dirty, and miserable, amid a pallid crowd of woe-begone
Japanese fellow-passengers, if possible more sick and
miserable even than ourselves. The rain was pouring in
torrents and a piercing wind chilled our very marrows as
we landed. After a good hot bath, a sound sleep, and a
very hearty mid-day breakfast, we walked round the

settlement, which had been thoroughly well washed down
by the rain.   Kobe is a modern " foreign "-built town,
with regular, well laid out streets.   The houses are usually
tinted in two colours, according to the Italian style, and
have a very pleasing appearance.   The settlement seemed
to be raised on a succession of broad scrub-clad gravel
terraces, and is closed in by a high range of hills crowned
with patches of dark wood and scraggy brushwood.   Close
by is Hiogo, a characteristic old native town, where there
is now the spacious terminus of a well-laid railway which
runs to Osaka and Kioto, and will yet, it is hoped, soon
reach Tokio.   A waterfall of no great volume—a " one-
horse fall " my friend termed it—is the chief attraction to
visitors about Kobe.   The dark vegetation surrounding it
was, however, very romantic and beautiful, and one or two
pious persons were shiveringly doing the " cold water
drip " penance—which I suppose is a religious substitute
for our honest British B. and S.—at a considerable rill
beside the main volume of water.

   After drifting about the settlement in rather an aimless
manner we took tickets for Osaka, which was then the
temporary terminus of the railway.

   The railway crosses at a high level a spur of the range
that encloses Kobe and then darts down towards Osaka,
straight as an arrow, by a series of alternating slopes and
levels which had rather a striking appearance from the
top of the incline.   The traffic even then was very good,
and seemed to bid fair for the ultimate success of railways
in Japan.   It is now, I understand, almost as great as that
on any line of similar capacity in our own country, and
the returns are good.

Osaka was formerly the chief commercial town of Japan, and is still a city of not less than 400,000 inhabitants, boasting of a very old moated castle of much historical interest, a modern mint, an arsenal, and a considerable garrison. Few foreigners live there, and those are chiefly either missionaries or government employés. It is situated not far from the sea, on the banks of a shallow river which must some day soon be deepened, and

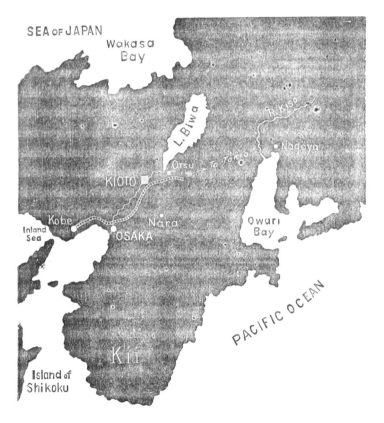

the city is intersected by numerous canals meeting at right angles. The houses which overhang the canals have a

very characteristic Japanese look, and reminded me
strongly of some quaint old illustrations in works of
romance.

From certain points a little above the city we could see
away out at sea white ˏspecks of sail glinting in the sun-
light, which recalled a famous voyage made ages ago by
a citizen of credit and renown—a sort of poetical Pepys
of the period, for an interesting account of whose old-
world diary we are indebted to Mr. Aston, our scholarly
Consul-General in Corea.

After roaming about the endless half-dead and alive
streets we found a French hotel and had dinner, which
combined most of the worst features of Japanese and
French systems of cookery, and a splendid cup of coffee
which almost atoned for all that had gone before. We
had brought with us a Japanese servant who amused us
with somewhat preposterous stories of his own doughty
doings in the great wars which preceded the Restoration,
and who described his marching as one of the guards of a
train of bullock-carts laden with solid gold, which he is
quite sure has been cleverly secreted somewhere by the
officials of the Shogun's time, to be unearthed when some
great crisis arrives !

This now peaceful warrior was sent to forage for
jinrikishas, and soon arrived, flushed and argumentative,
with a grand array of those useful vehicles and the
drawers thereof. It seemed as if such terms of payment
as the law gravely lays down had never once been proposed in Japan before, but we drove a bargain at last after
much forensic display ; for Mr. Mankichi was an accomplished amateur lawyer as well as an invincible warrior ;

indeed, his character was quite kaleidoscope, for we soon became involved with him in almost fierce discussions on astronomy and the ultimate causation of fossils. After lots had been cast by means of straws, a bargain was struck at the despised rate, and the crowd of disappointed candidates retired, grinning good-naturedly in Japanese fashion at their bad luck.

It is best in travelling in hot weather over dusty roads to avoid white linen clothes—some prefer Chinese blue flannel, others duck, with military collar to the coat. The popular white suit becomes hopelessly grimy and degraded-looking after a few miles. I find a most useful thing is a small snap-bag with provender, and a *kori*—a kind of basket woven of thin flexible bamboo laths—in two portions, the one overlapping the other like a grass or cane tobacco pouch, and so varying in capacity with the need of it. Others are made of willow. They can be rolled up in the tough, untearable, oil-paper of the country, and then strapped behind the hood of the jinrikisha. A satchel is useful to have across one's shoulder to contain geological or botanical specimens when on foot.

Two good runners will carry yourself and light luggage along, without undue fatigue, at the rate of about seven miles an hour, and will run with one or two short intervals for rest and refreshment for seven or eight hours in one day, or even longer in an emergency. For a short distance, in mild weather and on an exceptionally good road, very rapid work is sometimes done. I think, however, that tourists have often shown a tendency to exaggerate the staying powers of the coolies. When pitted against professional runners, Japanese jinrikisha-men have been badly beaten. I have myself drawn a loaded jinrikisha for a short distance, and the labour is less than one might suppose, when some momentum has been acquired.

The men do not suffer severely from their occupation, as far as a medical experience of nine years, chiefly in dispensary practice, enables me to judge. On the contrary, I think they are on the whole a very healthy class, and the broken-down members of it are chiefly those who have already failed in other spheres from intemperance or bad health, or idleness. Those men slink into by-lanes for hire, and carry priests, sick folk, and old women, bent on doing shopping, at lower than the usual fares. An active jinrikishaman can earn a fair wage, and has a reasonable prospect of living quite as long as is good for him. I know of no special diseases to which they are subject, but have seen some bad cases of rheumatism, bronchitis, and so forth, from exposure in bad weather, just as in the case of farming and other out-of-door work. I have also seen a few cases of varicose veins in the legs, but that affection is more frequent amongst English shopkeepers who stand most of the day, than amongst the car-drawers of Japan.

Soon we passed the old castle with its ivied cyclopean walls on our right, running along a low embankment through wide marshy tracts, interspersed with rice fields and closed in with beautiful blue-tinted mountains, lying low on the horizon below banks of gloriously-moulded silvery clouds.

When we reached a hamlet in the suburbs called Moriguchicho, the coolies became insubordinate, and an amount of unintelligible but eloquent slang was expended, that promised to leave little breath for the long pull before them. A formal appeal to the wizened, tremulous old "elder" of the community, resulted in a bargain being formally drawn out and solemnly sealed—signing is not a Japanese custom, The project was one which I have since found to be very common ; the city coolies hoped to sell out their contract to the villagers at a profit to themselves. It is rather disagreeable to have the consciousness of being *sold* in this way. Many are the reasons alleged for the breach of contract, such as a broken spring, mysterious spasms, or a thorn in the foot, and no one need wonder that the trick very often succeeds. After we got on our way again the sky was yellowing—it rather rarely reddens here—for sunset, and soon we sunk into a gloomy valley which night had already reached. Here we had to alight and walk through marshes, rustling with bullrushes, to an invisible ferry-boat which many farmers, hawkers, and others were very patiently waiting for. Dark shadows were now falling over the reedy flats, and the plaintive cries of various water-fowls quivered through the silent fen. The sun was now only indicated by an oval slanting glow like that of the zodiacal light, and one by one pale stars tremulously peeped forth from a marvellously clear sky. The conversation quite naturally turned on astronomy, and it was curious to hear how well-informed were some of the intending passengers regarding a system supposed to have been introduced into China 2000 years before the Star of Bethlehem struck chill terror into Herod's heart.

After crossing the ferry, to the rather rare accompaniment of a genuine Japanese song, we had a long ride through dim lit villages,—inhabited by rough and dangerous people as we were warned in one case,—dark hedgerows and dreary rice fields, and at length when we were fairly nodding with sleep, we passed through what seemed interminable miles of long dark streets, at every corner of which I felt that a bloody tragedy might fitly have been enacted. At last we stopped at a cheery well lit hotel, romantically Japanese in structure, but with much European comfort about it, and there we found right good welcome in the native fashion, and the best of good cheer.

On the morning we climbed a picturesque slope behind the hotel, through a winding woodland path, smelling of fresh pine resin, and visited the red painted Buddhist shrines and temples that cluster beneath the umbrageous foliage of many lofty and venerable trees. I made many notes on details, which, however, I am sure would not be very interesting to readers. The temple servants were just swinging the heavy wooden ram which does duty in Japanese temples for a bell-clapper, striking the bell powerfully from the outside, but with great softness of effect. We were really startled when the first sonorous boom of a bronze giant quivered through the leafy gloom in most musical waves, went echoing in ever mellowing tones down through the hot city, and trembled in fainter and fainter vibrations far away across the valley to the bosky shrine-crowned heights beyond.

Bells in Japanese temple grounds are often made of the molten contributions in hard cash of pious believers, and the custom seems to me a very suggestive and pretty one. It is from this cause, the priests tell us, that the tone of their bells is so notably sweet, for gold and silver enter in considerable proportion into the composition of some of their finest bells—a fact which has been confirmed by chemical analysis in one case at least.

With a fine combination of American push and Scottish prudence we had applied for permission to visit the Imperial Palace, which was not then usually so open to visitors as it afterwards became. We were therefore greatly gratified to have a visit in an hour or so afterwards from a most courteous official of the municipality, who favoured us with a special permit from the Chiji—a sort of perpetual Lord Mayor—of this grand old royal city of Kioto. I have little to say of the palace. It was spacious, costly, and severely plain in many respects; but there was little in it to interest any one but a professional tourist.

We spent the evening looking over the latest English and American papers we could find—none of them very fresh; and when the shades of evening fell rather suddenly over the valley in which the old city lies embosomed so beautifully, we were surprised to see the river's bed—which was almost dry—suddenly glowing into one wide ruddy blaze of light; while one long street, lined on either side with coloured paper lanterns, stretched away in two straight beams, till the lines converged into a vanishing point in the hazy distance. It was the annual festival of the river-opening in which Kioto, fortunately for us, is always to be seen in its best and most characteristic aspects. The contrast between the lemon-yellow sky, still luminous with the last rays of a dying sun; the dark wooded sides of the valley, and the ruddy glow of

torches and coloured lamps was as fascinating as any
fairy dream of a young school-girl after her first pantomime. We hurried over dinner and made for the town,
so as to see what the festive citizens were about. The
gait, dress, and manners of the Kioto ladies are much
more pleasing and refined than those of Tokio, and their
hair is always prettily dressed. There is generally
throughout the community more old-fashioned punctilious
etiquette, and the language is spoken with greater
fastidiousness both in respect to clear enunciation and the
choice of words and phrases. The atrocious nasal sound
of *g* which prevails in Tokio is quite unheard in Kioto.

Kioto is noted for its fans, so I invested in a few choice
artistic specimens for friends. One of them contained a
well-drawn fanciful group of the great classic authors of
Japan, male and female. Another very pleasing one was
composed of the different kinds of maple leaf known in
the country, and contained great variety of form and
colour gracefully contrasted. In lecturing on Darwinism,
I pointed out the fact that a Japanese artist had thus found
beauty in all the so-called accidental varieties, and so objective beauty might be considered as a phase of utility in
viewing the universe teleologically, as it was still possible
to do. This and similar illustrations, I found, had been
very effective, as addressed to a highly educated Japanese
audience.

We spent some time amidst the giddy throng in the
dry river's bed, listening to open air story-tellers, laughing
at mummers, indulging in sips of tea and peppermint
toffy, and chatting in a free and easy way to the world
and his very sedate wife.

As we retraced our steps, warm and weary, the hedges of mingled cryptomeria, privet, and fern, were mysteriously lit up here and there by the pale lambent green light of glow-worms, while now and again a star-like firefly floated silently amongst the foliage. I have seen much larger and brighter ones when travelling through Bengal, and I never saw in Japan, what is often a very striking and·mysterious phenomenon nearer the tropics, the rhythmic simultaneous twinkling of all the members of a single group of fireflies.

We were just in time to see, by the dim candle light of many paper lanterns, in the court of an adjoining house a grand display of old-fashioned court dancing, or rather posturing in operatic costume, varying with the nature of the piece to be performed. It was rather a dull performance, and far too artificial to interest even a Japanese.

Before leaving Kioto we paid a visit to a porcelain establishment, and were pleased to see artists painting extempore designs of great beauty with a firm, free hand. In a tank close by I noticed a great eft-like brute, which lay quite still. It was a splendid specimen of the gigantic Sala_mander of Japan. I obtained a dead specimen of a kind of tree frog called *Kajika*, a contraction for *kawa-shika* (river-deer), which is found at Arashi Yama, about four or five miles from Kioto—a district famous for its fine cherry-trees. Those frogs

Singing Frog (Drawn from Nature). are prized greatly for their fine musical voice, which resembles the sweet chirp of some tree crickets, and like them they are kept in cages. They

are fed on flies when in confinement. Similar frogs occur
in one or two other parts of Japan, and I had once the
good fortune to hear one in Tokio, chirping in a very
sweet and mellow tone, which I am not musician enough
to describe. We visited all that was to be seen in Kioto,
which left a very charming impression on me, so little does
it seem to differ from the Kioto one reads of in old world
tales of the feudal times that have fled for ever.

We walked on a rough newly-laid road to Otsu, got
caught in a deluge of rain, and in the circumstances had a
rather dispiriting view of the great fresh water lake of Japan, called Biwa, from its supposed resemblance in shape
to the Japanese lute of that name. We spent our first
night on the way to Tokio at Ishibe. The people were very
attentive, and soon after we retired for the night closed
our shutters, depriving us of every breath of air. We had
made a successful appeal against this arrangement when
an old night watchman appeared on the scene, and
roused the dormant echoes and inmates by a pair of loud
clappers, which he worked with painfully frequent itera-
tion. We ventured to expostulate, but were at once
offered our choice of either sharp horn—suffocation or
sleeplessness. Knowing the vigilance of the watchman
would soon succumb we preferred to have some air. Just
as I had expected, the worthy old guardian of our safety
soon quietly dropped off to sleep, but rose once or twice
suddenly ere cock-crow and made up for long silence by
an unusually vehement clattering of his sticks. It is so
always in Japan—the silent watchman is believed to be
asleep. He must attest his vigilance by audible evidence
of it.

We were soon passing curious raised river beds, which have been formed like those on the great plains of Lombardy, and sometimes like them break their bonds and rush upon the plain below.

We spent a quiet restful Sunday at Sono. Some villagers brought specimens of quartz with pyrites which they suspected might be gold. My friend, who had had some experience at the Californian diggings, was struck with the resemblance to auriferous rocks which some of those specimens bore. I went to the temple and found an old farmer enjoying a "crack" with the rector. No notice whatever was taken of my presence, but when I asked some questions as to the temple, civil answers were returned and the conversation opened up pleasantly.

Goyu was our next stopping place, where we had to ourselves a clean pretty little room, opening on a charming artificial garden, with a river bridge in the distance and a mountainous background of romantic loveliness.

After that we spent a night in a large empty house in Shiraska, whose custom seemed to be leaving it, judging from the oppressive civility we received. There were several "ironwood" trees in the garden, and nothing else. The mats were all edged with red cloth, the reason for which I did not understand, and I do not remember of seeing it elsewhere in Japan.

At Suta Gawa we got into a junk, and others joined us, so that we had a large company. The sails flapped as soon as we started, and then a dead calm with a sultry sky set in. I cannot recall another so dreary episode in my life as this voyage turned out to be. We were soon afflicted with violent cramps, which relieved the

M

monotony a little, but the natives even got irritable with
the heat and sense of helpless stagnation, and no one
could be induced to try an oar, lest a sufficient breeze
should afterwards arise, and there would then have
been so much dead loss of energy—don't you see?
In one vast shallow creek which we poled through there
were great shoals of tiny fish about the size of sprats, which
rose clear out of the water like flying fish. I could not
find what their nature was, and certainly I have never
seen large flying fish in Japanese waters.

The banks of the tributary rivers were carefully lined
with great " snake-baskets," which are made of tough split
bamboos woven in an open net-work of wide meshes.
They are filled with large stones from the river bed, and
seem like enormous sausages as thick as the body of a
man and from twenty to twenty-five feet long. They are
embedded in rows, silt soon accumulating about them,
and if not carried away vegetation springs up and still
further guards the banks.

The road is lined most of the way with venerable pine
trees, and the humble beggar in a Japanese novel always
looks to end his days, nameless and forgotten, under the
shadow of one of those great trees. The telegraph is seen
nearly all the way. In some places great spiders hang
tough threads over the path, which crack across your
smarting face with a twang almost like that made by a
piece of pack-thread.

Every few miles or so you find a tea-house, and in busy
places there may be several in one mile's distance, where
you may have a cup of tea and a quiet smoke.

As we dashed through Shidzuoka with its old ivied castle,

where the ex-Shogun now lives in dignified retirement far
from the din of the world, we passed some great hulking
over-fed giants in peculiar attire—one after another in
rapid procession, as if one were in a nightmare. They

A Cup of Tea and a Quiet Smoke. (Japanese Sketch.)

were professional wrestlers who were to perform in town
that evening. Soon afterwards we came to a turn of the
road where through a veil of mist we looked sheer down into
a boiling, foaming sea, and by-and-by a great plain opened
out to view, from which arose in ever steeper sweep the great
wood-embroidered flanks of Fuji, stupendous and seeming
to merge into heaven itself, as I have seen no other
mountain do, and not even Fuji from any other single
point of view.

We had to ascend Hakone Pass in cages. The price
agreed upon was declared to be too little, and our gentle
bearers began a series of mild persecutions, bumping our
poor weary bones and giving us constant cc asion to

change our position. I began to see that this little game was proving a very great amusement to our demure oriental friends, so I passed the word to my companion to take revenge, and a very sweet and prompt one we did take. By raising ourselves well up and rhythmically bringing our whole weight down smartly whenever a bump was planned for us, the poor shoulders of our bearers soon came to ache so badly that they "smelt a rat"; a loud but disconcerted laugh was the result, and then we all got on amicably like good Christians for the rest of the way.

We found the heights of Hakone delightfully cool after the sweltering heat of the plains, and then there are hardly any mosquitos there. The hills are softly rounded, and when not thickly wooded are covered with wormwood scrub. Goats seem to thrive on the coarse pasturage, but have not yet been bred to any extent. We crossed the ridge at a height of about 3000 feet. The little town is spread along the margin of a deep and picturesque lake which occupies the cup of an old volcano, and in which mountains capped with cottony clouds were reflected as in a mirror. The depth varies about two feet according to the rainfall.

We had some fishing from a little shallop, but were not very successful. I was told that the following varieties of fish were found in the lake :—*Masu* (which is the best), *akahara* (red-belly), *funa, namadzu, koi* (see design on the cover of this work), eels, and a kind of minnow. Newts and a lizard with a metallic tail of great brilliancy abound. There are toads with reddish brown spots, adders, and at least two varieties of snake, the *ao-daisho* and *Yama kagashi* or *Yama gachi*, as I have also heard it called. The latter bites angrily, but not fatally. Great water spiders were swimming about, and I saw many pale cream-coloured butterflies tinted with red on the hinder half of their wings. They were hovering over a sweet-smelling plant like our own honeysuckle, but with stiff, tiny, star-like flowers. Midges were gyrating in swarms as evening closed in, but I saw no swallows there, though they were numerous on both sides of the Hakone Pass below.

I was soon striding down the long stone causeway which leads to the plains, outstripping a very determined little policeman in plain clothes who gave in rather unwillingly to my greater length of limb, and I arrived at Odawara at night. On asking for a glass of water, I got one containing, *inter alia*, a very beautiful large specimen of earthworm *vulgaris*, which almost spoiled my appetite for a jolly dinner I was looking forward to next day in the Royal Hotel, Yokohama, after ten days' Japanese fare and a tough dyspepsia.

CHAPTER XV.

Japanese Philosophy of Flowers.

Simplicity of Japanese Bouquets—Artless Art—A Floral Calendar—Flower
and Tree Markets—Fruitless Sprays of Blossom—Place of Honour and
its Decoration—Allusive Obscurity—"Heaven, Earth and Man"—
Symbolism in Flowers—Art Training of the People.

WHEN you enter the guest-room in a Japanese
mansion of the better class you are at once
impressed with a subtle elegance and propriety not easily
explained. The room may contain but a very few
simple articles of adornment, and the chief or only one
may be a plant or a bouquet. By-and-by it dawns upon
the observant foreigner that the very same elements disposed by clumsy western hands in but a slightly different
way would deprive the room of half its charm. The
pleasing effect is surely then due to art and not to accident,
and if so, some rational exposition of the principles which
underlie it may yet be hoped for.

I was once greatly struck with the unique beauty and
effectiveness of a large and stainlessly white blossom of
peony, accompanied by a single pearl-toned bud, which
was thus made almost to furnish the drawing-room of one
of the highest government officials. A Japanese friend,
famed for plant-lore, who was with me, pointed out what
art had done in this case to single out and firmly accent
the best of nature's work for attention and admiration.
Now, if it be true as President M'Cosh has said, that there

is enough even in a single "pine cone to reward the study
for hours together of the very highest intellect," it may
not be uninteresting to observe the manner in which an
æsthetically gifted people have been wont to prepare the
beauties of the floral world as objects of cultured contem-
plation. For all their apparent artlessness is itself an art
bound by technical rules and based on carefully attained
principles.

In one—which, by the way, happens to be a *sermon*—
of Mitford's charmingly told "Tales of Old Japan"
there is an amusing account of the efforts made long ago
by an accomplished girl, the daughter of a self-made man,
to entertain a pious preacher of great celebrity. Amongst
other pretty doings she arranged bouquets of flowers and
wove garlands round pine torches. Now this old-fashioned
accomplishment is by no means extinct, and there are still
in Tokio many "professors" who gain a livelihood by
revealing its mysteries for a very small fee indeed.

A great deal is now even popularly known in western
countries of the Japanese love of plants and flowers. The
whole calendar is pervaded by festive seasons named after
particular flowers or plants, and the newspapers, for days
before a festival of this kind, record the local progress
towards perfection of the season's floral attraction ; picnic
parties are arranged, and the staid official or practical
merchant, with family all arrayed in their holiday best,
move to the scene with a sense of as solemn obligation as
westerns feel on the occasion of a religious service. On
certain nights, too, which in the stifling summer time
happily come very often, certain streets may be seen from
afar to gleam with the radiance of innumerable torches,

and, shades of Macbeth! whole uprooted forests often in
full bloom, are seen moving towards the open flower-
market. The pot plants and cut flowers are always very
attractive, and on those sultry or muggy nights during the
midsummer heat, one never tires of viewing the fresh and
dewy leaves and half-opened buds which make the dusty
thoroughfare into a cool forest retreat. The streets in
spring, summer and autumn teem with the trim and tasteful stalls of peripatetic flower-sellers. Indeed, they are
not at all unknown in winter even, for then the camellias,
holly, early plum blossom and several others are in
season. Such wares are in constant request even in the
very poorest localities ; and flowers are largely used for
religious offerings by the Buddhists—a custom which
seems to have existed from the very time of Shakya
Muni himself. To those who seek a philosophic explanation of all customs in soil and climate, it may here be
mentioned as of some interest that flowering plants seem
to blossom much more luxuriantly in Japan than in the
west; perhaps the decomposed lava soil may be a main
factor in the result, as flowers growing on the slopes of
volcanoes are proverbially notable for their bright colour.

The fact, at all events, is strikingly observable in the
case of certain plants brought from England. Near Tokio
most kinds of fruit—with only an exception or two
indeed—reach maturity with difficulty, and the blossom
has very naturally come to be esteemed for its own sake
rather than for the problematic benefits it might
afterwards procure. And so a Japanese instinctively
tears down great branches from a flowering plum
or cherry tree to the disgust of the inexperienced

foreigner who looks for something beyond its evanescent beauty. The art of arranging flowers, then, has perhaps somewhat naturally come to occupy a prominent place in Japanese education. Besides the living instructors already mentioned, cheap works containing lessons in the art are widely circulated. In one of them before me is a specimen which is simple and pleasing, while it approaches much more closely to our ideas of a bouquet than others which follow. It belongs to the beginning of this century. The elements which compose it are, a straight stem of single hollyhock, a bit of begonium, and a pink or two. I cannot discern in it any of that symbolism which, as we shall see, usually dominates the art. It is almost the only specimen in my collection of prints in which the vase and chief mass of the bouquet lie in one perpendicular line. It is well balanced, without undue emphasis of symmetry, and the lines present pleasing repetition, with some slight variety to break it. The vase was probably intended to be hung against one of those straight panel-like ornaments called "pillar hangings," which adorn the exposed interior posts of Japanese houses, and hence the shape of the bouquet would be appropriate. Simple often as are the materials employed—homely as the despised grasses of the field, with which Ruskin proudly adorns "The Two Paths" as a frontispiece—few Western ladies, I fear, could use them to so much advantage. Have we not then something yet to learn from the Japanese?

Beginning our systematic study of the subject, then, let us look first at the place of honour where the floral ornament is to be set. It is a shallow recess in the chief room, having a raised platform, and is called the *toko no ma,* which we find from old books to have been, literally, the bed-place, in old houses of Chinese style. While its original dimensions have been greatly contracted in modern times, its dignity has been much enhanced, and very lofty indeed is the *rôle* which it plays in the complicated etiquette of Japan. The taste and culture of the householder is brought to a focus at this point, and the fertility of invention shown in the adornment of this simple recess never fails to interest one in visiting Japanese houses. A curious and pleasing feature is the love displayed for inartificial or simply natural forms. The richest merchant or highest official may have the bounding posts of this recess made by preference of twisted and gnarled pine trees splashed with moss and lichen, or of smooth and satiny trunks stripped of their bark, or of beams of water-logged timber covered with barnacles, and honeycombed by the action of sea creatures. The plaster, again, may be mixed with many tinted sea-shells, or adorned with sea-weeds of many colours, irregularly but artistically arranged ; but space will not admit the bare enumeration of varieties even of common occurrence. After nine years residence, the study of this little region is to me ever full of fresh surprises. I have even seen a live cherry or plum tree growing outside, coaxed to yield some of its best branches to adorn the mansion within. Great ingenuity is shown in the selection and construction of a vessel to hold the flower. It may be a joint or two of bamboo, plain, smoked like a meerschaum pipe, or carved ; a basket, real or imitated in pottery of some sort ; a model junk, or a vase in bronze, *faience*, or creamy satsuma. There is in most cases a tray or stand of simple and—

according to Japanese ideas, at least—elegant design. I have often seen in the place of honour a bit of oyster-clad rock, or the gnarled stump of a dwarf tree, carved in broad wavy lines by the larva of a large beetle, or arabesqued with rich creamy orange or bricky scarlet lichens, and set in deep green many-tinted mosses, from the dank velvet of which a spray of tiny fern or feathery plume of some rare woodland plant would peep. Then, too, there are often most subtle relations of the flower itself to the form or colour of its containing vessel ; and here the refined instincts of the true artist best display themselves. Often, however, as we shall see, the sway of symbolism is too rigidly enforced.

The higher masters of the art usually affect to disclaim the use of anything but simple water for the preservation of cut flowers. Usually, however, morning glories *(con-volvulus)* are set in tepid water. Some flowers, again, are allowed good tea to drink, flavoured with a pinch of stimulating spices. The stems of peony and *Lespedeza* are put into hot water. The flowers should be invigorated by filling the mouth with water and squirting it over the leaves, as one may any day in Japan see the green-grocers freshening their wares for fastidious tastes ! All defective leaves should be neatly cut off, and the plant trimmed as desired. The number of chief branches allowed to remain is usually three, but tastes vary as to the precise number of blossoms which should be left. The number four *(shi)* is disliked because it sounds the same as the word for death. The branches should be held over steam till they are sufficiently flexible, after which they may easily be bent so as to retain the " set "

which is given to them.   The pupil—who probably in-
clines unconsciously to illustrate Sam Weller writing his
famous love-letter—is warned to keep his mouth closed or
the twigs are sure to be broken in the process.   When
bamboo sprigs are used during winter the backs of the
leaves should be smeared with sugar and water, but in
summer salt water should be similarly used instead.   The
root or end of the stem must be carefully and firmly fixed
in its place.   Japanese philosophy—which has chiefly
hitherto been that of China, from whence it came—
divides the universe into three grand realms, Heaven,
Earth, and Man ; and so in the symbolism which gives
technicalities to the art, the three bunches or groups of
twigs which are usually made prominent are named thus:
the central or "true" stem is Heaven, the "flowing"
or broad one is Earth, and the "stopped" or limited
one represents Man.   Sometimes they are also more
familiarly called the father, mother, and child.   The
art came from China, but was at first less rigidly
artificial, and was developed along with the extraordinary and elaborate etiquette which prevailed in
Japan in connection with tea - drinking in the good
old times.   There have been many styles of flower-
arranging, some nine of which, at least, are now all but
forgotten, and are indiscriminately referred to in common
talk as the *Kō-riu* or Old Style.   What is called the style
of Yen-shiu is so named from the region in which it origi-
nated.   It is now the most popular but is usually rather
too stiff and constrained for refined western tastes, although
some little latitude is allowed for individual fancy.   As to
liberty, three degrees are supposed to be admissible, and

these are named after the three modes of writing Chinese
characters : *Shin, Giyō, Sō,* which may be made partly intelligible by the analogy of our Roman, Italic and Script
characters. Flowers placed in front of Buddhist shrines
are arranged in symbolic flame shape. *Kake-mono* or
scroll pictures are often hung beside the flower, and these
have usually a symbolic or at least indirect relation to the
season to which the flower belongs. The contained allusion may be quite veiled to the foreigner, but is generally
caught up by any Japanese with some degree of culture.
To take some curious examples of such far-fetched suggestions. The pot flower is a chrysanthemum. Beside it
perhaps hangs a picture of a monkey suspended by one
arm from a tree and grasping at empty nothing with the
other, and from an allusion in a short stanza appended to
the scroll we find that he is grasping vainly at the reflected
moon. But both the moon and its reflection are purposely
omitted from the picture. Now in Japanese poetry,
wherein the words and ideas are narrowly restricted, the
moon—our own harvest moon *par excellence*—is always
associated with late autumn, to which season, in short, the
chrysanthemum in the pot belongs !

In another example which accompanies a chrysanthemum with *seven* blossoms, a rather boyish looking old
gentleman, who is the god of plenty, is pointing—not
directly to Heaven as the bounteous Giver of all good—but
to the invisible harvest moon of autumn again.

Again, we have perhaps a bit of plum blossom. The
companion picture contains pine and bamboo, and these
three woods, pine, plum and bamboo or " the woody trip-
let " are always found combined for the New-year's festi-

vities. The pine is hale and green amidst the cold snows
of winter, the plum blooms first in the year, or as the
Japanese poet martially describes it, "leads the
van with its serried hundreds;" while the bamboo
with its straight stem and regularly recurrent joints is the
fitting symbol of an orderly and well regulated life.
Their relative places may be interchanged, and so we may
have the pine in the pot and the plum and bamboo on the
picture, etc.   While Buddhists have a liking for the number eight, other Japanese, like the Jews, seem to favour
the number seven—for flower blossoms.   The vase or pot
usually rests on a stand or tray with four legs, and
Buddhist symbols are found in their ornamentation, as,
for example, elephants supporting an outspreading lotus.
Sometimes boxes are used instead of vases, while in summer baskets are frequently substituted.   Symbols of
waves and hares occur together, because the word for
spindrift in Japanese also means hare, an astronomical
symbol.

We come now to ask whether these and other
similar accomplishments are due to a special art sense or
instinct peculiar to the people of Japan, or are they the
result of a long continued training in that particular direction?   The one alternative does not necessarily and completely exclude the other.   Both elements have probably
existed in some degree, and both are required for any
full explanation of the result.   The latter in recent times
has certainly had prominence given to it.   On the other
hand, for example, I have seen an old metal mirror, dating
on the best native authority from the very dawn almost
of Japanese history, and on its reverse side is stamped in

relief the cherry blossom, speaking to its fair possessor in the language of the national poetry, of the fleeting nature of human beauty. Numerous examples, indeed, might readily be given to show that modern conventional types of natural loveliness have had a very persistent existence in Japan. On the other hand, as I have already hinted, much has been done in very recent times to popularize the knowledge of natural forms, and especially the graces of plants. An ordinary workman or schoolboy can in a bold, free-hand style, draw leaves or flowers that might shame many a Western drawing-master. Little books which contain masterpieces for imitation, are very cheap, and often not unpleasing to the most critical eye. We have nothing exactly like them in Western lands, and this might suggest a new field of adventure to enterprising publishers.

It must be remembered, however, that these booklets were created to satisfy a felt need for them amongst the populace. The natural fitness to use them was there, and hence the present capacity, I believe, for a further development in art that may soon arrest attention. If the cave men were Eskimo, and if the Japanese are descendants of them, both of which views have been held singly, then we find such a special art sense very far back indeed. An impression seems to prevail amongst some foreigners that the ability of the Japanese free-hand artist is limited to a few well chosen but strictly conventional forms. I am quite sure that this is not a fair statement of the case, and I now possess many original drawings of birds, insects, and other objects, in which unusual but life-like postures have been well caught and rendered. In one of these cheap little books published just after the railway was opened, appears a quite unconventional sketch of a railway train rapidly retreating behind an embankment.   The invisible engine with its trailing clouds of lightly whirling smoke and the retreating buffers give a sense of motion which to my mind is singularly lacking even in many of our best prints of the same subject.   Again, as has been mentioned in another chapter, there are in all the streets plastic artists often of very original powers, who for half a cent mould out of brightly-coloured candy or rice, any flower, animal—real or mythological—bit of still life, or active enterprise which ingenious urchins can devise.   And these urchins do manifest genuine wit in devising puzzles for the artist's creative skill, while it is quite evident to the bystander that the unhesitating worker does not go by rote, but reveals a natural capacity for art which, under scientific training, might lead us to expect much greater things.

The national taste coincides very frequently with the æsthetic principles scientifically expounded by Mr. Ruskin, Grant Allen, and other recent writers.   Most intelligently in their " education " of trees and flowers do the Japanese observe what the former writer calls " the awful, the fateful lines of branch and foliage," and in a popular Japanese newspaper I read a short time ago a paragraph in which the ideal education of a city Arab is compared to the gentle process by which a wild chrysanthemum is fitted to grace the place of honour in a tasteful drawing-room.

CHAPTER XVI.

The Language of Nipon.

A Japanese Writer's Lamentation—Some Common Misconceptions—*Pijin* English and its Uses—The *Lingua Franca* of the Far East—A Big Alphabet—Chinese Tones—Iconographs or Picture-Words—No Declensions, Conjugations, nor Pronouns—Imperfection of the Colloquial—Need of Linguistic Development—Capacity for Combinations—Suspected Sanskrit Affinities—Etiquette and Honorifics—Future of the Colloquial Language.

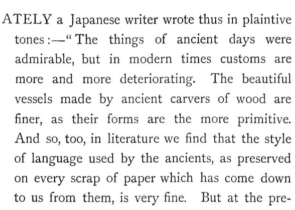

ATELY a Japanese writer wrote thus in plaintive tones:—"The things of ancient days were admirable, but in modern times customs are more and more deteriorating. The beautiful vessels made by ancient carvers of wood are finer, as their forms are the more primitive. And so, too, in literature we find that the style of language used by the ancients, as preserved on every scrap of paper which has come down to us from them, is very fine. But at the present time the popular language grows ever worse and worse. In the olden time people were accustomed to say 'Please, raise the vehicle,' 'Pray, favour me by elevating the lamp-wick.' Now-a-days they bluntly say 'Raise it,' 'Poke it up,' and thus in many ways the Ministers of State, and even what pertains to the sacred majesty of the Mikado himself, are spoken of in less honorific language than was customary in days of yore."

The fact is the wave of *aufklärung* which rose in France a century ago has now broken on the shores of those fair islands in the Pacific. Words and sentences are fossil thoughts. When organic nature rises to a higher level of being, effete forms are soon left to bury themselves in the preserving rocks. But words are not merely fossils. Even when buried in old books they haunt in ghostly form the busy throngs of men.

In China, Corea and Japan the Chinese written language is understood by all highly educated men, but I find a very common and erroneous impression prevails that the Japanese language is just a dialect—a slight variation of Chinese. The question is much more complex than many suppose, and another common misconception must first be cleared away. When two Chinamen from provinces not far apart meet, they cannot always converse together. If they are educated enough to be able to read and write they can communicate through the written language as adopted by the officials. Very often in settlements like Shanghai they may be heard resorting to the much maligned *pijin* or " business " English introduced by the " foreign devils."

Now, had he pronounced the name of the thing wanted according to any one or to all of the provincial dialects of China successively, he might have entirely failed to convey any idea whatever of what he wished to obtain. In short, the Chinese written language chiefly appeals to the eye, and in this way is more than the *Lingua Franca* of the Far East. It has also, of course, a sound associated with it, and here the real difficulty springs up. The sound is usually of one syllable. There are upwards of 30,000 characters, and necessarily, as we may at once see, the same single syllable, say *ki*, may suggest to the ear a great variety of dissimilar ideas, just as our sound—

we cannot here call it a word—*box* did to the bewildered Frenchman when on a visit to England. Well, the Chinese got out of the difficulty by having tones—rising, prolonged, falling, etc.—like those with which young clergymen studying elocution are driven nearly frantic. More correctly perhaps we may suppose that those Chinese tones are surviving indications of lost phonetic elements in the words thus differentiated. But there are no such tones in the Chinese of Japan, or at least they are not vividly preserved as an inherent and necessary part of the language. The lack of them, however, may turn out to be no real misfortune as we shall presently see. I have taken as an example the Japanese sound *ki* (pronounced like our *key*). A Japanese would quite instinctively ask you which *ki* you meant unless the sentence in which it occurred guided him clearly, and you would probably observe him drawing an imaginary series of hieroglyphs with a finger of one hand on the open palm of the other. He has learned to a great extent to *think* in Chinese characters. Now, let us take as an analogy our astronomical symbols, or our Roman or Arabic numerals. Clearly enough you will perceive that each represents the same concept or abstract notion to the French or German, Englishman, Spaniard or Italian, to whom it may be presented. It is also quite evident that the sounds associated with the one symbol may be very different to each of the nationalities supposed. In the case of Latin again, which was used so extensively in the western world during the middle ages, and is still so largely a medium of intercourse amongst scientific men in all parts of the globe, there are different schools of pronunciation, the Scotch and Continental, for example, and that of Oxford. So it is with Chinese. It is certain that many of the Chinese characters were at first what is termed iconographic, representational or imitative, simply *pictorial* in other words.

As writing was more and more used in the daily intercourse of men briefer modes of representation were followed, and instead of a completed picture we find a mere hurried stroke or two of the pen indicative of the artist's intention, for an artist rather than an author he must have been at this early stage. Soon the various stages of the process might become obscure to later observers from the very great ease and rapidity with which the evolution of the written language would now take place.

Sometimes a part only would be made to express the whole. Thus in Chinese (and in Japanese also) the iconograph of a tree thrice repeated stands for a forest. There is a very strong analogy between the Chinese and Egyptian modes of expressing ideas, but it would be quite misleading were I to give the impression that any traces of historical continuity have as yet been detected between the two languages. It is somewhat striking, however, that the Egyptian root *ka* "form," has at least an analogy to the *ka* in Japanese (and Chinese ?) which is found in such words as *kage*, shadow or reflection ; *karada*, body ; *katachi*, form, shape, etc., etc.

Leaving out of sight for a little the historically imported Chinese alphabet, and dealing as far as may be possible with the pre-existing elements of the language, we find that it belongs to the agglutinative Tatar or Turanian type. Words are not declined or conjugated.

Ideas are brought into mutual relation by intervening

preceding or following particles. There are no pronouns in the language, strictly speaking, although practically very good substitutes for them exist. The distinction between singular and plural is not quite clearly or directly brought out, nor has gender any genuine place in the grammar. Now, when the Chinese system of writing was introduced—and there are no reliable specimens of writing prior to that period—the fifty odd simple sounds of the Japanese language seem to have had assigned to them one, and unfortunately sometimes many, Chinese hieroglyphs used phonetically—that is, simply to express the Japanese sound. Then as Chinese culture in Japan advanced, others were used iconographically, and finally the same character might be used both ways, to the utter confusion and bewilderment for all time to come of all sensible people who don't think pedantic memories betoken the highest attainments of intellect. At present it is perfectly certain that no sane person—and *à fortiori* no insane one—completely understands and is master either of this system or of Buddhist mythology,—the two most meaningless freaks the Oriental want of imagination has ever produced. A speech addressed to an educated Japanese audience, or an official document containing a public announcement, departs from the simplicity of the earlier language, and is quite as intelligible to ordinary natives as a document written in lawyer's or doctor's Latin would be to schoolboys who have only learned the declensions. I have seen a political lecturer—of specially popular gifts, mark you—address a great popular audience, and every now and again an assistant had to hold up a placard containing a catch-cry or striking phrase in Chinese characters !

The inconveniences resulting from all this complexity and obscurity are very great, and various measures have been proposed, chiefly since the Restoration, to meet the urgent need which has arisen for a simple and more effective mode of conveying thought in these days of telegraphs and telephones.

Fortunately the monosyllabic Chinese terms so largely adopted lend themselves very readily—as readily as Greek or German ones do—to combination. Take the word *jin-riki-sha*, which has occurred frequently in the earlier chapters of this work. A Chinaman seeing the characters on a sign-board which the Japanese pronounce in this way, would at once know that it denoted an office for the hire of "man-power-carriages," although he might not know how to ask for one in words. The sign would be quite as clear to him as that of a finger pointing the way under the effigy of a Highlander taking snuff would be to us. And to the Japanese all obscurity of sound disappears at once on the combination of several signs. The somewhat recently coined medical and chemical terms are very expressive and useful for the most part, and represent the stage of physiology and anatomy we have now reached. A nerve, for example, is very beautifully and expressively called a "soul-thread," and many of the anatomical terms explain themselves, instead of being named after some ancient physician who first discovered the objects they denote.

The late Prof. Lenormant and Dr. Sayce have supposed that the Tatar group is connected with old Chaldean or Accadian. I should think, on many grounds, that this is highly probable, although the supposition cannot, perhaps,

in the nature of things, be very fully verified. Undoubtedly
there has been pouring into Japan a constant stream of
Chinese influences even from early times. Special Chinese
eras have left their traces on the language of Nipon, even
as regards style of pronunciation. To the present day a
Chinaman is called in Japan a Nankin man, pointing to a
period when the south of China was dominant.

Another early foreign element which has hitherto been
ignored, is Sanskrit. It is obvious enough that many
terms might be brought from India along with Buddhism,
which, however, did not come directly to Japan. But
apart from this, I have the impression that a closer study
might reveal some affinity hardly yet suspected. As
examples of terms which are perhaps of Buddhist origin,
the following occur to me, but the list might be very considerably extended. It is to be remembered that
Buddhism sprung from an Indian tribe which was probably of Turanian origin.

> *Sewa,* Sanskrit, service, attendance, worship.
> *Sewa,* Japanese, service, help, duty, business.
> *Shin,* S., spirit, soul.
> *Shin,* J., spirit, soul, pith of a tree.
> *Sahae,* S., help, assistance.
> *Sahai,* J., oversight, help.
> *Kusa,* S., sacred or sacrificial grass.
> *Kusa,* J., grass.

Such proper names as *Yama,* the god of judgment—the
Pluto of Indian mythology—which is Yemma in Japanese,
are of course quite numerous.

There are many examples of what some may term
merely false analogies, but some of them are striking

enough, and the number of examples is really considerable. The following may suffice as specimens—

Na, S., negative, not.
Na, J., negative.
Hin, S., deficient, destitute.
Hin, J., poor, wanting.
Han, S. (pronounced *ha* with nasal sound), yes, aye.
Hai, J., yes, aye.
Mudha, S., deprived of reason.
Muda, J., useless, vain, ineffective.
Kanaka, S., gold.
Kane, J., money, metal.
Shikār, S., hunt, chase.
Shikari, J., hunt, hunter, sportsman.
Nak, S., nose.
Hana, J., nose.
Bin, S., lute (nasal sound of *n*).
Biwa, J., lute.
Hans, S., goose.
Gan, J., goose.

I shall now mention, and very briefly for lack of space,
some of the more striking and interesting features of the
language. There is a tendency to make etiquette supreme
even here, and it requires great alertness to keep oneself
right, in addressing different classes. In speaking of the
members of one's own household, humble terms are used ;
while you must needs grovel to the man who is hardly
more than your equal.

In the earlier years of my stay in Japan I blandly asked
an official how his brat (*segare*) was. This would have
been the appropriate and modest term to apply to one's
own child, as he at once showed by saying, with a smile,

the *brat* was very well indeed. The *honourable* country, or hat, or stick, at once indicates, in spite of the Japanese horror of pronouns, that your native land or personal property is referred to with laudatory deference.

Terms of an evil meaning are rarely used directly in courteous conversation, and words of a similar sound, with a different meaning, are also studiously avoided. *Shi* means death, and also four, but it is better to use another term to express four. The same dread of words of evil omen is widely spread amongst nations in a low stage of culture, as for example, in Samoa (see Turner's *Samoa*, p. 33).

The Japanese use water greatly, and I was not surprised, therefore, to find that their vocabulary is marvellously rich in expressive terms connected with rain, hot water, cold water, and the like. So it is with rice culture, navigation, fishing, and other industries which are prominent in the country; the terms connected with them are numerous, and full of fine distinctions, illustrating the value of what Dugald Stewart called "attention."

I venture to doubt whether some have not spoken a little too deprecatingly of the colloquial language. It does indeed occupy a very ignoble position in Japan at present, but there are new and powerful forces now in operation, which must inevitably raise its level somewhat. It is necessary only to mention the growth of public speaking, which will, I am sure, become more and more a necessity as the liberal movement towards popular representation becomes realised in living institutions. When the colloquial language, which is a necessity in the senate and on the platform, becomes a powerful political engine, it will speedily come to be associated with the grandest and gravest thoughts in the minds of the people. Even now one might almost detect some rising perception of the ridiculousness of the inflated style now in use amongst the educated classes. In a colloquial newspaper which is said to have by far the largest circulation in Japan, a writer argues that the sinical authors, that is those who write in Chinese, are like artists whose sketches of dragons and other fabled animals, which nobody ever saw to compare them with, seem wonderfully accurate and beautiful, but when the same gentlemen condescend to draw anything from real life their failures are very conspicuous. He ends by very sensibly advocating greater care on the part of colloquial writers in securing fidelity to the facts of nature. The idea may perhaps be thought suggestive of the future prospects of this part of the language.

Some writers on the subject ignore the existence of works of a grave cast in colloquial Japanese. Not to speak of volumes of well-known sermons by different Japanese authors several minor Christian publications have already been issued and circulated widely, and many others are projected.

One or two lucid and lively little scientific brochures have also recently got into print, and been widely circulated amongst an intelligent class who cannot read books in the Chinese style, and who crave for something more solid than romances of the old school, or the blood and thunder of the half-penny dailies that circulate largely in Tokio. A strong crusade has been initiated against Chinese as a medium for scientific purposes. Those who have distinguished themselves chiefly in the advocacy have unfortunately not enjoyed any great reputation as Chinese scholars amongst their countrymen in Japan, but nevertheless the time has now come when it may fairly be raised as a practical question whether Japanese progress is compatible with the fetters imposed by such a complicated system as the use of the Chinese characters involves. English has also been proposed for adoption, and it is easy for foreigners to learn because it is blunt, truthful, straightforward. An excellent business man—a German—told me that his countrymen in the far east greatly preferred to carry on their correspondence in English even with other Germans!

It has been proposed as a kind of compromise to use Romanised transliterations of the Japanese characters. The difficulties in the way are great. An accurate orthography sacrifices the practical benefit of an agreement in the spelling with the prevailing pronunciation. Nikkō would be spelled Nitsukuau, while Tokio would be lengthened into Toukiyau. Were the Japanese to adopt the Italian vowels and spell their words as good speakers now sound them, it is dreaded that we might make one or two mistakes as to how those words were spelled many centuries ago—a catastrophe too appalling for us seriously to contemplate! My only fear is that the love of complexity is too deeply engrained in the Japanese mind for us to hope for immediate great benefits from any new system. Japanese learn to write our script characters with great elegance and clearness. But in the main street of Tokio there is a gilded sign-board gracefully written in English letters, but so cleverly obscure that almost no " Anglo-Saxon " could tell what it is meant to convey.

CHAPTER XVII.

Schools.

General Diffusion of Education in Japan—Educational Influence of Buddhism—Statistics—Duration of School Period—Genuine Accomplishments—Heroes of the School—Pens, Ink, and Paper—Introduction of Arabic Numerals—A Japanese Writer on Girls' Schools.

D URING my whole residence in Japan, I was meeting daily with large numbers from the lower strata of the people, but I can only recall one or two clear instances in my experience of Japanese people having been unable to write and read. The fact struck me very much even in the first year of my sojourn, that the people have all had at least a fair elementary education. On the authority of the American Consul-General, Van Buren, and which my limited experience quite confirms, the small peasant farmers can nearly all read, write, and keep accounts. Curiously enough, the same impression was made on my mind while living amongst the Nepâlese and other Himalayan tribes. I am disposed to believe that the cause may be Buddhism—not that the Nepâlese are all Buddhists, but I think the schools probably owed their origin to that humane religion. In China what we western people loosely call Confucianism has long been noted for its intense devotion to education ; but even there a question rises as to the *rôle* played by that new and genial enthusiasm of humanity which came from India. We have hardly yet, I believe, fully compre-

hended the vast influence the swordless creed of Shakya
has exerted over the world. It everywhere taught the
unity and brotherhood of man, and so literature could no
longer be maintained as the peculiar possession of any
caste of mere priests or princes.

There are probably at present some 30,000 common
schools throughout the empire, and these are attended by
about 3,000,000 of scholars, or about an average of 100
scholars to each school. More precisely, the records
show :—

	1883.	1882.
Common Schools, ...	29,081	28,908
Scholars,..................	3,004,137	2,616,879
Teachers, ...	84,765	76,769

Steady improvement has of late been observed from year
to year. The various schools in connection with Pro-
testant, Greek, and Roman missions—which are now
numerous, well attended, and in several cases very
influential—are probably not included, I think, in the
official statistics. A large number, also, of the better-off
class have their children taught privately at home.

Now in Scotland there are about 14·92 per cent. of the
people attending school, while in England there are 15·87
per cent., yet those figures do not really imply that the
people of England are better educated than those of
Scotland. The contrary is perhaps nearer the truth ; but
the simple explanation is that the infant schools which
are so popular in England have not yet met with much
favour from the cautious people north of the Tweed.
Well, the average attendance in Japan is undoubtedly
lower than in this country. I think we might suppose

twelve to thirteen per cent. to be somewhat near the truth. Are their children, then, not kept so long at school as ours? This question resolves itself into two others—Do they begin as early? Do they remain as long? Educationalists are coming to agree [pretty well that the age of seven is physiologically soon enough to exercise the growing brain. Our own children, unfortunately, go much earlier than this. A Japanese child is often suckled till he is four, and he rarely enters school till he is at least six. Fully as many hours a day are spent in study by a Japanese boy as by one of our own; the amount of mere memory work to be achieved is greater, and the pure active recreation is very much less. I do not think they remain so long at school, and this is more especially the case with girls, for several social reasons on which I need not enter here. Of course the quality of the education given opens an entirely different question.

A famous preacher once rebuked the then fashionable taste in education in a striking way. An accomplished young lady who had paraded before him all her gifts and graces, was first highly flattered, and then asked, to the horror of her well-to-do papa, if she could shampoo. The irate sire answered for her, with severe dignity, " I may be poor perhaps, but my daughter has not had to stoop to shampooing yet." The rabbi replied, smiling, " If her father-in-law or mother-in-law should become sick, plaiting flowers and artistically making and presenting tea will be of little, avail," and so on, to the confusion of his well-meaning host. Since then great educational reforms have been carried out both in regard to matter and methods.

The general impression one receives in travelling all

over the country, with eyes and ears open, is that education is very highly esteemed by every class, and that some
genuine sacrifice will readily be made to obtain it for their
children. In a very popular *half*-penny dreadful, a writer
addressing the lowest possible class of readers, complains
of the neglect of their offspring, shown by many parents
in this respect. A child, he says, when left alone becomes
a poor prairie flower instead of a magnificent spray of
blossom to grace the chief vase in a drawing-room. At
present the poorest child in the remotest hamlet may
hope, if mentally qualified, to become a European or
American-trained Tokio professor. One of the greatest
heroes of boyish imaginations is the hard-working peasant
lad who, when too poor to buy oil for his midnight lamp,
learned to read the classics by the soft green radiance of
fireflies which he imprisoned in cages of rush. Another
mythical model for imitation is Ono no Tôfu, one of the
most famous penmen of antiquity who, like Robert the
Bruce under the teaching of a spider, was stimulated to
noble and courageous perseverance by watching the long
continued struggles of a frog which was trying to climb a
willow tree, and which was at last successful.

The hardships a Scotch student will endure in trying to
convert the wholesome national porridge and kail into
theological metaphysics or calvinistic marine-engines of a
rather workable kind, could hardly excite greater admiration than those I have often witnessed to be most
patiently borne by students of medicine in Tokio. Every
teacher from the West speaks with favour of the capacity
for memory work of the Japanese student, and the college
records of Europe and America can now show a fair amount

of original work done by them.   Dr. Delaunay says the
young Japanese at Paris excel the French boys up to the
sixteenth year, and I believe a similar result would be
found in a careful comparison with British or American
students.   Unfortunately this favourable verdict could not
be repeated at a later stage in their career.   Most natives
of Japan skilled in educational matters are ready to reverse
it in the advanced stages of a life which consists of study.
While the reason may be largely physiological, it must also
be remembered that there is not the same social stimulus as
in our countries after college associations are broken up.
In old-fashioned schools—and these necessarily are still
very numerous—the classics, or rather selections from
them, are rhymed over, and the sounds which are at first
perfectly meaningless to the pupil, are committed to
memory, in a very peculiar and never-to-be-forgotten
sing-song falsetto.   Each sentence ends abruptly, as if
the pupil's head had been suddenly cut off by a guillotine.
When a doubtful word or character occurs, the last note
is sustained in a quavering way till the clue has been
found.   The shrill notes of half-a-dozen children in a
household are very striking when you are walking about
the by-streets of Tokio in the evening.

There is no such thing as expression in reading the
classics.   How could there be?   And yet their story-tellers
are perfect masters in the art of modulating the voice.   The
passages read are afterwards explained just as our Scriptures are in Sunday schools, by the aid of popular com-
mentaries, and strange to say, the commentators do not
always agree.   I think this is done much more carefully
and frequently than many suppose, and as a matter of

fact, the writings of the great Chinese moralists are pretty well known to all educated people.

Penmanship is laid great stress upon, and there are many different styles in use. Beautiful models, like our headlines for copybooks, are to be found in all stationers, and are usually on a much larger scale than we are accustomed to use—wherein lurks a useful hint to our own educationalists. The paper used is the ordinary unsized tissue paper, commonly called Chinese paper in this country. The Japanese make many different qualities of it, quite unlike that made in China. Chinese ink is used, and it requires a great deal of moisture and much laborious rubbing down before the pupil can begin work—facts which contain untold worlds of comfort to an urchin who loves to do anything but study, and yield many amusing subjects for the caricaturist. The pen used is made of a reed in which a well-made cone of stiff paper is inserted and covered with goat or antelope hair. It is called a *fude*. The pupils learn to draw, or rather paint, the Chinese and Japanese script characters with such hair pencils in a bold, free, sweeping hand—the action not being confined to the wrist so much as with us. Writers' cramp has been declared by a distinguished German writer on medicine to be due to the modern use of steel pens. I have seen a very well marked instance in Japan, in the case of a person who had never used any but a Japanese *fude*. Steel pens are now being introduced, however, and are called *penu*, while our ink is called *inku*, which shows the fallacy of arguing that pens and ink were only introduced into Ceylon when the foreign words which name them were first introduced.

The use of the pencil in this way naturally leads to a sweeping free hand style of drawing which possibly may not have been entirely favourable to scientific precision of detail, in which some pretend to find Japanese art lacking. The lack is somewhat imaginary, however. In Tokio there is a sacred Pencil-Mound or *Fude-dzuku*, into which school children solemnly cast the stumps of their used-up hair-pencils ; but in Japan there is no special sacredness about printed or written paper as in China, where it is always solemnly consumed by fire—a good rule which might well be more extended in its application.

The black-board is used in all schools now, and the artistic tendencies of the people are often well displayed on it. Colours and forms are very generally taught by the use of appropriate objects on the modern method, and sheets of object lessons are hung around the walls. Slates and slate-pencil are now manufactured in Japan itself, and are seemingly as good as those imported. The Arabic numerals are fast displacing the old Chinese system, which is quite as clumsy as the Roman. The *soroban* (abacus) is always taught, and is used for the most trivial calculations by hucksters, shopkeepers, bankers, and official treasurers, all through the country. It affords time to meditate as to the capacity of the purchaser, and is, in fact, indispensable to the orthodox Japanese or Chinese man of business. Mental arithmetic has been introduced, but it has not been taken kindly to, and it is not at all uncommon to get the wrong amount of change even at the Imperial Post Office in Tokio.

I close this short chapter by a few lines from an interesting essay by Shioji Takato (one of the Japanese stud-

ents sent to America by the Government), on the Co-
Education of Boys and Girls.

" In music, there are a thousand instruments, each differing from the other in its pitch and sound. The object,
however, is not to separate them, but to unite and har-
monize them, so as to produce an enchanting melody,
which can never be obtained from any single sound. So
the object of God in creating all things and beings, and
giving them forms and characters differing from one another, is, no doubt, to unite them and produce a temperate and accomplished whole. The burning wind of the
tropics uniting with the freezing blasts from the poles,
causes the mild and temperate clime, where spring flowers
smile and spontaneous products grow. God has given
the man a character bold and strong ; the woman, one
mild and gentle, differing one from the other as the
piercing sound of the flute from the soft tones of the harp.
His object is evident in itself, and requires no solution.
Look at the nations who are treating woman as a slave or
as an instrument of their sport, they are very low in their
civilization, and like wild beasts, are constantly biting and
fighting.

" From the law of God, and the instances furnished by
those nations, I see then, clearly, that the characters of
the sexes must blend and help each other : or otherwise
great discord in the music of nature will be the result.
Female colleges and academies are excellent and important institutions ; but they have nothing to do in the matter of tempering the characters of the sexes. Only in co-
education of the sexes can we secure both ends at once :
the cultivation of their intellects and the harmonizing of

their characters, . . . the saucy mischievousness of
the boys will be tempered by the gentle politeness of the
girls, and the vain fancy and timid weakness of the girls
will take on the primitive simplicity and determined
steadiness of the boys ; and, at last, a moderate, accomplished, and unblemished virtue and culture will be attained by both the sexes."

He goes on to deal with the objection that evils may
arise from the joint education of boys and girls, and humorously meets the case by the example of two country
people who caught a pair of young foxes. One of them
brought up his amongst the barn-door fowls, and it never
did them any harm, while the other timorously kept his
poultry out of his young pupil's sight, with the worst
results in the end.

CHAPTER XVIII.

A Glimpse of the Land of Neglected Education.

The Carlyle and Thackeray of Japan—Bakin's Idea of the Genuine Gentleman—Geography of the Land—The Natives and their Strange Ways—
Bad Schoolboys in Japan—Apprenticeship—Coddling and its Consequences—A Family Scene—Breaking the Indentures—On the Streets—
Moral.

Y favourite Japanese author, Takizawa Sakichi—
at once the Carlyle and Thackeray of Japan—
better known by his *nom-de-plume* of Bakin,
published the work from which the following
extracts are translated, in 1809-10. It is based
on an older story of mystical adventure like
Sinbad the Sailor, and is a powerful and
clever satire on the manners of the author's countrymen
at the beginning of this century. The following is part
of a translation which I contributed to the *Chrysanthemum*
a few years ago, and has probably been seen only by a
very few in this country. I had hoped ere this to have
issued a complete English edition of this interesting and
valuable work, but a tedious illness intervened which has
led to delay.

Bakin belongs clearly to a modern and yet powerful school of Conservative Radicalism, which keenly
questions everything as to its right to exist, but with

o

which thought and progress is not essentially a mere crude process of demolishing whatever is.

No one, he says, in looking at the *flayed* (unclothed) mass of clay which was once a living man can tell what its rank had been, but the true gentleman, he elsewhere shows, is the honourable man of *reading and culture*, who modestly but strenuously does his duty in the world, though his robes be threadbare and his sword rust-eaten.

GLIMPSE OF THE ISLAND OF NEGLECTED EDUCATION.

"This land lies amid the surging tides of Good and Evil, in the bone-strewn Ocean of Coddling, and its title is announced on a pillar of stone.

"When you look into the condition of those who are born in this place, you find that from the age of seven or eight to the sixteenth year, inclusive, may be deemed their special period. During this time the clothes are tucked in at the shoulders and skirts, 'lost-child tickets'* are attached to the amulet bag, the hair is shaved away at the crown in a patch shaped like a *koban* (an ovoid gold piece), while it remains long all round. The hair may also be dressed in what is called from its shape the 'dragon-fly,' with its four tassels ; or the clean shave all over, called the 'poppy-head priest.' However, as the natives of the island heartily hate having the stubble shaved or the hair knotted in any way, the prevailing fashion is what may be called the 'unkempt mop.' . . . They climb trees like monkeys, swim in water like

---

* Those contain the name and address of the child ; the practice is one which might well be imitated.

kelpies, hide in grass like hares, and take their bath like crows. They care nothing for nail rents in their clothes, nor for raw wounds in their limbs. They rejoice to brandish about big sticks, and to set dogs a-fighting ; they dote upon mice, and keep them confined in cages jingling bells. In spring-time, forgetting all about the dinner hour, they scatter with their kite-strings the neighbours' plum blossoms ; in summer they catch cicadas, beat down bats, and delight in the sinful taking of life ; in autumn they chase dragon-flies in the fields ; in winter they smash the ice about the back door and roll up great snowballs, and although they may sometimes collect fire-flies wherewith to make a lantern, they are by no means fond of reading books by its aid.

" As for the one only *duty* they have to perform, they sit opposite a desk from eight o'clock till two, and although they take a hair-pencil in hand they do not learn to make therewith a single dash or dot. When tired of drawing men's heads they slobber over their tissue-paper copy-books with moisture, so as to make an appearance of work before the teacher.* They lick their brushes as if they were applying tooth-blacking (like their mammas), and besmear their hands and faces till they are inkier even than their copy-books. They wipe their noses on the sleeves of their robes, and run about naked in the porch. When they are made to show themselves to visitors, they bite their thumbs and slip away backwards like a cat from a bag ; but they push themselves readily enough in front

---

* A Japanese copy-book is a kind of complicated palimpsest, being written over and over again. New and moist letters as they dry, fade into the general blackness.

of those weaker than themselves, and with tongues like razors, call them ugly names. Sometimes they plunge with full intention into puddles, and don't mind dirtying their sandals a bit. They poke holes in the paper lanterns, playfully dig into the wall plaster, eat earth or even ransack the family altar and gobble up the incense. . . . Rewards and punishments are not strictly administered there, and so when there is anything eatable in view the natives stick to the spot and are ever prone to snatch and swallow. Peaches, persimmons, pears, grapes, musk-melons, water-melons, and oranges of all kinds they devour like so many hungry monkeys. Pumpkins and sweet potatoes they esteem as special luxuries. They are addicted to dumplings and bean-cake, or coming lower down in the scale, they revel in all sorts of hard-bake and cheap buns, but rarely do they indulge in tobacco or beer.

" Once only in a twelvemonth, when the new year pine-trees still remain before the doors do they don their holiday robes of fine hempen cloth, put on the airs of the big folks, and for a little while walking on from gate to gate, do they look consequential ; but on the way home, all in their pompous dresses of ceremony, they weariedly crave to be carried pick-a-back.

" At the festival of the fox spirits who guard the rice fields, they eat and drink like hysterical tabby-cats, and for two or three days together never think of returning to their homes. On the fifth month, when the sacred flags are set up before the gate, they brandish about the leaves of the iris for sword blades, hang dangling from the piles that prop the flag-staff or climb the pole itself, hand over hand, sending a cold shiver through the livers of frightened onlookers.

.　　.　　.　　.　　.　　.　　.

"Writing does not take more than three years to master, and so, when two or three copy-books have been gone through, such a one, supposing himself to be already of some use in the world, and that the son of a poor man does not need to go very deeply into anything, gives the teacher his dismissal. But when he is sent off to serve an apprenticeship, he finds that it is not just the same thing as playing about at home.

"He can't wait for the two annual holidays usually allowed, but while going a message he now and again drops into the parental dwelling in passing; and when, perchance, being sent to accompany his master home with a paper lantern, he peeps in, the old folks are set quite purring with delight, and exclaim: ' Now, now, there will be lots of time before sundown, so you can stay at least to eat a little rice before you go I'll boil some of the pumpkin you are so fond of, deary. But, O gracious! how much thinner you are than when you lived at home, no doubt from the badness of the food they are giving you.' And so saying, the mother takes the greasy boxwood comb which is sticking in her hair and smoothes the recent stubbly growth on her boy's temples, while he himself is delighted down to the inmost layer of his frame; and so thinking this is rather a jolly state of affairs, he begins to tell how his workmates bully him, how the foreman boxes his ears daily, how the mistress makes him peel radishes, how the master once bade him draw water, and how whilst he was going to do

so he slipped on the slimy well-planks, how he barked his
knee-pans, how he never said as much as that it pained
him, and how he was then scolded and called a " useless
piece,' and, 'Boo—hoo—hoo! I ca—ca—can't help it;
but—boo—hoo, for a, for a lo—lo—lo—ong time back,
boo—hoo!! I haven't eaten my three daily meals at all
we—we—*we—well ! ! !*'

" And so as he is grumbling through his long list of imaginary grievances, as if they were real, crying and sobbing
all the while, his mother no longer able to restrain her
feelings begins also to wail, saying :—

" Since he was quite a little boy he has always been *so*
subject to headaches, and I am sure that even had he been
a Lord Buddha of the hardest metal he would not forget
it were he to have his ears boxed in that way every day!
As for his master,—*master* forsooth! making these little
eleven or twelve years' old arms draw water! I would
master him! He might think of his *own* pet child a bit,—
and—then—he—would—p'rhaps—have—a—little—more
—sympathy—*peeling—Radishes !!!*—They are such horrid
things to peel, too! Why—how—ever—in—the—world
—could even a big man in cold weather help letting them
slip from his fingers—and not a word of setting him to
learn the real business of the shop either ; and what's
more too, setting him to stand before the kitchen fire
cooking, was a think never mentioned in his contract!
Well, smashing the poor little knee-pan must have been a
dreadfully sore thing!

" Come, deary, I will put some ' White-scented Dragon '
ointment on the place. ' Show me your knee,' on which
the urchin displays a tiny scratch. The fond parent for

whom, according to the proverb, 'the needle has grown into a crow-bar,' never dreams, however, that the wound was really acquired during a wrestling bout in the recreation room of a public bath-house!

" However, after having silently searched the drawers of her needle-box, and taken out from thence a shell containing some ointment, she screams out in a voice like to burst herself, and frightening away the neighbours :—

" ' Oh, how very patient the poor child has been up till now! No; it will never do to keep him there another day; that it won't! You,' to her husband, 'just go away smartly, and get him released; off with you now at once !!!'

" The father, not at all liking the commission assigned to him, nevertheless gets his boy released from his indentures to a ,painstaking master who, quite aware of the youth's propensity to cheat him out of the price of many a feast was fondly hoping that time might improve him.

" ' Seeing that we have now taken him back,' reflects the father, 'people's tongues would be sure to be set a-wagging were he to be allowed to play about again. Look here, now!' says he, turning to the hopeful youth, ' in summertime you may now go about and try your luck at selling peaches. I'll do all the marketing for you myself, and you may keep for pocket-money all you can make. Only mind you don't sell below first cost. I won't take anything back from you at all, so you may buy whatever you've a mind to.'

" From that day forward the urchin does just as he likes with himself; learns the various uses of small cash, is prematurely knowing about sundry questionable matters,

hangs about the dancing-saloons, swallows voraciously at
drinking matches, and soon forgets all the useful things
he may have seen or heard.

"There are many parents in this Island of Neglected
Education who, after having failed to lend a helping hand
to their offspring, blame the companions who associate
with their children, as if *they*, forsooth, had been their
bitterest enemies. . . . .

" Let a restive horse have nothing else for its legs to do,
and it will be sure to kick some one ; but if you ride it
about skilfully, curbing here and checking there, and
giving it no rest for its limbs, there will be no more
attempts to fling.   Now, the human heart is just such an
unruly colt as this.

" If children are from early infancy taught reading,
arithmetic, literature, and military science, to as advanced
stages as may be possible in the station of life to which
they belong, and are pulled in day by day from one exercise and guided to another—while in the intervals of such
instruction they are brought to the parental home, and
taught to hand round tea and conduct themselves pro-
perly in society ; then, from morning to night there will
be little leisure left for their minds to wander into evil
paths."

CHAPTER XIX.

My Garden and its Guests.

A Dull Look-out—From Chaos to Cosmos—Shower of Frogs (?)—A Rare
Hedge of Roses—How the Japanese treat Sick Trees—Painters and
Pine-trees—Pine-boring Insect—Some Curious Spiders—A Fable fresh
from Nature—Ants and Aphides—An Entomological Pharisee—Nest of
the Mantis—Sons of the Prophets—A Flight of Dragon-flies—Moles
and Worms—Curious Superstition—Committee Fever and Dame
Nature's Soothing Syrup.

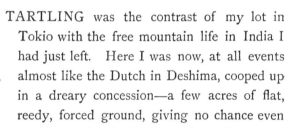 TARTLING was the contrast of my lot in
Tokio with the free mountain life in India I
had just left. Here I was now, at all events
almost like the Dutch in Deshima, cooped up
in a dreary concession—a few acres of flat,
reedy, forced ground, giving no chance even
when duty permitted of enjoying a rustic walk without
first crossing monotonous miles of uninviting streets. The
prospect was especially dreary to one who, though in no
sense a naturalist, has always found in nature a chief
recreation and pleasure.

So to console myself I set about to cultivate a garden—
not a frame wherein to set trim Italian parterres, but simply
a place to group trees, shrubs, and plants, leaving them to
grow pretty much as Nature herself had trained them to
do. The soil was damp, and when you dug down to a
distance of two feet the trench filled with water like sand
at the sea-shore. This water was brackish, too, and in-

creased with the pressure of the rising tide, rising some time after it rose, and sinking tardily with the ebb. I examined it frequently in the microscope, and found it to be swarming with minute organisms of many kinds. This fact had a very important relation locally, I thought, to two epidemics of cholera which visited that crowded district, carrying off many victims in quite a systematic way.

Great multitudes of frogs haunted this reedy flat, and one day when crossing a portion of it, after continued drought, there was a sudden heavy fall of rain. A few minutes afterwards I saw that the ground was teeming with tiny frogs, and one would naturally have supposed that they had rained from the clouds. I found, however, that they were radiating in tens of thousands from an old marshy spot in Tsukiji—the district in which the concession lies—had quite recently been filled up. After I got our bit of ground drained, frogs disappeared never to return.

When our patients grew too numerous for the little waiting-room to contain them comfortably, the garden was a great boon on hot midsummer afternoons. Some of the sick folks were heartily glad to sit down under the cool shadowy greenwood, and chat or smoke while awaiting their turn. To help the drainage, which was naturally bad, and could not be aided much artificially, I got some great pine trees *(Pinus Massoniana)*, from a kind of mall up the river, and had them successfully transplanted in the dispensary ground, where they are still flourishing grandly. To these in course of time I added some varieties of *Eucalyptus*, a hedgerow of wildly mingled roses, camellias, *Cydonia Japonica*, holly, and other plants which

I cannot name ; and by-and-by a good Christian friend,
Mr. Tsuda Sen, as well known in Japan for his scientific
zeal as for his philanthropic enthusiasm, planted a hedge
of fine American rose bushes all along the front of our institution, the richly blushing beauty of which for a month
or so was one of the recognised wonders of the district,
and for a week or two after their glory was gone the road
was thickly strewed with their crimson-pink petals. The
rubbish left over from the building was decently interred
by a gardener in several mounds of severe geological
accuracy, covered over with smooth-shaven turf, and
finally crowned with tastefully gnarled pines, which any
one would have been ready to affirm, in the newest and
most solemn fashion, had been growing there undisturbed
for a quarter of a century at the very least. One of those
pines sickened and threatened to die—it *pined* away in
fact. Our gardener prescribed a barrel of the best *sake*
or rice-beer as an infallible remedy, and when the colossal
" eye-opener " was being tenderly administered I overheard two of our carpenters lamenting that human beings
should so seldom receive similar kindly treatment. The
remedy was ineffectual, however, and the tree died—a
western expression, by the way, which, when literally
rendered, sounded quite uncouth and laughable to the
Japanese, who nevertheless have sturdy survivals of tree-
spirit worship in their midst to-day.

Japanese artists have usually caught very well the
aspects of their national pine trees—the crooked, gouty
elbows of the great branches, the knobby angularities
of the finer ones, the general massing of the pine
needles, which vary in style with each species, and the

ruddy flesh-toned trunk with its bark cracking and
scaling off in great many-angled plates, which are
rough and frosted over with pale whitey-green or
silvery-grey lichens.   Amidst the crevices I often
found little white webs of downy silk, fastened down at
the corners, in which *saltici* or hunting spiders had deposited their eggs.   On the grey twigs were often myriads
of curious grey plant-lice *(aphides)*, which imitated the
colour and texture of the bark so closely as to make it
difficult to observe them even when pointed out.   A
boring insect was very destructive to the growing twigs
of the *pinus massoniana.*   I am sure this insect alone
costs Japan many thousands of pounds annually, but,
strange to say, in the very excellent display made by the
Government in the Forestry Exhibition at Edinburgh
this year (1884) I saw no reference to its existence or
work.   A small fly drops a maggot at the tip of a growing shoot from the middle of March to the middle of May.
The maggot soon pierces the epidermis and works downwards through the heart of the growing twig, and gains
strength and rapacity with the nourishment it gets.   The
twig bleeds resin in great drops, and soon is nothing but
a brown hollow cylinder filled with *débris*.   By watching
the first shrinking of the bud, nipping its tip off with the
contained maggot, and burning it, some good might be
done.

A curious spider used to haunt the pine trees, chiefly, I
think, in the later summer months and in autumn.   It resembled in colour and texture a collection of remains from
a spider's banquet on a large scale, and always lay buried,
and to all appearance dead, amongst the ruins of former

repasts. A scholarly Irish friend of mine on having it pointed out as a curiosity in natural history, wittily described it as "just like Paddy himself asleep in the midst of his midden." So far as I have observed, it always has the concealing rubbish arranged longitudinally, and it lays itself out carefully in the same direction. Its dusty grey-coloured body is warty, but some of the projections are pointed and symmetrical, and there are some minute spots of deep red also symmetrically arranged. These spots are decidedly adverse to conceal-ment from human eyes, at all events, and I learned to look for them when in doubt as to the presence of a living spider. I suppose they may be of service to the species as beauty marks.

The hunting spiders in my garden were numerous and very interesting. I was looking at the buds on a fine camellia bush one misty morning, when I saw on the leaves what I took to be a large jet-black and very glossy ant. I don't know what passed through its little cerebrum, but it looked at me quickly with a very un-ant like and sinister expression which at once arrested my attention. When I moved it moved too with all the alert vigilance of a Japanese policeman, when you are doing nothing wrong. I took to watching it carefully morning after morning, and found that our demurely-attired and industrious-looking little friend was a most atrocious villain of a hunting spider in the meek disguise of an ant, and I afterwards discovered a number of similar kinds. Nature is full of fables far more fascinating than anything poor old Æsop ever palmed off upon an innocent world as his own. Many ordinary hunters or *saltici* were to be seen daily, and I think they were more expert than the others who lived by stealth. It would be interesting to know more of the mental qualities of the insect game pursued by each species. I have often seen a little silvery spider of gobular shape, and I think its *rôle* is to look as like a glistening drop of dew as possible. I have seen them most frequently on the morning lying quietly in the centre of their webs and shining just like a rain-drop in the sun. There is a little spider with scorpion-like claws which probably now represents the earliest type of the race, and that I have seen only once in Japan, and in proximity to a recently-opened parcel of drugs from home. I have never attempted to enumerate the varieties of ants found in my garden, but I think I have seen nearly all the varieties—or ants resembling them very closely—that we have in England, and several others besides.

During one long rainy season a strange thing happened which I had never witnessed or heard of, though likely enough it may have been described before. Ants, as many must know, take an extraordinary interest in plant-lice or green-fly. They nurse them, tend them as we do sheep or cattle and, I believe, as others also have long ago observed, *milk* them. Now there was a fine young tree which began to fade, having been attacked by a host of purply chocolate-coloured plant-lice. I had been trying what effect on the growth of bark the removing parasites from particular twigs would have, and had often observed how much worried the ants appeared to be with the liberties I took with their herds. Well, going morning after morning, I was once surprised to find an elaborate arcade of

clay, made by the ants, winding round the stem of the
tree up to the spot where the leaves gave shelter from the
heavy rains to the browsing insect cattle! In another
spot I found, in the same season, that a colony of similar
ants had constructed a similar tunnel on a ledge of rock
to the base of a pine tree on which *aphides* (plant-lice)
were feeding very unlike the others just mentioned. The
larvae of lady-birds preyed on the aphides, too, just as
they do in England. Another deadly foe to other insects
was the *mantis*, or preying insect. It preys on its neighbours also, and is so voracious that while I was about to
impale one alongside of a fat locust, it turned upon its
companion in tribulation and began to munch at its eye
quite complacently. Its nest is curious, and looks at first
like a large oval splash of clay. It is carefully adapted
to its position, whether in the hollow of a split bamboo or
the convex surface of a branch, and is not very prominent
in appearance. I kept one of those nests till a crowd of
about a hundred hungry young "sons of the prophets"
emerged on the 28th of June, and began at once their
career of hypocrisy. As soon as they emerged they began
to sway to and fro like orators about to begin a speech.
A cold wind arose, and most of them perished. Japanese
boys keep those fierce insects and set them to fighting
like game-cocks.

In the hot season the dragon-flies used to be a feature
in our garden. Very often, indeed, was I able to verify
the marvellously vivid description of our greatest modern
poet :—

> " To-day I saw the dragon-fly
> Come from the wells where he did lie.

An inner impulse rent the veil
Of his old husk : from head to tail
Came out clear plates of sapphire mail.
He dried his wings : like gauze they grew :
Thro' crofts and pastures wet with dew
A living flash of light he flew."

We had several varieties of them, and our boys grew very expert in capturing them.   One Sunday early in the summer of 1882, the wind was blowing gently from the east, like our sweet west wind, when great armies of crimson-scarlet dragon-flies spread in pairs all over the city, and continued to come for the greater part of the day.   Where they came from, where they went to, or what their end was, I never knew.

Red-bellied Dragon-fly.

The branches of a tall *Salisburia adiantifolia*, with leaves like those of the maiden-hair fern, overhung our quick set hedge, and in autumn its smooth little nuts and pale golden leaves fell in showers about our path.   I have often heard strangers go into rapturous admiration of this kind of tree, which often grows to a great height ; but I think it is most ungraceful in the general massing of its foliage, and cannot compare for a moment with our own birch,

elm, oak, beech, or ash. I suppose when any one sees
the leaf for the first time it appears so strange and beautiful that the conclusion is jumped at that the tree itself
must be grandly shaped. Nature, however, does not always build up her work in this way, and so the *Salisburia*
has great sprawling awkward branches, which seem not to
know quite what to do with themselves, and often give
up life in despair when there is a high wind. In far back
times trees of similar foliage grew in certain of the isles
of Scotland, as their fossils show.

Cryptomerias, which thrive so well in Japan generally
did not thrive with us, for what reason I never found
out. Sometimes from crevices formed by the longitudi-
nal splitting of the outer bark, a curious juicy cocks-
comb-like growth protruded and increased to great dimensions in moist weather. It was of a golden yellow
colour, deepening at the tips into orange, or even into amber
brown, and was quite elastic. In the microscope it was
seen to be composed of large yellow cells, resembling in
shape the metallic capsules used by artists to contain oil
pigments, having a shining metallic skin, and being in-
dented just like them. They were, however, much shorter
in proportion to their length, and often tapered to a point
at one extremity. This parasitic growth soon over-
mastered the trees on which it appeared.

Moles used to work some devastation, and often there
were long irregular tunnels near the surface, which were
said to be the work of shrew-moles. The Japanese place
near mole-hills a piece of wood shaped like this **T,** for
owls to sit on at night, and they make special efforts to
destroy them in March and April, when the nests are found

in the larger mounds, at their base and on a level with the
ground, or just a few inches below it.   Once when I was
putting a snake into a bottle of alcohol it disgorged a large
shrew-mole which seemed quite beyond its capacity.
I was led to notice the effects of the work of moles, or
the peculiar shrew-mole *(Urotrichus)* of Japan, in burying
objects lying on the surface.

Great fires sweep over Tokio in the winter time, leaving
wide patches strewn on the surface with bits of roof tiles.
By and by spring comes round ; moles throw up mounds,
and the rain washes them down to the common level.
Grass and weeds spring up and catch the dust.   Another
year passes and the process is repeated, so that in three
or four years there is an inch or so of soil above the layer
of brick-bats, with luxuriant vegetation of rank grass or
wormwood scrub growing atop, as if man had not at all
recently visited the spot.

I have watched the work of earth-worms in different
parts of Japan, and found them to have the habits so carefully observed and described by Mr. Darwin.   Glass
has not been very long used in Japan, but I was surprised
to find how often small particles of glass were to be found
in their casts.   In Japan, too, they often have the paths
to their subterranean mansions tidily paved with tiny
pebbles.   On the whole I think moles may have greater
influence in certain localities than earth-worms, in slowly
and unintentionally burying superficial objects, and the
amount of soil turned up by them appeared to me very
striking as observed while on railway journeys in Scotland
during the springs of this and last year.

A curious superstition prevails in Japan that certain in-

juries—to the skin chiefly, and of a superficial and sudden
character not easily accounted for—are due to the malev-
olence of an animal called the *itachi.* There is such
an animal, and I have seen them several times in my garden, and heard their curious eerie scream. One evening, when about to hold a meeting, an *itachi* met me on

a shaded path. It was
screaming loudly, and in a
very extraordinary manner,
and did not desist when I
went close up to it. Japa-

Teeth of an Itachi.

nese patients and others shouted to me to beware, but I
got a broom and "went for it," a compliment which it was
evidently about to return. I paused, reflected a little—and
found it was just about time to open my meeting. However, the nasty brute kept whining away for some time.
I suppose it to be allied to our Scotch stoat, and it
changes its colour in a similar way.

Japanese Stoat (Itachi), Drawn from Life.

Several salt water creeks or canals intersect the "foreign
concession," and some of them run up close to our ground.
Many a time when coming from a series of committee
meetings—and on Saturdays we had sometimes three
or four of them—feeling flushed and heated (this was

in summer of course), and growling to myself something in this fashion :—" Now, there's that beastly fellow
Jones : they say, indeed, that he left the prospect of a fine
west-end church to come out here—umph ! Pity of the
west-enders if he had stayed, that's all I can say ! and as
for the Greek and Latin that his friends brag about, why
he always adds *r* to idea ; and I have heard him leave out
his *h's* twice at the very least ! ! The fellow's a fool, and
perhaps something worse ; and to go and smash up my
well-planned motion by that dirty dodge of an amendment
of his ! ! ! Well, I'll make it warm for that leering fellow
Smith and him yet, or," etc., etc., etc.—then I would sit
down in a favourite little lower-step of a ruined landing-
place, where I was hid from the world, and feel the fresh
sea breeze play on my burning temples, and the gentle
lap of the wavelets soothing away all care ; then perhaps a
little dipper would mysteriously emerge from the depths,
shiveringly send a little fountain of silver drops about it,
look at me with a comic look of sudden enquiry, and dip
again to leave me in deep suspense as to which point
of the compass it would next emerge from ; and ah !—
there's a sooty shag dashing into the creek a little further
down.

Great numbers of a kind of sea-slater—not the
borers I have already described—are crawling over the
shingle and large stones which line the canal banks.
A sparrow, just like our English sparrow, runs after
some of them in a way quite absurd and improper for an
orthodox and well-bred sparrow to do. Poor little slaters,
or whatever you call yourselves, you have your amusements, too, for I have watched you gambolling, humor-

ously wrestling and tumbling about like a pair of young lizards or boys, or anything else that lives and moves and has conscious being.

A rat peeping around makes a very circuitous route to its hole and darts in suddenly, while swallows are careering close to the surface of the water, and a kind of gull, which breeds not far off, seems almost to be imitating the circular flight of kites high up in the air, the cry and straight flight of crows, the short circular journeys of groups of house pigeons, and the ways of ducks on the water,— truly a versatile bird is the *miako-dori*, or bird of the capital! High above is a great wavering wedge of wild geese, from which peacefully floats down to earth a mellowed and musical chant; five or six ibis-like birds forming a similar wedge follow at a lower level; a stately snow-white crane alights and stalks grandly about for a little, then spreads its broad pinions, strenuously flaps them to the time of the " Dead March in Saul," and, spurning the mud, rises into the blue ether with the dignified solemnity of an archangel.

CHAPTER XX.

Japanese Art in Relation to Nature.

Absence of Degraded Conventionalism—An Exception Proving the Rule—
Outlines of Fuji--The Bamboo in Art—Simplicity in Composition—
Flight of Birds—Spider's Web in Wood-work—Want of Truth in Greek
Art—A Japanese Picture Gallery.

S O MUCH has already and so ably been written
on the subject of Japanese art, that my only
apology for the few pages which follow is the
hope I have of inducing a still wider circle to
become interested in the problems it has done
so much both to suggest and to solve. We all
know the painful effect produced upon our
minds when lying sick, by the wall paper
pattern of our bed-room transforming itself
into a series of faces. Those faces are after all
often objective realities ; the pattern designer has
betrayed the decadence of his art, for his fanciful designs
are not unfrequently the descendants of earlier and higher
attempts to portray the human face divine. Common as
this later phase of degraded or conventional art is in most
countries, it is hardly to be detected in Japan at all.
The one solitary instance I have observed, at all events, is
this bit of carving on the end of a sort of towel rack, and
the exception tends to prove the rule, for the specimen
was obtained by a friend from an Aino who produced it.
I shall be happy to hear of other examples, and I suppose

*Conventional Carving of a Bird's
Head, by an Aino from Yesso.*

there may be many. On the whole, the impression left on one is that Japanese art strives after fidelity to nature, and succeeds pretty well. Nature is complex, however, and technical skill is limited on many sides and must grow by stages. Art struggles to fix one view of nature's many-angled prism, and so it tends to lose another. An object viewed artistically has form, size, colour, light, perspective, texture, motion, and where life is, expression. No one medium or method can overtake such a task as to fix and freeze all those phases at once. And Japanese artists have never attempted to do so, but in the directions in which they have seriously tried to advance, there have been few ignoble failures. The success in regard to inanimate objects has been very signal and general, where geometrical perspective does not enter prominently.

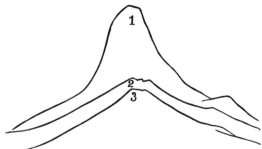

Outlines of Mount Fuji—
1. From Miss Bird's *Unbeaten Tracks ;* 2. From an old Japanese
Drawing ; 3. From a Recent Photograph.

In the above outlines we have (1) that of the view of Mount Fuji, presented to her readers by Miss Bird, in p. 13 of the first volume of her *Unbeaten Tracks in Japan*, with which, though in sight of Fuji almost daily for nine years, I have never seen anything in nature corresponding; (2) is from an old native drawing of Fuji, giving the usual conventional shape ; and (3) is from a photograph taken recently. The two latter outlines correspond wonderfully well, and the graceful logarithmic curve of such volcanic mountains is caught in the second one, though not quite accurately. It is often rendered much more correctly.

The simplicity of the means whereby in wood-engraving a certain end is gained is very admirable. The sketch underneath has perhaps not been quite successfully reproduced,

The Coxcomb Plant (Celasia Cristata).
(From a Japanese Sketch.)

but when printed on the soft flabby paper of the country, the texture of the crimson coxcomb plant *(Celasia cristata)* is very wonderfully rendered by the simplest methods. It is a favourite garden plant in Japan.

I have observed that in Siebold's figure of *Pinus densiflora* a slight mistake is made in regard to the curve of the pairs of needles, which is not shown, nor are they represented as of equal length, as they are in nature. On ob-

serving this, I turned at once to a Japanese drawing, and
found the rendering to be quite correct and natural in
that respect.

The bamboo is one of the greatest boons to sub-tropical
and even tropical man, and is devoted to an inconceivable
number of uses.   It is largely employed in Japanese art,
and is capable of being turned about in all sorts of ways
so as to yield every graceful variety of form.   I had in
my bedroom a Japanese wall paper composed of bamboo
sprays twining and curving so as apparently never to re-
peat themselves, and the eye never tired of it.

Sometimes the foliage effects are produced by single
strokes for each blade. The subjoined sketch is boldly and

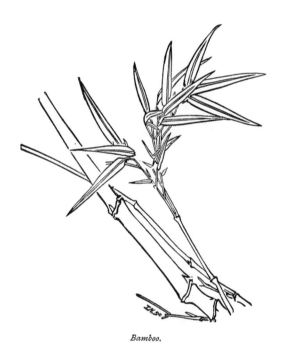

Bamboo.

effectively brought out by swift continuous strokes, the pencil hardly being lifted from the paper.

One of the greatest feats an artist can perform is to

draw, say, a horse at the gallop, with flowing mane and waving tail, with one dip of his pencil in a given number of distinct strokes—the fewer the more wonderful the achievement.

Here, in another style of execution, is a sketch of the same beneficent plant. There is some attempt to indicate shading, and the veining of the leaves is shown simply but quite as effectively as need be. The stunted twigs, the lines of fracture of the thick main stem, the varying lengths of the internodes, and the nibbled blades, are all quite characteristic and true to nature.

Another favourite plant is the cherry tree, and from the earliest times it has figured as a chief ornament on various

Another Sketch of Bamboo.

articles of furniture.

This is a modern specimen, by Shunzan, in his characteristic style :—

Spray of Cherry Blossom, by Shunzan.

A style of pictorial ornament very much in favour, and partly founded on the floral philosophy already described, is illustrated in the next cut. The combination of ele-

Fish, Fruit, and Flowers.

ments is not quite accidental. Each part in the composition has a meaning usually in relation to the other elements of it, and it requires a certain amount of familiarity with Japanese modes of thinking and ways of looking at things to enter fully into the enjoyment of such simple and pretty designs.

A student of ornament will find much which is worthy of his attention in designs even of such austere simplicity, and specially worthy of note is the direction of each dominating line in relation to associated lines, in regard to which Ruskin has said much, the truthful force of which every Japanese designer would at once feel.

Snowy Egret.

A pleasing object which often meets the eye in the country is the egret or paddy bird, of snowy white plumage and graceful form. The wading birds generally are favourite themes of the Japanese artist, and are found in every form of ornamental work— on painted screens, fans, hanging scrolls, and bronzes. To the crane belongs special sanctity, as it is a well-known symbol of long life and constancy.

The flight of cranes is often wonderfully well portrayed, and I think in a manner truer to nature than some of the recent illustrations on the subject of the flight of birds. The curves in Marey's

book are often both wrong andunartistic, while those of
Pettigrew are stiffly correct but ungraceful.   On a folding
screen which I had there was a great flock of cranes in
flight, descending and in every conceivable attitude.   The
eye was closely carried down the canvas—shall I say?—
till you felt the whirling flight make you almost giddy,
—a genuine triumph of art.

Here is a specimen which seems to me also to be true
to nature and full of grace and suggestive hints of the

Wild Goose descending.

natural environment of the subject, conveyed with ex-
quisitely simple sincerity.

Even in wood-work natural forms are most skilfully
rendered subservient to the purposes of ornament, while
nature's blunders are triumphantly made to yield an element of new beauty.   I have seen a screen made of cane
arranged as a spider's web.   Now, I can imagine how a
skilled British workman would grasp the conception and
at once give us in cane a severe problem in Euclid.   The
Japanese artist does nothing of the sort.   He looks at nature again and again, but he does not allow ideal forms

to dissipate its truth. This web of cane, then, was not
rigidly geometrical, but as if broken and in process of re-
paration by a spider (in bronze) placed near, but, of course,
not quite in the centre. There was nothing in the least
offensive in the design. The twin aims, beauty and utility,
were thoroughly harmonized without any sacrifice to the
truth of nature, and the very faults in nature's model were
made to break in upon the hard conventionalism of a
mere geometric form. Classic art has taught us the
beauty and dignity of reposeful human forms, but in many
respects it led us far astray. Art often loses in beauty
what it loses in truthfulness. There is an old Greek
Cameo which represents Jupiter hurling some large cigars
at a few frightened giants, who are trying vainly to flee on
legs composed of snakes, each governed by an indepen-
dant cerebrum. Hence they are tumbling about in ungraceful and meaningless attitudes. One wheel of Jove's
chariot is running along a celestial cable—a kind of tel-
ferage on clouds, while the other rests on space. The
horses are not visibly attached to it, nor are their muscles
strained as if by the resistance of a weight. It is difficult
to understand why they should rear and prance unless the
snakes have frightened them—an altogether unworthy
conception of the steeds of the mighty thunderer. The
impression on one's mind is necessarily confused and un-
satisfactory, and to a thoroughly modern mind vulgar and
ridiculous.

In the year 1882 there was a very large exhibition of
paintings, supposed to be entirely in pure Japanese styles
of art. I went with great interest to examine the
pictures, which were all on the usual scrolls. One

prominent department contained very severe but pleasing
drawings on warm chocolate with gold—in a rather Indian
style, however—of Buddhist saints, by Hose of Kioto and
others of the same school. They were all sold a day or
two after the opening of the exhibition, and brought
very high prices.   There was also a good painting of
Amida Buddha by Nakajima, and of the Goddess of
Mercy, Kuwanon, by Akimoto. Those pictures showed
that even in sacred art there had been change, and
that it was still being maintained; but on the whole, it
had the savour of " death unto death."   It was impossible,
however, to ignore evidence that western criticism of
former productions had not been without beneficial results,
especially in regard to drawing.

Passing by the conventional groups of flowers in
Chinese fashion, many of which were infinitely more
attractive however than those which are sent over to this
country to the curio shops, my interest was drawn towards
pictures of a new realistic school, such as that of a group
of pups by Hibino ; a cormorant, evidently studied from
life by Furukawa ; a bear and cubs by Hara ; a heron by
Yamamoto ; plantain leaves ; a grim skeleton overgrown
with toad stools—powerfully drawn ; swallows sitting on
a telegraph wire—nearly all looking one way as they are
seen in nature ; an owl and a ragged tramp with monkey
dressed in bright robes and surrounded by a crowd of
village youths. The last picture showed very clearly the
effects of the stimulus given by photography even to
" pure antique Japanese art," in securing better drawing,
truer shading and firmer acquaintance with the anatomy
of expression. It, I think, was the chief popular attraction

of the exhibition, if one might judge from the pleased crowd which was always around it, and marked a new stage in the art progress of Japan, full of hopeful prognostication.

CHAPTER XXI.

The Philosophy of Heaven and Earth in a Nut-Shell.

Why Some Birds Fly Well and Others Badly—Guesses at Protective Imitation —A New Version of the Sphynx—Analogies of Nature and Man— Casting Away of Passion—The True Gentleman—The Eight Virtues— Some Wise Sayings.

THE following translation appeared in the *Chrysan-themum* some years ago. The stand-point of the author, Bakin is that of the Chinese sage Chwangtze, who lived some centuries before Christ. The Universe is an orderly product of Mind, and that Mind apparently is One. There are two great polar influences at work in all things, which we should term the negative and positive. The terms *male* and *female* are nearly equivalent in the philosophies of China. It is curious to observe this attempt, made some seventy years ago, to give a rational account of protective mimicry.

It would be easy and pleasant to make a finer translation. I have endeavoured simply to let my readers know what the original author wrote.

THE CREATOR'S POWER.

The eggs of wild-birds are brooded over by the male as well as by the female, and therefore these birds have great power of flight, but in the case of barn-door and other domestic fowls only the female sits, and hence their power of flight, as in ducks, is limited.

Now this fact arises from the influence of the *female principle*, and we find analogies even in the case of human children. Thus boys who are brought up in the midst of females till their sixteenth year resemble girls, and the result is due to the overcoming influence of the female principle. We find another example in the case of those birds and beasts which are developed in uncultivated mountains. They resemble herbs and trees, for the bodies of those birds are covered with feathers which correspond to the leaves of the trees; while beasts have a furry covering quite analogous to grass. Fish are born amidst *water* and so their bodies are covered with *wave* like scales. Unclean things which grow out of mud in drains and filthy places have numerous *feet* because they devour mud *(earth)*. Again, because birds are products of the male principle and have *round* eggs resembling *heaven* they soar aloft. Fish are products of the female principle and having square eggs they bury them deeply in the *earth*. Trees and herbs grow from the earth, but the wood of trees yields *fire ;* so, too, grass becomes *hot* in summer, and again, the buds of trees and the sprouts of grass are alway *rounded* like *heaven*. Man receives his human form from Heaven and Earth, and therefore he resembles Heaven as to his head which is round, and earth to his feet which are square.* If in Heaven there are Five Elements, viz., Fire, Water, Wood, Metal and Earth, in man there are also the five corresponding viscera :—

---

* It will be borne in mind here that the underlying thought of classic cosmogony is that Heaven is round and Earth flat and square, as symbolised by two famous altars dedicated to them, at which the Emperor of China yearly offers sacrifices to the Divine Ruler.

lung, heart, liver, stomach and kidneys ; if in Heaven
there are the five planets or stars, viz., the Fire star, the
Water star, the Wood star, the Metal star and the Earth
star, in man we find also the five fingers and nails ; if in
Heaven there are the four seasons, the twelve months,
and the three hundred and sixty days, man displays
also the four limbs, twelve great joints and three
hundred and sixty minor articulations ; if in Heaven there
are the six spirits and six *fu*, then in man too there are
six viscera (the spleen here taking the place of the
stomach and the ovaries being added as one) ; if in
Heaven there are the five influences or spirits, Heat, Coolness, Cold, Drought, and Moisture, in man, again, there
occur the five excretions, tears, nosedrop, sweat, saliva,
and expectoration ; if in Heaven there shine the sun and·
moon, in man there are eye and ear; if Heaven and Earth
rouse winds and clouds, in man too there is respiration,
noise, song, weeping, and groaning. [*Note* (by the
Japanese author). In man five voices exist, viz., of calling, speaking, singing, weeping, and sighing.] The clouds
are paralleled with the gall-bladder, the atmosphere
(or ether) with the lung, wind with the liver, rain with
the kidney, and thunder with the spleen. When Heaven
and Earth meet and sweetly mingle, the heart is lord,
but when the male and female principles clash there is
the flashing of angry passion, and when the man is angry
his voice rises. But the voice is produced by the sun,
and is a male (i.e., positive or active) spirit or essence.
Sometimes in Heaven frost and dews descend and so man
also frequently perspires. Sometimes Heaven pours forth
rain and snow and not unfrequently man sheds tears.

Again, if in Heaven there are the constellations, in man we find that there are freckles; if in Earth there is soil, in man there is solid tissue ; if water produces soil, blood evolves flesh ; if the soil produces rocks and these rocks give forth gold and iron, flesh too begets bones and the bones develop teeth and nails. If in Earth there are herbs and trees, in man there is the hair of the head. When the female and male principles are separated, strength and tenderness fashion the forms of all things, and while the troublesome or headache spirit * becomes crawling things, the subtle delicate spirit becomes man. Hence, when his body is first being framed, the troublesome spirit produces abdominal parasites, teeth-worms, and lice, while the delicate spirit becomes his blood and flesh. When the good and bad spirits or influences develop in Heaven and Earth the sun and moon are eaten up (i.e., by eclipse). In man when there are the two spirits present diseases are generated. When water fails the soil becomes sterile, and so when the blood diminishes the flesh wears away ; or, again, if the soil dries up, plants and trees wither, and so, too, when the blood fails, the hair of the head falls of. In stagnant water deposits of mud become heaped up into mountains, and so when the blood does not freely circulate the flesh becomes massed into tumours. If mountains contained no rocks to give them firmness, they would be much subject to landslips : and if the man had not bones he could not have a body. When the female principle overcomes the male principle

---

* Such a spirit is referred to in carly writings in other lands.

frost and dews descend, but when the male principle
asserts itself sweat pours forth (i.e., there is heat).

These are the general facts of the case.   Man is called
the Microcosm (=Little Heaven and Earth).   Heaven
and Earth are truly devoid of selfishness, for when spring
comes it is warm, when summer comes it is hot, in autumn
it is cool, and in winter, cold, nor is there anything which
receives not seasonable nourishment.

It naturally flows from this that all who follow Heaven
(i.e., God or Providence) prosper, while those who oppose
it surely come to ruin.   If any human being is of a peaceful
disposition at his birth, he is so by reason of his heavenly
nature.

The activity of one who has obtained perception of anything is the passion of his nature.   When an object is
present, the pursuit of it by the soul is a movement of the
consciousness.   When consciousness and its objects come
in contact there arises desire or dislike.   Desire having
taken form [in action ?] the consciousness passes on to
something else ; but if one cannot return into himself the
principles of Heaven are overthrown.   This returning
into oneself is what is called the casting away of human
passions.   If man, having an external form resembling
Heaven and Earth, cannot bring his heart into accordance
with these, it is because there is an exceeding of passion's
dictates.*

Therefore, the superior man (or the true gentleman),
does not barter Heaven for self, but whatever external ob-

* The idea seems to be that there is a legitimate gratification of healthy
appetites and affections.

jects may come into synthesis with him, he does not lose his true disposition, but excels in the Path.

Those are up to the ideal standard who, ripe in religious erudition, bestow deeds of goodness on their fellow men. If it is true that sagely wisdom cannot be comprehended, it is no less true that Heaven and Earth cannot be grasped by our understandings. When ordinary men attempt to compare their ordinary attainments with the minds of the sages, mistakes are apt to occur. We cannot indeed see the whole pale sky through a narrow tube. The swallow cannot fathom the purposes of the *taibō*.† Any one who knows of the purity of U may yet hate his fondness for the cup, who after death was recognized as the inventor of wine—not very becoming work for a sage to engage in, methinks.

Everyone knows of the vileness of Ketsu, but nevertheless his manufacturing tiles and leaving the art of making them behind him is recognised by everybody as a redeeming virtue in the character of an evil man. For the sage is one who dislikes to see fine purple replaced by common turkey-red ; who dislikes to hear fine singing and music rendered discordant by an unmelodious voice, and who dislikes to see men of brilliant parts overthrow their own house and country. It was said in the ancient times that man was the type of all things. Birds and beasts differ from him, and the difference consists in his alone possessing the eight virtues of humanity, righteousness, politeness, wisdom, loyalty, truthfulness, and filiality.

If he forgets these eight virtues, however, he becomes

---

† A fabulous bird with wings several thousand miles in length.

still more degraded than the brutes or even the vegetable productions of nature. Again, even amongst the animals there are such rare beings as the phœnix and *kirin;* * while amongst vegetable growths there are such honourable trees as the pine and the oak, and the herbs contain the *ran* and the chrysanthemum.

Men who themselves have but a modicum of wisdom had better refrain from laughing at fools, for a man may be indeed a thorough simpleton but if he be honest withal he is not making the mistake of throwing his life away.

If a man of intellect does not frequently listen to the opinions of others, his blunders will be many. Men having gifts of genius balanced by but little learning, are liable to have their hearts go astray. Knowledge itself is not really difficult ; it is the hard study required to obtain it which is the real difficulty. Rikusan-zan says :—

" Purity is the most honourable thing ; not the rich but he who is righteous in conduct is the higher in rank. The vilest man is he who hears not the Path.† There is no one lower than he who knows no shame." And saith Hōkōhō :—

" The ripe man is he who spreads abroad the truth of the Path."

I have felt most deeply the weightiness of these sayings and so, too, have felt profoundly the depth of my own folly.

---

* A mythological quadruped supposed to represent the giraffe.

† I prefer to follow this rendering, leaving " way " for the teaching of Him who is "the Way, the Truth, and the Life."

CHAPTER XXII.

Homes of the People.

Moated Castles in Miniature—Bird Rest or *Torii*—Grim Gateways—Keeping the Wolf from the Door—Primitive Stairways—Pebbled Courtyard —*Hara-kiri*, or the " Happy Despatch "—Wells and Water—A Poet and the "Morning Glory"—Paper Lanterns, Pillows, etc.—Mosquito Nets—Rats and Cats—The End of the Home—" Fire ! "

I SHALL endeavour in this chapter to give my readers as clear a conception as I can, consistently with extreme brevity, of the dwelling-houses of the Japanese. Rich and poor live side by side, although in Tokio there are caste traces still of the feudal age, and there are also growing tendencies in the rising mercantile and monied classes to separate themselves from the common mass. There are now great portions of the capital densely populated by the working classes only, and quite destitute of any open spaces of practical value for health or recreation.

I have had many opportunities of seeing the interior of houses tenanted by Japanese of every rank in life, and I shall try to describe things just as I have really seen them.

The proverb, "every Englishman's house is his castle," might very readily be appropriated by the Japanese, whose home, however humble it may be in all other respects, is always guarded by a moat! In Charles Dickens's *Great Expectations* there is painted a lawyer's clerk of sober, severely legal disposition, who has yet a

streak of romance in his constitution, and whose humble
residence is guarded, when office hours are over, by the
severest military precautions approved of by novel-writers.
Such a pathetic survival of ancient manners is well illustrated by many little points about an ordinary Japanese
dwelling.

In a feudal mansion the moat was usually deep enough
to prove a genuine obstacle.   While it is still almost uni-
versally retained, the muddy water is hid in summer time
by duckweed or the broad leaves of the lotus, and from
the long edible roots of the latter plant in some cases
some revenue may be derived.   The smaller gentry ape
the grandeur of those a scale or two above them, and
when at last we come down to the lowest level we still
find a miniature moat—which is often dry—of a foot or
so in breadth, and at most about two inches deep!

I have already spoken of the custom of sprinkling the
streets with water from those dirty ditches, which in
populous places are made to run into each other like
drains, but very irregularly.   The better class of houses
have them lined with layers of stone, built somewhat like
cyclopean work, in receding layers.   At the angles larger
stones are used.   The humbler habitations have their
moats lined by thin pine boards pegged down into the
ground.   As their sides and bottoms are of course per-
vious, and as the surface sewage all passes into them, the
sanitary results are sometimes rather startling.

The soil in such a neighbourhood I have found to be
peculiarly rich in microscopic life, and the people who
reside there are specially susceptible to cholera.   Classic
conquerors used to pass a plough over the site of a cap-

tured city. I trust no such process will ever be performed over Tokio, but if it should be, I think manure might at least readily be dispensed with for a decade or so.

The above account of the origin of the moat-like drains of common houses is that which is received by learned native antiquarians. It is, however, worthy of note that in Fiji the natives are said to build themselves a small house on certain occasions, and to surround it with a moat, believing that a little water will neutralise the charms which are directed against them. May the Japanese custom not have come down from the time when lake dwellings were so much used, perhaps originally—as illustrated in some parts of Central Africa at the present time—for a defence against insects of formidable kinds, which may now be unknown to our race?

Torii or Bird-rest in front of a Shinto Temple.

In China there is a curious superstition called *feng-shui* on the basis of which the site and aspect of every house is determined. It may possibly, as some have ingeniously supposed, have arisen from crude untrained observation of the effects of soil emanations and other agencies of nature on the residents of ill-chosen dwellings. You can find everywhere in Japan many little books for sale filled with engravings and minute directions how to place your dwelling favourably, but I cannot say that I have observed amongst the people any very solid evidences of the existence of *feng-shui* as a current belief.

Approaching the gate we are awed by a massive arrangement of black wood, reminding one of a hideous sable structure we saw many years ago, on a very memorable dull grey morning, in front of a Scottish jail. Its form in some cases approaches that of the so-called "bird-rest" in front of Japanese temples.*

The wall or fence may consist of bamboos, whole or split, or of thin wooden planks blackened with a mixture of Indian ink and the juice of the unripe persimmon, which is highly bitter, astringent and antiseptic, preserving the wood for a long time.

In houses of some pretensions there is an embankment behind the moat, topped by a quick-set hedge of either holly, privet, camellia or the like. Behind this there is either the fence already described, or a wall composed of thin tiles laid horizontally, with much white shell lime ; or a bamboo lath and plaster wall, sometimes covered by diamond-shaped tiles, the joining lines of which are

---

* In some archæological drawings in my possession, very ancient native pictures of such structures are shown, and above them are two birds something like pigeons, poised in the attitude of those usually painted in the familiar old Chinese willow-pattern plate.

concealed by diagonals of white· lime laid on smoothly, rounded and as thick as three fingers. This has a very pleasing appearance, quite characteristic of Japanese architecture. I have seen such a wall crowned by a line of old bayonets, forming a picturesque and rather formidable *cheval de frise.*

As the name of the street is not to be found at the street corner as with us, it is repeated on every door-way. The towns are divided into wards and blocks, and the numbers of the houses are often confused and misleading. A slip of white wood is nailed on one of the posts of the gate, and is inscribed with the name of the street or block, the number, name of householder, numbers and sexes of household. Besides this combined street-sign and door-plate there is often a charm to keep away the *wolf* from the door, an animal which literally, in times not very remote, was known in the vicinity of Tokio, and was greatly dreaded. Yellow placards are put up when there is any plague or infectious disease there, such as cholera. Within the porch there are racks for halberts, and other grotesque instruments of formidable shapes, which we might call "clutches," such as the ever vigilant gate-keepers might find useful when aiding the apprehension of brawlers, beggars, or unruly partizans. The halberts and other weapons have been removed, but the racks still remain to attest the existence of rougher, ruder times, but recently passed away. Just outside the outer gateway posts are inserted in the ground wherewith to support the tall flag-staffs used at festivals, and sometimes other smaller ones for the cords on which lanterns are hung during illuminations. These costly rejoicings are exceedingly frequent, and though pleasing to visitors are a heavy burden to householders, and a constant theme for grumbling.

The gates of the larger houses are heavy, are adorned with verdant copper or bronze mountings, and often studded with large nails.

When you enter by the gate you generally find a court from several sides of which the open verandahs of the building are approachable. The verandahs are high, and there is a special entrance by heavy wooden stairs. In some temples you often find that those stairs are composed of great tree trunks placed at an angle of about forty-five degrees, in which the steps are carefully notched. I have seen precisely the same kind of work in the Himalayas, but in a much coarser style of carpentry, and as the same construction is shown, I think, in a Greek caricature of the Delphic oracle, this may perhaps represent an early form of our familiar wooden stair. The court is sometimes paved with large water-worn stones, larger than the egg of a goose ; sometimes it is of level, weedless, perfectly well swept earth ; and in either case there are lines of smooth stepping stones where they may be required. There is not the same horror of publicity as in India—not by any means, but usually the court or garden is very well fenced in, either by wooden walls or a well trimmed hedge. A garden in Japan is never laid out in flower plots like the approved carpet patterns of the Italian school. Sometimes flowering plants are purposely allowed to grow in sweet confusion, but the ground is chiefly taken up with close cropped, bristly turf—which turns rather yellow in winter—and carefully trimmed trees, often dwarfed and trained with more skill than eye for beauty.

I have already alluded to the miniature landscape gardening, in which the Japanese so greatly excel, and need add little more here on that subject. One great aim is to secure an idealised, flawless woodland effect in a small space, and every ton of sheer rubbish and fragment of shapeless stone can be prettily turned to account.

In the grander mansions there is a space which in olden times used to be strewn on certain awful occasions with white sand. When a member of a knightly family had been found guilty of a serious offence, he had, sitting there, to bare his abdomen, and taking the smallest of the two swords which every samurai carried, plunge it into his belly and carry it across. Usually in later times a mere skin scratch sufficed, and whenever this act had been formally done, a relative, who stood behind the unfortunate knight, and who had probably been chosen as an expert swordsman, severed the head from the body by a swift stroke with a weapon edged like a razor. Thus was honour maintained and justice satisfied.

Miss Bird is unfortunately quite wrong in supposing that *hara-kiri* (not *hari-kari*, as our newspapers persist in styling it), is entirely extinct, though indeed it is becoming rarer every year, and science has introduced the Japanese to much more elegant ways of " working one's self off."

The gardens even of somewhat humble mansions are often graced with carved stone lanterns. The well, placed near the kitchen, is surrounded with a platform of green and slippery planks; it often has a rim of stone around it, and the bucket is raised by a beam with a

stone attached to one end, like the Egyptian shadoof, or
by means of a rough rope working on a large pulley.
Sometimes it is simply attached to the end of a long
bamboo like a fishing rod.   A Japanese poet prettily and
wittily sings of the "morning-face"—their name for the
convolvolus or morning-glory—which he sees at break of
every day twining its fair arms afresh round the well-
rope ; and Japanese painters love to picture graceful girls
engaged in drawing water.   At the well, too, many a sad
history ends.   A love-sick maiden often fills her wide
sleeves with stones, and sinks to what is hoped may be
rest.   In Tokio there is a full supply of fine clear water,
but during a great cholera epidemic I discovered, and, I
think, demonstrated, that the method of distribution is
such that the mains become necessarily more and more
polluted as the water nears its outlet in the bay, and I
suspect that the mortality keeps very close pace with the
increasing impurity of the water supply.   Nothing is so
urgently needed in Tokio as reform in this direction.

The roof is of black tiles made out of a clay, dark with
organic matter, which is obtained from the bottoms of
old canals foul with putrid sewage.   Sometimes in the
poorer houses, and in the outhouses of the greater ones,
wooden shingles only are used, and very frequent pro-
clamations are issued forbidding their use, on account of
the danger of fire, but without much effect.   Under the
eaves, and even within the house, which is quite open in
warm weather, swallows build their nests within easy
range of the hands of the residents.

In front of the doorway there is a small space unfloored,
called the *doma*, where you take off your shoes after

announcing yourself in the words, *O tanomi mōsu*—" I
beseech you " ! or by banging a gong suspended by the
door-posts. Looking above, you are struck with the
ponderous size of the beams that support the roof, and
you are perhaps not quite prepared to accept the reason
given—the desire to avert the evil consequences of earth-

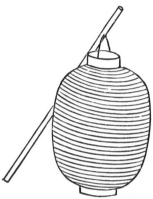

quakes ! The walls are hung with
paper lanterns, and there is a
range of white wooden fire-
buckets all stamped with the
crest of the owner. Some of the
lanterns are quite cylindrical, open
out like a concertina, are suspended from a ∩ shaped stick,
and are like those used in ancient
Egypt. A favourite form of
lantern for carrying about the

*Paper Lantern Used by Pedestrians
at Night.*

streets at night—and in Tokio every one must carry a
lantern lighted even on moonlight nights*—is that shown
in the cut. The crest or cognisance of the owner is
generally painted outside in large dimensions.

There is often only one storey in Japanese houses, and
very rarely more than two. The stair to the second
storey is very steep. The ceilings are composed of very
thin broad planks, and are lower than we are accustomed
to, but it must be remembered that the people do not

---

* The students of Tokio having once been reminded by their *proctors*—
shall I say?—of this regulation, did purchase, and, in conformity with its
terms, carry about " a lantern " of colossal dimensions, to the disgust of all
legal-minded persons and pedants.

sit on chairs, and have no high beds or tables. Doorways, or rather the grooved lintels in which the screen-doors slide, are very low, and the Japanese, who are always bowing for some reason or another, seem to enjoy having an unusual number of them to pass through in extensive houses. No room is completely walled in, but opens on two or more sides completely into the garden, the street, or the adjoining rooms, so that eavesdroppers do not need to hide behind the dear old arras. Sliding shutters, with tissue paper windows, the carpentry of which is careful and exact, move in wooden grooves almost on a level with the floor, which is covered with padded woven mats of rushes. Those mats are of uniform size, six feet by three, and this fact dominates all architecture in Japan. Estimates for building houses, and the cutting of wood, rest upon this traditional custom.

As a protection against the severities of the weather, rain-shutters are also used, which are slid into a box-like recess with alarming noise early in the morning   The floor underneath the mats is like the wood of which band-boxes are made, and I have had the experience, once more common in Japan than it now is, of a robber moving underneath the floor and noisily seeking an entrance.

In a recess is rolled up the soft cotton-stuffed mattresses which constitute beds in Japan, while alongside are placed the wooden paper-padded pillows. Sometimes each one contains a little drawer in which to put a lady's jewelled hair-pins. I never knew a " foreigner " who cared to dislocate his neck by using them. This form of head-rest may perhaps have arisen in connection with the elaborate and costly hair-dressing common in some of the Pacific isles, but a pillow of similar shape was used in ancient Egypt, and the one used by the late King Cetewayo, as figured in the illustrated London papers, was also similar in design.

In the walls are recesses with sliding doors, into which the bedding is thrust in the day-time. Clothes are kept in plaited bamboo boxes usually covered with black or dark-green waterproof paper. The furniture is very simple ; there are often in the best houses no chairs, no stools, no tables, no bedsteads. There may be some low short-legged side-tables of characteristic Japanese pattern, and one or two costly vases or other ornaments, a few scroll pictures which are changed in deference to guests and seasons, some flowers or dwarf trees in vases, and a lamp or two. Often you may now find in one room of the house a good and costly western carpet, some chairs, a table, a photographic album, and a copy of one or other of Herbert Spencer's works—two-thirds of which is probably uncut.

In one part of the house is the altar-shelf on which images of saints or sages or pictures of ancestors may be seen, with incense tapers burning before them by day and lamps at night. I have often seen photographs of the dead honoured in this idolatrous way.

I must not forget to mention the dark closet for naughty children—the severest punishment usually resorted to in Japan.

As mosquitoes are exceedingly troublesome in summer on the plains, curtains of a dark green hemp are placed above the sleepers at night and over the baby's cot in day-time to exclude them. They are smoked out at sundown by the burning of a kind of scented grass. On the 8th day of the fourth month portions of the same herb are also hung up within the paper lanterns to act as a charm against those most irritating bloodsuckers.

According to the scholarly Mr. Satow, peasants place bundles of the dried stems of tobacco in the space between the walls of their cottages and the eaves, to keep out rats and mice, which are very troublesome. The stoats also tend to keep them down greatly, and great is the noise of scurrying and screaming behind the thin wainscot when one of those pugnacious animals makes an entrance at midnight. Cats are kept for the same purpose. They are very fond of fish, do not seem to care much for cow's milk, and have a curious short, stunted, and deformed tail. It is supposed by many foreigners that the short tails are due to the Japanese practice of cutting them off. The fact is the majority of Japanese cats are born with this deformity, and it is often so ungraceful that the practice of cutting off what remains is certainly quite common. When English cats were brought into the country many years ago, their long tails were greatly admired, and it is almost impossible to retain a long-tailed cat many days, so eagerly are they sought after.

At the New-Year, when all debts are paid and a new life begins, every corner of the house is gone over, the mats are raised, the furniture washed and polished, and the cobwebs swept away.

I need hardly describe the outhouses in detail. In large mansions there is usually a partially matted fencing room, in which all kinds of juvenile racket and mischief are carried on, without danger of injury to furniture or person. The poorer classes indulge in the public hot baths very frequently, and the dressing room is the nightly resort of neighbouring gossips. The sexes still bathe in common in many parts of Japan, and in spite of many efforts on the part of government, indecent publicity is by no means rare.

In summer, a well planned Japanese house is the very ideal of coolness, grace and comfort. In winter it is the acme of misery. There are no fire-places, and there is unmitigated ventilation. People keep themselves warm by holding their palms over some morsels of red hot charcoal in a brazier, and frost-bite is very common. No one goes out if he can at all help it in wet or very cold weather. At night, when cold dry winds blow, a heating apparatus is put beneath the heavy cotton coverlets. It often gets overturned ; a watchman from his ladder-like tower sees afar-off a dull red glow, a bell suddenly clangs, another, and then another, and soon the vast city is in an uproar, friends rushing madly to congratulate or commiserate, or help ; poor householders careering along with their *lares* and *penates*, and a few mats ; and here and there firemen bearing along ghastly shapeless charred burdens which move and groan. The roar of the ruddy rapidly onrushing waves of flame, the crackle of dry wood and the loud pistol like "pop" of hollow bamboos filled with heated air, tend quite to unnerve the coolest person. In a few hours a great fan-shaped gap, as the morning papers show in red-coloured maps, has appeared in the city. You go at day-break to find the scene of horror, but it has already almost disappeared. New sign-boards are erected intimating that the premises will be reopened, etc., in a day or two. Crowds of carpenters have rushed in from outlying suburbs and far away villages, and have already done much to re-erect on the hot and smoking ruins wooden houses nearly as good as those last night's fire and fury swept away.

CHAPTER XXIII.

How the Japanese Amuse Themselves.

Artistic Toys—Cheapness, a Hygienic Advantage—Gardening in Miniature —Archaisms of the Toy World—Tough Picture-Books—Early Kinder Gartens—Dumb Oratory—Puppet Shows and the Drama—Wrestlers and their Rewards.

MY FIRST impression on seeing the Japanese face to face, in their everyday garb, was that they were a people exceedingly earnest as to the routine duties of life, sober-minded, good-natured, and ever ready for a laugh at any trifle, but just on that account not requiring and not seeking for any great amount of artificial amusement.

Well, I was not quite right then, and may even be wrong now ; my more experienced judgment may still require correction ; but I do now most assuredly think that a very large amount of time, and an excessive amount of money is devoted to amusements of an exciting kind, and that in this respect the Japanese have perhaps gone somewhat beyond most other modern races. Japanese children have always had a great variety of toys to choose from ; and now, when our own highly civilised nations are not slow to adopt the happy thoughts of the Far East, many would be astonished to find how very rapidly western ideas are appreciated and imitated by eastern toy-makers. I remember once of pointing out to a passing tourist a new and very ingenious toy which was selling at every corner in Tokio, and seemed to be thoroughly Japanese alike in conception and construction. He rather astonished me by saying that the same toy had really appeared in Paris twelve months before as a new invention and, sure enough, the Japanese had borrowed it from the West.

The artistic breadth and firmness of purpose we now tend to associate with Japanese ornamental work of all kinds, is fully displayed in the toy department, as may be witnessed on the occasion of any Buddhist saint-day. With a bit of common clay or coarse *papier maché* deftly daubed with paint, an object will be fashioned, pleasing enough for any child to play with, and artistically far beyond what the same money would be able to purchase in any of our own village fairs.

On returning to Europe I have been much struck, however, with the wonderful improvement the last decade has effected on our European cheaper toys and picture-books, both as regards taste and ingenuity. The cheaper *papier maché* ones of Japan, proverbial as they are amongst native authors for their frailty and transitoriness, have a special hygienic value, as I often found when attending little fever patients. A copper or two—in Japan they even condescend to iron—would buy a hatful of them in variety enough to fill the little sick one's heart to overflowing with happiness, and you felt no compunction in speedily consigning their ruins to the fire.

A very simple and charming toy of which my little patients did not readily tire, consisted of a neat little box of white wood containing many kinds of fish in coloured porcelain, all very wonderfully like nature, fresh and lively looking. Each had a tiny ring in its mouth, and there was supplied to the young angler a little fishing-rod armed with a hook, with which he would dexterously whip out a finny captive from the transparent depths of a tea cup. I think each of those boxes cost about three-farthings sterling to a foreign retail purchaser. For how much less a smart Japanese small boy could purchase one is still a mystery which no foreigner is ever likely to fathom.

I have already alluded to the mud-pie instinct. In Japan it is diligently fostered and guided as it ought to be. There are always certain shelves in the toy-shop of the poorest hamlet devoted to what might perhaps be called the "properties" requisite for miniature mud-pie gardens. There are little terra-cotta bridges, rustic bowers, huts, trees, storks, oxen, and cattle ; and the children learn to range them with a good eye to landscape effects. I think I should like to endow a professorship of this infantile art, which has perhaps done as much to promote æsthetic culture in Japan as all other means put together. I should be told, of course, that the instinct is there already. Very true, but according to modern teaching, not quite Darwinian, perhaps, instincts can be quickly created when they are wished for very much.

Did you ever notice the frequent archaisms in the world of toymakers ? Not long ago the soldiers in the realm of toys were dressed in armour. They are still usually clad in uniform a few decades old. No such loco-motives are seen in active service as the toymakers continue to supply. The same thing is true of Japan. You find the old world of pre-Restoration days perpetuated for the children.

There is also what city men would call "a strong line" in picture-books. I do not intend to speak here of those that are educational in their tendency. Well-drawn but too gaudily coloured sheets of object-lessons in endless variety are to be seen on every bookseller's shop-front—windows are only a recent innovation. I have in my possession many most useful productions of this kind, showing the various cereals, vegetables, etc., which have been issued at somewhere about one farthing each, and they seem to be exceedingly popular with the little folks. A finer style of work contains very excellent' and well-selected drawing lessons for home study and amusement. And here I may state that the old friend of our infancy, the transparent slate, has found in Japan alert imitators and a ready sale.

The low-priced picture story-books remind one very much of those common in this country some thirty odd years ago ; but in Japan they are usually printed from blocks with four or five colours. In the better class of books the effect of colour in drapery, armour, plumage, etc., is often very prettily heightened by a simple embossing process which indicates texture effectively, and does not seem to add very much to the expense of production. A thick and, in ordinary circumstances, indestructible paper is used for such works. I believe it would be useful in this country for a similar class of picture-books for children, and I sincerely trust some enterprising publisher will try the experiment.

Bakin, a Japanese writer already quoted, says that from

olden times there were many games which brought out the faculties of young children, and he commends especially such amusements as scene guessing, in which cards containing pictures have to be correctly named. Another game is the pairing of clam shells, which keeps little eyes and fingers well and quietly employed for a long time. His remarks show that he had fairly grasped the principles of the *Kinder-garten* so far back as seventy years ago.

The dressing of dolls is a great pastime for girls, and much money is spent on them. A game which is very popular is for one to imitate by set signs some object, animal or person, on which his opponent must promptly simulate something more powerful and so outwit him or lose the game. At wine parties, with drinking as the forfeit, the fox, gun and master are set forth by signs in this way. It is a silly affair altogether. The ancient Italian game of *moro* is one which is common also in Japan—so many fingers are briefly and quickly displayed and must be counted correctly. A good deal too much strong rice-beer is absorbed on those occasions. The same game is very much played also in China, as I have observed on two occasions when passing through Hong-Kong, the shrill quick cry and answer of players being very noticeable. There are multitudes of home amusements which I cannot here find space to dwell upon as I should have liked to do.

During the New-Year holidays the streets are always gay with bright dressed parties of young people of both sexes, playing at battledore and shuttlecock, or bouncing pith balls. I have already spoken of kite-flying, which is almost a fine art. Hand balls are used greatly, but football is unknown, and athletic exercise is chiefly found in the fencing saloons, which are very greatly patronised at all times, but especially when political feeling runs high.

The story-tellers are a great attraction to people on the streets who have nothing special to do, and many of them are really accomplished elocutionists. They blow loudly through conch shells at certain passages, and utilize the fan in a thousand ways to aid their action and emphasize their oratory. They are entering now a new field, and indulge in political tirades, somewhat thinly veiled.

One of the most curious feats I have seen in public —speaking, shall I say?—is what may be called dumb oratory. The story is acted on the streets in pantomime, and without any adventitious aid from beginning to end, but it is astonishing how quickly the audience responds. by smiles or even in rare cases by tears, revealing a new phase of the eloquence of silence.

Foremost of the public recreations, of course, is the theatre. The Chinese drama, which like our own began with marionette shows, and from which that of Japan springs, is supposed to have begun in the period of the Han dynasty (B.C. 200—A.D. 200) in a very strange way. The story, as told by Mr. Giles in his charming and scholarly *Historic China and Other Sketches*, was this :— The imperial founder of the Hans had been attacked by the Huns, and closely shut up in one of his own cities. " His Majesty, acting under the advice of a crafty minister, sent a messenger to the Hun chieftain, and offered. him the present of a very beautiful girl on condition of being allowed to pass unharmed through his lines. The

Hun chieftain, suspicious of treachery, repaired by agreement to the foot of the city wall, and there beheld a charming young lady moving about among a circle of attendants almost as lovely as herself. His suspicions being thus allayed, he gave orders to open a passage to the Emperor and his suite, who promptly made the best of their way out. At the same time, the Hun chieftain entered the city and proceeded to the spot on the wall where the young lady was awaiting him, still surrounded by her bevy of handmaids ; but on arriving there, he found, to his infinite chagrin, that the beauty and her attendants were simply a set of wooden puppets which had been dressed up for the occasion, and were worked by a concealed arrangement of strings. Overcome with rage and mortification, he instantly started in pursuit of the flying Emperor, who, however, succeeded in making good his escape "—having, of course, no Manchurian pig-tail, like poor Commissioner Yeh in after years.

From that time till the present day marionette exhibitions have been as popular in China as in Italy, where they seem to have amused Charles Dickens intensely.

In China people of public spirit provide the entertainment for the village community, and the show, like that of our own venerable " Punch and Judy," is set forth in the open air.

A Character Dance.
(From an ancient Japanese Engraving.)

Restrictions are placed in China on the representation

of royal characters or great public officers, even of the remote past; but there is no intention, the law declares, "to
prohibit the exhibition upon the stage of fictitious characters of just and upright men, of chaste wives, and pious
and obedient children, all which may tend to dispose the
minds of the spectators to the practice of virtue."

The introduction of the drama proper into Japan was
very late. The first public performances are said to have
taken place in Kioto, the old inland capital, in the year
A.D. 1467-8. Very much earlier than this certain religious
mummeries were performed. Instead of having a stage,
those performances took place under a shed on a carpet
of grass, and so the Japanese word for theatre is still
Shibaya, or turf-house.

I do not think that the sacred Shinto dances are in any
way related to the drama, although some dramatic elements may have accidentally become mingled with them,
and "character dances" date almost from the beginning
of history in Japan.

The Japanese theatre is open from very early in the
morning and lasts till six in the evening. The introduction of gas has favoured night performances of late. It is
of interest to remember that in Shakespeare's time the
theatre was open from 1 to 5 P.M. Women players are
hardly known in Japan, except as special companies acting by themselves, and their grade is esteemed much
lower. I have never been in a Japanese theatre during a
play, but am familiar with many of the favourite pieces
performed in Tokio as literature, and their tone is much
higher than I had expected—a perfect contrast to those

of India, and probably above that of some recent plays which have been immensely run after in England.

Wrestling seems to have a great fascination for the Japanese, and nothing is so common as for spectators, in a rapture of excitement, to throw off their own garments, layer by layer, to a favourite combatant, and, if the caricaturists may be trusted, to seize those of their neighbours also without saying by your leave !

CHAPTER XXIV.

Japanese Manners and Customs—Negative and Positive.

Degraded Religions—Origin of some Fetishes—Superstitious Customs.

I AM becoming more and more convinced that a great many of our familiar everyday customs, such as fashions in dress, etc., are derived from what are usually called superstitions, and that these, in turn, are quite commonly degraded survivals of once high religious thoughts and emotions. Once, for example, I was told of a stone in Japan which changed its colour when a thunderstorm was impending, and, on going to see it, I found that it was archæologically and historically simply a Buddha of great antiquity, the features and limbs of which had long since been "weathered" away. And such I have often found to be the history of so-called fetish development. It is not for me to assert that all fetishes are of this description. Possibly some of them may have been aerolites in reality, or have been mistaken for such, and perhaps the descent from heaven of such a stone as the Kaaba at Mecca, may have really given the first conception of a fetish to star worshippers in the old times. However that may be, I myself have never seen a "fetish" which did not clearly point to a past and higher faith. I once pointed out to the Asiatic Society of Japan a curious example of this. Some larvæ, like those of the caddis worm, make little cases of large sand grains, which resemble the human form as rendered by Buddhist sculptors. Those are collected, named after certain divinities, and worshipped. A pre-existing belief has been attached to them ; they did not give origin to it.

And so I have found it to be with many customs that seem at first sight in no way related to thought or to the reality of life's conditions. They are often the clear results of mental activity frozen into unthinking habit or fossils of burning religious ideas evolved and quickened under conditions long since passed away. Many of those survivals are quite unconscious and unintentional. According to a London interviewer, even Mr. Spurgeon has a great horse-shoe over his stable door !

My limits strictly forbid my entering here upon the religions of Japan, without a study of which I think no adequate account of the customs of the country can be given.

It may interest not a few readers, however, who seek for early affinities to other races, to learn that in the earliest faith of the people of Nipon there was a great primal trinity of spirits or gods, from whom all things flowed. The first of these is called Lord of the Centre of the Heavens and Earth. The progenitors of the Japanese race are named Izanami and Izanagi.

Here are a few superstitious customs which may have arisen by the process of degradation, although the process cannot at present be definitely shown.

Certain priests of Japan exorcise by cutting imaginary letters in the air with sword-blades. The figures are very greatly modified Sanskrit letters, and the rites came through China, probably through the influence of Taouism,

IZANAMI AND IZANAGI,
The Progenitors of the Japanese Race.

(By a Japanese Artist.)

which, although usually deemed a Chinese faith, is really, I believe, a heresy from Buddhism which came from India. It was easier to cut bad Sanskrit letters in the air than to read the language or to master its grand philosophy.

When children in some parts of England are ill with whooping-cough, they are sometimes passed through the fork of a tree. Herbert Spencer thinks this custom to be a survival of tree-worship. In Tokio, children solemnise a promise or bargain, especially at the New Year, by applying a pine branch to the foreheads of the contracting parties. Sometimes, also, they seek out a tree with a narrow crevice, anoint the place with some oil, and make a vow in language now unintelligible to most people. Should one of them break the promise, he is bound to go through the hole, which, of course, is impossible. This custom I have not found to exist in the country north of Tokio.

Miss Bird, in her *Unbeaten Tracks*, speaking of the superstitions of northern Japan, says—" If a stalk of tea falls into the teacup and stands upright for a second, a visitor is expected from the direction in which it falls." I have never heard of this custom, and it seems to be quite unknown about the neighbourhood of the capital. It is a very common thing in Scotland to hear people joking about "visitors" in their teacups in this way, and possibly the idea may have been imported along with tea from China by our sailors or merchants.

Holly, along with Japanese sardines, is hung above the door at New Year time to protect the dwellers from demons. When the Duke of Edinburgh paid a visit to

Japan, the evil spirits were carefully and solemnly exorcised from the "Palace on the Strand" which was appointed for his residence. Of course, the officials meant it only for a mark of care and respect, and were no doubt greatly amused as they went through the process.

I come now to deal with the family life in relation to customs. There are, strictly speaking, no castes in Japan in the Indian sense. Still it is clear to my own mind that when Buddhism came it brought with it reminiscences, so to speak, of the four great castes and of the outcasts, which are themselves a caste, of India. Hence we have in Japan the old distinctions still living in the popular imagination, and there are Knights, Farmers, Workmen, and Shopkeepers, and till lately an outcast race, the *Yetas*, who acted as executioners, curriers, and the like, where the taking away of life, a Buddhist crime, was concerned.

The names of the people help to mark the distinction. The merchants or citizen-shopkeepers are rising rapidly in their social status since the Restoration has broken the feudal system and given them security for the fruits of their skill and industry.

I cannot here enter fully into details, but will mention briefly the leading facts in an average individual life.

From birth the navel-cord is carefully preserved. It is placed in the amulet-bag worn with other relics. During infancy the hair is completely shaved away, which has hygienic advantages; it is afterwards allowed to grow in a ring, like figure 2, then as in figure 1, and finally as in figure 3 (p. 285). Some examples of the mode of dressing the hair of women occur in the earlier illustrations of this work. Children are suckled much longer than with us, and often they are not weaned till the fourth year. Coloured rice and beans are presented on the hundredth day after the child is born. Tattooing is very common, but I cannot find evidence that it was

customary amongst the early Japanese. I have seen some magnificent examples of the art, and showed a living specimen in the Japanese Asiatic Society which has perhaps never been equalled. With the exception of the face and extremities, every portion of the body was covered with a beautiful damask-like design in three colours, so fine that the punctures had blended perfectly, leaving no space uncoloured. It cost a great sum of money and a lifetime of pain.

Japanese married women blacken their teeth—to make them unattractive, some say. Really, however, the women have only conserved a custom common to both sexes in ancient times.

The usual Japanese robe is loose like a dressing-gown, folding over in front, and fastened by a girdle. It is open at the neck. The sleeves are wide and are used as pockets. The Japanese, therefore, naturally girds his loins and tucks up his sleeves when about to put forth energy. In place of handkerchiefs, paper is used, and is hid in the sleeves. The sleeves are used to hide the mouth when laughing, to wipe tearful eyes, and when life is too burdensome they are filled with stones while the wearer seeks a watery grave. I have already described the clogs,

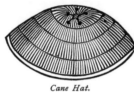

Cane Hat.

sandals, and pattens in common use. Hats are not much worn by the better class in ordinary weather. The above is a common form, but there are many varieties, and felt hats are now greatly worn.

Woollen underclothing and knitted scarfs bid fair to become of universal necessity in winter, and as sheep cannot be got to thrive there would seem to be promise of a growing trade in such materials.

Marriage is usually arranged by consultation with the relatives, but love affairs of a spontaneous kind form a large element in the romance literature of Japan. There is an old pine tree in Tokio where betrothals are wont to be made. After the relatives have formally agreed, presents are made publicly, and then, as in China, certain symbolic acts of eating and drinking are gone through, after which domestic duties begin. The wife owes filial allegiance of a very severe kind to the mother-in-law. Occasionally, as in India—and in certain high strata of

English society—children are appointed by the relatives from birth to marry each other.

According to a correspondent of the *Japan Gazette* (April 3, 1878), if a woman is unfaithful to her husband she is made to stand before the house with her arms tied in front of her and her head shaven, while an inscribed

Japanese Mangling.

board is hung around her neck. As I have never seen an example of this custom in my daily duties, which have carried me everywhere, either the custom must be nearly obsolete or domestic felicity is very general.

To enter upon the consideration of burial ceremonies would imply some study of Buddhism, which I must reserve for another work. Both incremation and inhumation are practised in Japan.

Japanese faith in immortality has survived the long

continuance of a Buddhist teaching which seems to many
to deny it.

A native paper published in Osaka, in April of 1878,
relates the following incident :—"Inouye of this city has
made a life-size figure of a daughter of his who died.
The friends of the family were feasted some days ago on
the occasion of the image being completed.   It is now
always attended by two maid-servants, and in a few days
it is to be taken to the Shinto 'Cherry Temple' to see
the blossoms."

A Studious and Dutiful Girl Shampooing her Rheumatic Father.
(From a Japanese Story-Book.)

When a believer of the Monto sect dies, a copper is
put in the coffin to pay "Granny of the River of Death,"
just as the Greeks paid for old Charon's services to their
departed.

The Japanese do not buy their own coffin-boards and store them in their drawing-rooms as the Chinese do, but they used to retain the dead in their own dwellings for a long time—a custom which is happily being given up. The dead are buried in cemeteries, as with us, and are not scattered about the country singly as in China—a fact of great practical significance in relation to railways in Japan.

The Japanese are as fond of proverbs and pithy sayings as we are, and some of them are very happy hits in the original, though translation weakens them. Not a few of the proverbs which have been noted by writers as current in Japan are of very recent introduction into that country, and the process of absorption of such racy and memorable condensations of Western thought and experience is still going on. Some few of those which follow may be traced to other lands, but they are sufficiently well-known throughout the country to be esteemed Japanese proverbs.

The Japanese Mrs. Partington attempts "to drive away a fog with a fan."

An allusion to the once universal vendetta, or personal revenge, is contained in "When you curse look out for two graves."

The sweetness of contentment and the wide hat I have already described give rise to "Live under your hat."

A democratic growl is now heard in "The voice of the crane is louder than the chirping of sparrows."

Aristocratic ignorance is sneered at in "The tree that vice grows on."

A fool is asked "Can you boil potatoes?"

Beni, or vermilion, is greatly used by the ladies to

redden their lips, hence "Who fingers rouge becomes red."

Of the dead, with us, nothing but good must be spoken. In Japan, where the tiger is, of course, known only as a rare foreign animal, the expression of a similar kindly feeling is "Spare the skin of the dead tiger."

The system of irrigating the rice-fields by cross ditches at successively lower and lower levels leads to "Taking the water away from your neighbour's field."

That domestic felicity is sometimes interrupted even in Japan is illustrated in "A three-inch tongue can kill a six-foot man."

The following require no elaborate commentary to explain them :—

"The borrower smiles like a saint, and the repayer scowls like Old Nick."

"Even monkeys fall from the tree."

"The frog in the well knows nothing of the high seas."

"A tiger in the streets."

"The bad artist blames his brush."

"Frog spawn becomes frogs."

"Egg-plants do not spring from melon-seeds."

"Don't seek fish on trees."

"There's no escaping the net of Providence."

"Blind men fear not snakes."

"To draw tears from the very devil."

"Making an idol does not give it a soul."

"A good preacher gives a short sermon."

"There is no professor of poetry."

"Every one has his wen."

"As much esteemed as the bat in the birdless village."

CHAPTER XXV

General Survey : What I Think of Japan.

Growth of Population—Promise of Improved Physique—" Bafe " Tea
and Blankets—A Reasonable People—Over-Legislation about Shipping
—Usurpation of the Shoguns—Growth of the Daimiates—Questionings
—Japanese Whigs and Tories—Dread of Socialism—The Clan Unit—
Moral Progress—Revisal of Treaties.

INCE returning to England I have very often
been asked in this country—what do you think
of Japan ? The question has been put with
such varying motives, and by so many different
classes of people, that I now find it exceedingly
difficult to attempt any answer at all. However, I shall put down here, fairly and
reasonably I trust, some conclusions to which
I have come, not altogether hastily and
without thought.

Japan, with its thirty-seven millions, must soon become a most important factor in the history of the East.
Infanticide and other causes have long kept down the
natural growth of population. Those causes are now
ceasing to act to an appreciable extent, and so I think
the growth of population in Japan will now be rapid.
The physical stamina of the people will also speedily

improve. Smallpox has been almost completely stamped
out. Cholera is understood now by the authorities, and
has been coped with pretty efficiently. Chest diseases
are being better guarded against. The Japanese have
always been given to cleanliness under peculiarly ineffective conditions. The genuine principles of *medical*
cleanliness are being studied and followed now amongst
the better classes. Buddhism has long restricted the diet
of the people to vegetables,—fish and wine being winked
at,—but that system has no longer a strong hold upon the
intelligence of the community. Milk is now greatly
appreciated everywhere for sick people and children.
Beef is becoming a common article of food, and " Bafe "
tea is an article known and appreciated in all households
throughout the treaty ports and larger towns. Cod-liver
oil is manufactured and consumed in large quantities.
Woollen clothes—shirts, comforters and blankets—are
now considered even by conservative people to be useful
in warding off chest complaints which are common and
fatal in the country. The empire is now peaceful, and
the majesty of law is rapidly replacing the bloody
principle of the vendetta. Recreation and physical
exercise are more insisted upon for school children, and
there is the same movement as in our country to throw
open parks and gardens to the poorer classes of the
community. The railway and steamer routes are being
used for pleasure trips as well as for business, and an
unexpected source of revenue has thus been opened up
which may yet be augmented a hundred-fold. All these
influences strongly tend to make the population healthier
and more numerous. There is sufficient waste land

within the empire to supply the wants of "colonists," as those who enter uncultivated territory are called. The Island of Yesso is being rapidly colonised in this way, and it may supply the desire for openings to young men of enterprise for a decade or two to come ; but soon the time must arrive when, under the new conditions of her higher life, Japan must expand her influence and assert herself beyond her present narrow bounds.

Going back even to Xavier's time the Japanese were declared by one of themselves, very correctly, to be a reasonable people. They have ever been ready, at all events, to respond appreciatively to influences of a healthy and useful tendency. From China, India, Portugal, France, Holland, America and England, successive waves have borne in upon their shores germs of thought which have taken natural root in the soil, and promise to become indigenous. It was from a not unreasonable dread of the mysterious and deadly influence of Rome that the country was so long and closely sealed against foreign intrusion. Even the ships of so daring a race of navigators had then, by legal enactment, to be so built that they could hardly risk heavy seas, and it was almost superfluously made a capital crime for any one to leave the shores of Japan in one of them for a foreign country. Feudalism and a fertile soil made such regulations possible, and in result they were quite effective.

With a rapidly growing and more heterogeneous population, with a totally cultivated or even less fertile soil, the problem would not have been so simply solved. Japanese patriotism—the *Yamato-damashi* or Soul of Old Japan—has ever been keen ; the danger to the State from

the threatened ascendancy of a foreign political hierarchy
was real and immanent, and when the word had been
given of a powerful and cruel military autocrat whose will
was not above law, for no true law existed, the people had
little to say. Had Cromwell succeeded in establishing
a hereditary dynasty of military autocrats, it is hard to
say what might have been the next chapters in English
history, but Cromwell's soldiers had the Bible—the Old
Testament at anyrate—in their bosoms, but in Japan
there was no Bible nor any very feasible substitute for it,
and so wrong triumphed through the danger of a worse
wrong.

It must not, however, be supposed that from the middle
of the seventeenth century, when Japan became sealed by
the great Shogun or Generalissimo Iyeyasu against all
foreign intercourse (save with China), till 1868, that abso-
lute stagnation of thought reigned amongst the thirty odd
millions of the "black-haired." Admitting, as we must
meanwhile practically do, their ethnic homogeneity, there
were already in the land and in its literature, systems—
Aryan, Turanian,—and shall I even venture to say Sem-
itic? *—which could hardly fail to have various fertilising
interactions in the seething process of social evolution
which we now begin to see, somewhat dimly only as yet,
to have been going on in the long dreary interval of darkness and silence.

There was, first of all, an ominously silent and

---

* The Nestorians may just possibly, through China, have influenced the
leading modern Buddhist sect of Monto. It is indeed somewhat hard to get
rid of *a priori* grounds for some such influence, which is also—speaking from
a historical standpoint—quite within the range of possibility.

stealthy but gradually significant questioning in liter-
ary circles as to the usurped authority by which the
act of isolation had been decreed, while it is not
clearly evident that at first the great common sense
of the country at large dissented from the severe
measures taken to secure the validity of the decree
itself. There seems indeed to have been a wide-spread
conviction amongst the intelligent portion of the population not converted to mediæval Christianity, that however
hard it might be in detail for individuals, the safety of the
state demanded the immediate and vigorous exercise of
capable authority.

There followed, by gradual stages and at long intervals,
the decline of the hereditary shogunate, and the simultaneous growth in wealth and influence of the great clan
chieftains or daimios (*dai-mio* = great name). Often the
power of the daimio really lay in the hands of some
shrewd retainer of even the humblest rank, who had
mastered the subtle oriental arts of secret wire-pulling
and the caucus. The Cabinet of the present Mikado after
the Restoration was very largely composed of able but
plain men, who had made an entrance into the mysteries
of statecraft in this humble and informal way.

By-and-by arose a disposition cautiously to question
publicly the wisdom and finality of the act itself. The
wide world outside was always sending in through some
newly-discovered chink a ray of knowledge that was felt
to be only good for man.

Nor were there wanting now and again adventurers
who would risk even life itself for one sweet bite of the
forbidden fruit. The light at last dawned, and when the

"Black Ships" first came, the people were really far better prepared to welcome them than we have been wont to suppose. The Shogun's party then began to move, and, of course, the Mikado's party then asserted itself as essentially conservative. The conservative cause, too, included the rowdy military element, in which the masterless two-sworded men or rōnins played a bloody and conspicuous part. *They* were ready at least to lay their lives down voluntarily rather than see Japan stained by the footsteps of barbarians.

Whig and Tory.
(From a Japanese "Dialogue on Political Economy.")

New blood was infused into the old veins of the political organism. Men of the people, as we have seen, made themselves felt, and the progressionists who sided with the Shogun were outbid in Radicalism by those who "ran" the boy Mikado into power once more—power that was now to be formally supreme, and almost as much that of the people themselves—although this is hardly visible yet, as is the authority of the United States President. The preparedness of the people is apparent from the suddenness of the change. Such a transformation may seem easy and natural to those who derive their notions of Oriental history from the translations of the Arabian Nights; but in Japan, as, I believe, everywhere else, such free movements are effected by measurable dynamic influences which the patient historian may hope yet to analyze and record.

But what of the large and ferocious party who had for years made the fertile plains and valleys of Japan ring with the sound, "Expel the barbarians!" Their conversion was very easily effected. It was clear that razor-like blades were no match for bomb-shells, bayonets, and rifle bullets. If they were ever to fight the barbarians it must be by patiently learning their arts and purchasing or making their weapons. This suggestion when made was heartily resolved upon. Arsenals were founded, steamers were bought, and professors were engaged to teach every science known in the West, and a great deal more that was not science at all. For many years the original purpose was doggedly maintained, but happily broader and more liberal views now prevail. The reign of the present Emperor restores the spirit of toleration that prevailed in ancient times. It is said that the peaceful direct reign of the Mikados of Japan has never been stained by an act of religious persecution, and the statement is almost literally true.

T

The London *Times* in 1859 predicted that " the Chinaman would still be navigating the canals of his country in the crazy old junks of his ancestors, when the Japanese was skimming along his rivers in high-pressure steamers, or flying across the country behind a locomotive." The railway is now, in fact, stretching its iron tracks across hill and dale; the telegraph is spreading her web all over the country; tramway cars are to run on the quieter roads as they now do in the large cities; the printing press is heard rattling merrily in every moderate sized county town, and the Japanese, who have always read much, now read ten times more than ever they did before. Technical education, of that higher kind which no system of schools or colleges can quite accomplish, is telling upon the people, and many works are now undertaken from which the authorities would have shrunk a year or two ago as being impossible for them to grapple with. The roads are still far behind what the Empire needs, but there is enough of criticism going on to give us the hope that they will soon be mended. A Japanese newspaper says that " our Government differs from that of other countries in this— that the Government itself leads the van of progress." Of course this can hardly be true of any government, and is essentially untrue of Japan. No step has been taken forward without the most strenuous popular discussion, which in Japan unfortunately has hitherto always threatened to end in civil war.

Far back in history there are traces to be found of the now more familiar *toku-sei*—equality of condition, or socialism. The authorities know well that Christianity is at present the one effective restraint upon the growth of this dangerous social heresy, the genuine counterpart of which it professes to expound. The teachings of scientific atheism, which have been attentively weighed, are therefore not greatly in favour at present, on account of their supposed tendency in the direction of levelling all social and traditional distinctions. Possibly it might be shown that genuine science has done much to accent the very opposite doctrine of special fitnesses in nature for lower or higher functions. Apart from this question, the influence of the modern scientific spirit is immense, and ever growing. Photography corrects the bad drawing and false perspective of an art from which we have yet much to learn. The telegraph post with its caps and wires is now a conventional subject in decorative work. The social influence of the railway is very extensive.

The late able minister from Japan to St. James's—Mori Arinori—is reported by an interviewer of the *Pall Mall Gazette* to have marked the absence in our country of that "sense of brotherhood which binds together all the members of one family, and which extends from them to all dwellers in one district," and which, I may add, keeps the number of paupers in Japan down to a very low figure. It may perhaps be that this blood and local tie does not imply that a very high stage of civilization has yet been attained in Japan, but it seems to be an admirable basis for the growth of larger and more complex social aggregates, and it works fairly well in Japan, tending, however, somewhat to hinder individual progress and aggrandisement, perhaps too much to be altogether for the good of the State.

Miss Bird has stated seriously (*Unbeaten Tracks*, Vol. II., 347) that—

"The nation is sunk in immorality, the millstone of Orientality hangs round her neck in the race in which she has started, and her progress is political and intellectual rather than moral ; in other words, as regards the highest destiny of man, individually or collectively, it is at present a failure."

Now this seems to me, after nine years of daily and most intimate intercourse with all classes except the very highest to be an extremely harsh and erroneous judgment. The recent intellectual progress of the Japanese people has been very striking, though not as yet so general as many have supposed ; its political progress has perhaps been unprecedented ; but I think that on the whole the moral elevation of the mass of the people within the last decade has been still more striking and noteworthy. The judges will not now I am sure accept a bribe any more than an English magistrate would do ; obscene images and pictures are rarely to be seen in public—unless imported from Christian countries,—and the women are far more modest in their clothing and outward demeanour than they were a few years ago. I speak what I know to be the opinion of enlightened natives when I say this, but an appeal to the daily newspapers would show the existence of a higher tone in the political and national life—a nobler sense of honour, a truer, kindlier regard to the rights and wishes of others in the hard struggle for existence. Truly there is a vast amount of impurity and evil to deplore, but there is more of it on the surface, and therefore visible to every passing tourist, than is found to be the case in other eastern countries.

Confucius does not speak to the times we live in, as even an infidel or pagan Japanese editor feels that Christ does. Buddhism, with its lofty asceticism that can promise no reward, has forgotten its old clear cold message, and indeed has almost reversed it all. Christianity, bathed in blood and charred to very dust, has sublimely risen out of the long cold embers, and speaks to the land in a voice which every one now listens to with some trace of respect and admiration. Through its translated Scriptures, its pure literature, its vernacular and higher schools, its stimulating lectures and sermons, and its medical missions, it has done much directly,—it has done very much more indirectly,—to leaven public opinion with lofty and manly sentiment.

The mere contiguity also of a higher civilization has tended to raise and purify the people, and to justify and emphasize what is best and noblest in the teaching of old systems long and deeply rooted in the country.

The Japanese Government, echoing the unanimous voice of their people, have been agitating for a relaxation of the terms of our treaty made in 1858. At present the British subject living on Japanese soil is under what are piously supposed to be the laws of his own country. As a matter of fact these laws can be made and unmade pretty much at the discretion of a British minister under strange powers conferred on him by an Act in Council. The foreigner cannot go into the interior without a passport binding him down not to trade in the country, and his reasons for going must be either pursuit of health or

scientific research.   His rights of residence without a
passport are limited to the treaty ports and a very narrow
radius around each of them.   If he offend, he must be
tried before one of his own officials.

The system does not work well; but what of that
which it is now proposed to substitute for it?   It is
not long since photographs were on view, taken from
life, of a poor crucified native criminal being tortured
to death by spearing.   Other forms of torture of
a hideous kind have but recently been abolished, and
very naturally enlightened foreigners who are warmly
in sympathy with Japan urge caution in placing ourselves
under a system of jurisprudence of such sudden growth.
A great deal is said about torture in this connection.   I
have seen in my ordinary practice several of its results,
but I have never seen a recent case, nor have I even
heard of any well-authenticated one within the last six
years.   But for my part, I think that while this dread may
now be ignored, it would be more satisfactory to secure
some better guarantees that foreign interests will not be
interfered with in a multitude of petty ways.   This fear
is the true nightmare that broods over every foreigner
who contemplates residence in Japan under native jurisprudence.   It may only be a nightmare, but its existence
must be taken into account by any one who discusses the
subject gravely.

The subject has very recently assumed a novel
aspect.   It has been urged with effect, that till Japan
becomes a Christian country, Western countries will not
consent to submit their citizens to her jurisdiction.   In
nature there are curious laws of organic life which tend to

perpetuate struggling species. One of them, first enun-
ciated by the distinguished naturalist, Mr. Bates, is that of
" Protective Mimicry." A great Japanese educationalist,
who has deserved well of his countrymen for his patriotic
services, and who has been one of the most popular ex-
ponents of Spencerian agnosticism, catching up the phrase
with his usual keen, practical intelligence, proposes to
utilise the conception by advocating a " Protective Mimicry" of Christianity. The proposal is, of course, quite
suicidal, though I believe well meant, and by no means so
cynical as it may seem, and is not ill-calculated to fall in
with the prevailing cultured eclecticism, which is not an
entirely new feature in the national *geist* of Nipon. The
march of men, we trust, is ever onward, and as we have
already seen the " Protective Mimicry " of Western arts
of warfare end happily in a large development of the arts
of peace, so it may not be altogether vain to hope that
a false and faltering step in the right direction may
ultimately lead to genuine and germinal reform.

As I write these closing sentences, the announcement
reaches me that while the official priesthood—both Shinto
and Buddhist—is being finally abolished, the peerage is
being re-erected with greater lustre than before. It is
now clear to most moderate Japanese that such a regulator
will be needed in the promised National Constitution of
1890 as a partially hereditary House of Lords will afford.
Not a few strong and enlightened democrats in Japan are
of opinion that a true democracy alone possesses the
guarantee of good manners and fair intellectual discussion. May the people of Nipon and their enlightened
and progressive ruler long continue to advance, true to

the glorious symbol of the Rising Sun which blushes so
hopefully on their standard.

For EU product safety concerns, contact us at Calle de José Abascal, 56–1°, 28003 Madrid, Spain or eugpsr@cambridge.org.